ADVANCE PRAISE

"Todd Wilkinson has written a deeply researched book describing the wonderful interconnected and mutually dependent tapestry of biodiversity that makes the Greater Yellowstone Ecosystem unique in the world and 'America's natural miracle.' Sadly, because of thoughtless, hubristic and ignorant management we as stewards may fail in our responsibility to pass the 'miracle' on in better shape to future generations. Every man, woman, and child in this country needs to do everything in their power to honor the wisdom of our forebears of protecting this miracle."

—**Ted Roosevelt IV**, noted conservationist, investment banker in New York City and Managing Director and Chairman of Barclays Cleantech Initiative; a hunter, angler and visitor to Greater Yellowstone, he is committed to protecting wildlands wherever wildlife lives; great-grandson of American President Theodore Roosevelt

"Todd Wilkinson is our essential witness to wildness and wilderness in the Northern Rockies. His sharp-edged prose take us to the knife point of why the Yellowstone ecosystem matters to the soul of America, ecologically and spiritually. It is the white-hot center of wildlife protection from the survival of grizzly bears and wolves, to trumpeter swans. Wilkinson shows us repeatedly how the health of Yellowstone National Park is a microcosm of the health of our planet. Diversity matters. Restraint matters. Unchecked human development and solipsism creating an irreplaceable loss of biodiversity in the midst of climate collapse are at the core of Wilkinson's concerns. In a cascading moment of all we stand to lose, what we gain by reading *Ripple Effects* are insights into a community of committed citizens from brave biologists to business visionaries who care. If hope is a force field, Todd Wilkinson creates a force field of stories capable of true change and cultural transformation in the service of the wild."

—**Terry Tempest Williams**, educator, conservationist, activist, and author of fourteen books including *The Hour of Land: A Personal Topography of America's National Parks* and *Refuge: An Unnatural History of Family and Place*

"Yellowstone is more than a park, as Todd Wilkinson reminds us in this deeply reported, important, passionate book. Yellowstone is more than an ecosystem. Yellowstone is a grand idea that America had, a hundred and fifty years ago, and retains: that nature, big and wild, is an essential part of our country. That idea can't survive without defenders."

—**David Quammen**, author of fifteen books including *The Tangled Tree, Spillover, The Song of the Dodo,* and *The Reluctant Mr. Darwin*; his articles have appeared in *Outside Magazine, National Geographic, Harper's, Rolling Stone, The New York Times Book Review, The New Yorker* and more

Ripple Effects

Ripple Effects

How To Save Yellowstone
and America's Most Iconic Wildlife Ecosystem

TODD WILKINSON

Wyatt-MacKenzie Publishing
DEADWOOD, OREGON

Ripple Effects

How To Save Yellowstone
and America's Most Iconic Wildlife Ecosystem

Todd Wilkinson

Hardcover ISBN: 978-1-954332-45-4
Trade Paperback ISBN: 978-1-948018-73-9
Library of Congress Control Number: 2022934353

Cover art by A.D. Maddox.
Bart Koehler lyrics used with permission.
1872 Map of Yellowstone restored by bauhau1000 | iStock by Getty Images

Proceeds of this book go to *Mountain Journal* ~ Supporting Truth and
Defending Wild Nature with Journalism.
mountainjournal.org

A portion of all proceeds go to Yellowstone Forever.

~

The publisher dedicates this project to Jeffrey Todd Haight,
a science teacher who inspired the best in everyone, and who found
great joy in advocating for Yellowstone National Park.

Wyatt-MacKenzie Publishing
DEADWOOD, OREGON

www.WyattMacKenzie.com

Dedication

To Yellowstone, and all who try to save it.

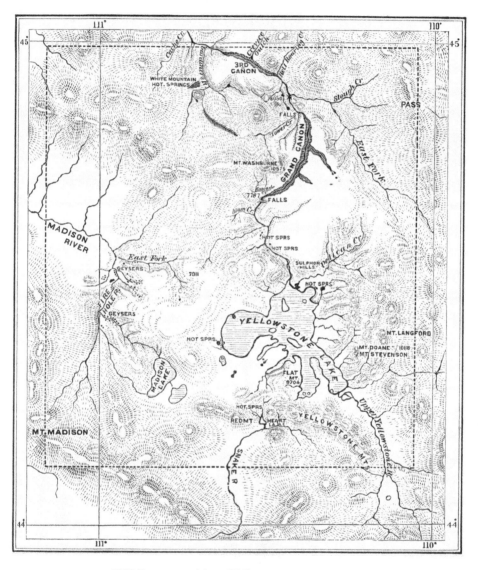

1872 Engraving ~ Map of Yellowstone National Park

Contents

Prologue

Anatomy of a Wake-up Call

by Thomas Spruance

WE CONTINUOUSLY TELL OURSELVES there's no point in changing. Either we are too old to make a difference or too young to alter the trajectory we are presently on. Once upon a time, I subscribed to this belief, too.

And then the other day, I read a quote posted in the online conservation journalism site, *Mountain Journal* that came from Dennis Glick, an expert in community conservation who has been tracking the kind of epic changes bearing down on the Greater Yellowstone Ecosystem, the last best wildlife-rich ecosystem in the U.S. Lower 48.

Mr. Glick was quoted as saying, "Many people have relocated to Montana and Wyoming and Idaho from Colorado ski resort towns because their once-intimate connection to nature has vanished from the bustle that has overtaken those places in the Colorado Rockies."

I am one of those people and here is my confession:

I am a recovering seeker of the American dream who pursued it blindly, without reflecting upon my own impacts and what they meant for vanishing wild places. If all of us became more ecologically aware we could stop repeating the pattern of thoughtless destruction, but it will require inconveniencing ourselves. More difficult is that we push ourselves out of our comfort zones and see nature as being far greater than ourselves.

I, too, was drawn to the interior West as you no doubt are. At the age of nine, my father introduced me to the wonders and beauty of the wilderness as his father had done for him. After fly fishing for salmon on the Miramichi River in New Brunswick, Canada, and hiking the endless trails above that river for many summers, I, representing the third generation of my family to do so, was "hooked."

But it was more than just the love of the wilderness and fishing.

My grandfather who designed our 100-year-old ancestral home located in the historic Brandywine River Valley of Delaware also spoke to his love of nature. Many who visit comment on the feeling of our hunting lodge with the large moose head above the walk-in fireplace, which towers 20 feet to the ceiling and includes a surrounding balcony. Four remaining fireplaces are all accentuated with deer-head mounts. In earlier eras, one way of coveting wildness was to possess it, by taking the lives of wild creatures, having them artfully turned into a work of taxidermy and then displayed, as if the spirit of the animal continued in the confines of our own dwelling spaces.

The premise was that wild places existed to provide habitat for the animals we hunted. They existed to serve our desires; the conservation ethic advanced by Theodore Roosevelt and others was premised on this notion. Little thought was given to the survival of the non-hunted animals that certainly have their own intrinsic worth as products of the same evolutionary processes that gave rise to us and which we are incapable of engineering.

My father continued a family tradition of supporting conservation by placing the 25 acres that surround our home under conservation easement, thus assuring that the land will remain in its natural state in perpetuity.

His gesture left an imprint on me; it's in my genes because in the late 1970s, I built my own little lodge in Eagle Vail, Colorado, two miles west of Vail, Colorado. The skiing was great but it was the summer trout fishing, the hiking, backpacking, and the tranquility of the surrounding wilderness that really drew me to the area. The highlight of my first Christmas in Eagle Vail was a herd of elk wondering through my front yard.

Of course, Eagle Vail appealed to many others who came. What followed was an incredible expansion of development around my one-wilderness home. The meteoric growth included 12-plus golf courses stretching down the valley; shopping centers replaced the peaceful grasslands where the elk once grazed; and then came the opening of the Beaver Creek and the Arrowhead Ski Areas. I never saw another elk. I doubt that the skiers who came in winter and the mountain bikers who now throng there in summer ever reflect much on what they are not seeing, or what's been lost: an essence of place that once it is covered in human infrastructure can never be regained. And the fact is that most wild places have gone in that direction.

Although my magazine publishing business in Vail continued to prosper as well as the rental of my home to those who longed to experience "the magic of the mountains," the ceaseless wave of development and growth ate at the core of my original dream of mountain living. Thus, I sold my home in Eagle Vail and started visiting Big Sky, Montana with my son, Preston, who was nine years old at the time.

I was on a quest to find an area that would not turn into "a Vail" as noted by Dennis Glick's comment above. Indeed, there is a prevailing conceit that if a place gets destroyed all we need to do is pack up and move to a less-developed place. Sadly, there are no great places left and I've had a personal awakening that the Greater Yellowstone Ecosystem is, in very literal ways, the last one still standing.

My goal was to pass along to Preston a home in a local town that would provide the unique experience of the natural wilderness with all the wonders that came with it—including the indescribable feeling that you are entering a world that belongs to non-human life forms. And in the case of Greater Yellowstone, it means a region still holding creatures that have vanished from almost everywhere else.

The infection of conservation starts with doing what you love and then letting that love transform you into being a protector. Preston's very first Montana trout was a brown trout caught on the Firehole River in Yellowstone National Park. A picture of Preston proudly holding that brown hangs prominently in our kitchen today along with other pictures of trophy trout from the Gallatin, Madison, and Yellowstone rivers. Preston, like me, was "hooked."

At first, Big Sky looked and felt like something special, "the place." But instead of buying another home immediately, I thought it best to first join some local organizations whose mission was to preserve the natural essence of the Gallatin River, liquid gem of the Big Sky area. As a member and contributor to several environmental/conservation organizations, I planned to assist in fundraising and furthering the importance of sensitive development in hopes to avoid the calamity I witnessed in the Vail Valley. Our many summer and winter visits gave me the opportunity to experience firsthand the path that Big Sky was thoughtlessly taking.

Unfortunately, I began to observe the conundrum that faced many business members of the local community and their families: the lore of the personal financial benefits brought on by growth and development outweighed the need to maintain the "wild things" that created an appeal and brought the development. There grew a divisiveness within the community between those who supported more growth versus those who wished to maintain the extraordinary sense of place, as represented by the presence of wildlife, and the tranquility of mountain living for people.

Preston and I personally witnessed the effects of the growth with the increased "fishing pressure" brought upon the Madison River. Our once-sacred father/son fishing floats on the river evolved into sharing the day with a flotilla of fly fishermen, many of whom measured the satisfaction of their day on number of fish and not on the ecosystem that enabled a fishery to thrive. While hiking the surrounding trails of Big Sky, we noticed they were inundated more and more with off-road bikers and ATVers who did not notice the animals they were displacing. The decline in quality wildlife watching was disheartening and I realized it wasn't merely about my inability to see animals, but also the question of why they were being displaced from their homes.

History was repeating itself and that pattern is spreading across Greater Yellowstone and the Rockies. Thus, I decided not to purchase a beautiful Gallatin riverfront lot located near Red Cliff just south of Big Sky, an investment in retrospect that would have been very profitable, but financial profit was not my motive. Call me crazy, but I wanted to leave a natural legacy for Preston and it meant reflecting on my own impact. You may think this was just another tale of paradise being lost.

There actually is a silver lining from our experience in Big Sky. Preston and I had the fortune of meeting JD Davis of the park non-profit support organization, Yellowstone Forever, during the early years of our visits to Montana. In 2011, the Spruance Foundation II, along with many others, contributed to Yellowstone Forever's lake trout removal program in hopes of seeing the return of the native Yellowstone cutthroat trout left imperiled by the introduction of exotic lake trout into Yellowstone Lake. Action, combined with patience and persistence, prevailed and the Yellowstone cutthroat numbers in Yellowstone Lake and the streams that flowed into the lake began to increase. The incredible success of that project led to our meeting with author Todd Wilkinson. Thus, the embryo of *Ripple Effects*, which you hold now in your hands, was conceived.

This is a book that speaks a compelling, at times alarming, but ultimately inspiring message, and it echoes the message of Dr. Seuss's famous environmental fable *The Lorax*—unless someone cares, nothing is going to get better.

I would like to share another personal and symbolic experience that has reinforced my efforts in the Yellowstone Cutthroat Trout Restoration Program.

Preston and I always enjoyed dry fly fishing the upper Yellowstone River just north of the town of Gardiner, which is the northern entrance to Yellowstone National Park. Our last float together in this area was in 2013. During that float, I experienced an event that has stayed with me. We had just put in at the Yankee Jim Canyon area of the Yellowstone, and I was casting my dry fly close to the bank allowing it to float into a calm pool just below a large boulder. As the fly entered the pool, a large Yellowstone cutthroat trout rose from the depths to take the fly. And yes, in my excitement, I tried to set the hook too soon and the fish disappeared back into the dark water. I never forgot that frustrating image, an image that replayed itself over in my mind for many years thereafter.

The next time I floated that area of the Yellowstone was the fall of 2020. Same place, possibly the same pool. Both my guide and I were watching my fly as it drifted into the pool and much to our excellent amazement a large Yellowstone cutthroat trout rose and took my fly. This time, a little older and wiser, I hesitated for just a moment and then lifted my fly rod to set the hook.. Upon boating the cutthroat, a wave of closure came over me. I had finally brought to an end the repetitive episode of losing that trout.

My conservation work had been done to help rescue an imperiled fish but it was the cause of getting involved and succeeding that rescued me—that turned my winnowing hope around, convincing me that all hope is not lost until we give up.

I later reflected on all the great work of Yellowstone Forever in Yellowstone cutthroat trout restoration program and felt that this was truly a sign to me that our efforts were not in vain. A "thank you" and a "symbolic encouragement" to keep up our work, not only for the cutthroat trout and many creatures linked to its survival but also for the many challenges that face the Great Yellowstone Ecosystem.

I share these stories with you and remain undaunted in my journey to find and maintain that wilderness hideaway for Preston. A similar opportunity exists in your family and among your friends. Along with advocacy groups like Yellowstone Forever, we desperately need environmental entities like *Mountain Journal* and I encourage you to support it.

Ripple Effects provides the road map to a time and place where mountain communities will share the wilderness with all its many occupants in a cooperative manner but we must remember that often we are visitors to their home. Understanding this is the only way the wildlife wilderness will remain healthy for Preston, your own version of Preston and their future generations.

There is a responsibility that all of us have to consciously make space for nature in our lives. I reflect on my journey to this point in time and realize more than ever that we all need to avoid the wholesale consumption of nature. As a Dad, a businessman and self-proclaimed steward of our precious wildlands, I hope to leave a legacy of one who let the natural wonders that surround us better than I found them.

We have to open our eyes. As responsible people no matter where we reside on a political spectrum, we have no other choice. As you read the pages that follow, I am hopeful that Todd's incredible thoroughness and insight provides you with the inspiration and confidence that our taking action will turn around the seismic forces that threaten the Greater Yellowstone Ecosystem and beyond.

Ripple Effects gives wildlife and all its members a seat at the table. Come join us on this incredible and promising journey that taps into the rich, natural pleasure from recognizing our place in Nature.

Casting the First Pebble

I T'S TIME TO PLAY AN AGE-OLD GAME. For fun, side-arm a flat stone into a calm lake or stretch of river. Watch it skip and skim. Challenge your friends to a contest of who can notch the most rings. Now, *think*. Think hard. Devote just 60 seconds of time to this thought: Count the number of times you can make the rock leapfrog across the water, casting off ripple effects of overlapping circles, watching them emanate wider until they ebb and eventually disappear. Now, imagine that *you* are the stone and the circles represent how you might affect the world around you. Yes, how *you*, we, *us* try to make our gift of life count for something.

We can effect change, positive and negative, and it is vital that we become conscious that our actions are not without consequence.

Ripple effects happen in Nature and can assume many different shapes and forms. They happen in the human-dominated world we now call the *Anthropocene*. They can appear as cause and effect, trophic cascades or they might appear as falling dominoes. Each of our own actions ripples collectively and individually. You ripple. What you *do* impacts others, including non-human beings, in overt and unseen ways.

Where and how you build your home—one of the most important decisions you will make—ripples across the landscape. How you spend your money. Where roads and trails are built ripples. The kind of cars we drive ripples, the food choices we make, the people we elect, the worthwhile charities we support. The places we go to get reliable information, such as *Mountain Journal* (mountainjournal.org)—the non-profit environmental news organization I founded as a watchdog for Greater Yellowstone, matters and is based on the premise that you care.

This book was written for people who love Nature. It will take you into a realm of topics possessing gravity and interest as standalone yet interrelated chapters. They involve places and things that have global prominent and whose fate will be determined by what you do or don't do.

So, let this question be a first stone tossed. The ripple is a question: What. Is. Yellowstone?

Certainly, you know about the place, but ponder it by thinking outside the box of its rough geometric dimensions and reputation of being a kind of wild Disneyland.

You can approach it three ways:

What is Yellowstone? What *is* Yellowstone? What is *Yellowstone.*

Yellowstone itself as a concept is a human invention, handed an identity based upon an arbitrary notion imposed finitely upon an arbitrarily selected area of real terra firma. The land itself did not evolve with hard "boundaries"; nor did the inhabitants—human and animal—have any inkling of being "inside" or "outside" of it. In fact, wildlife are not able to read artificial maps or signs, including informational brochures informing us that approaching bison, bears and elk is dangerous. Animals also do not comprehend invisible human delineations.

Until the arrival of technology and with it the return of the horse to the North American continent, guns, cars, ATVs, mountain bikes, e-bikes, planes and various kinds of other machines, people and non-humans were on, relatively speaking, more equal footing. It's poignant that Yellowstone, as a demarcation, was codified as a set-aside of Nature on March 1, 1872, around the time that the most transformative time in human history, which brought our domination of Nature to a new accelerated level, was just getting started. Today, another product of technology, social media and the ability of people to post a photo of a place along with the geographic coordinates, can on the day of its sharing celebrate Nature and in the next summon a mad rush to experience it—and sow its destruction. The ripple of a seemingly innocent, benign gesture, can mean the difference between an animal in need of space, security and food to raise its young surviving, and that same animal being displaced by an onslaught of us.

Yellowstone as a conception of place is made up out of thin air and yet the late noted writer Wallace Stegner pointed to U.S. national parks, which started with Yellowstone, as the best original idea America ever had and which is still being emulated around the world. Despite this,

Yellowstone today remains being viewed as an "other"—as if it's a bastion for real nature and what's outside of it is less wild. Of course, there are some of us who also disparage it as a glorified drive-thru zoo all the while they will never venture farther off the road than the hotel where they'll check in for the night.

To further bedazzle your brain, consider these ponderances: What if Yellowstone were suddenly to no longer exist? How would that alter our conception of wild nature and orientation to "the West"? If Yellowstone had *never existed* or were she to perish, would we have a system of nature preserves in the 21st century? If not, would we have protected still-wild species as we know of them today?

In this moment, ask: What would be lost or missing if Yellowstone ceased to exist as a beacon of hope? How would our construction of what is possible for protecting wildness in other regions be different if this bright light were snuffed out—a bright light that serves as an illustration of why it is important to protect all of the essential known pieces of an irreplaceable jigsaw puzzle if the goal is having a healthy ecosystem? With that in mind, imagine opening your mailbox and receiving this note, or maybe, as an expression of these times, getting pinged with the following text.

Yellowstone:
AN OBITUARY

Dear Citizen,

With regret I inform you Yellowstone is dead. Our first national park, born in 1872 and the most iconic nature preserve on Earth, passed away quietly. I wanted to let you know because you and your family were shared owners. I imagine her death may come as somewhat of a shock. The exact cause is under investigation. Results of a full autopsy are pending.

Emergency responders, I am told, were summoned to the scene but desperate resuscitation efforts sadly proved futile. Yellowstone died of multiple causes. Concerns about the park's deteriorating vital signs and that of the larger Greater Yellowstone Ecosystem had been mounting for some time. Eventually, Yellowstone's bodily functions—related to her heart, lungs and circulatory system—suffered a variety of converging, irreversible failures.

Scientific investigators, who specialize in ecological forensics, believe the most lethal contributing factors, besides the lacerating impacts of too many people bringing crushing impacts in and outside the park, were, ironically, a combination of human apathy, ecological illiteracy, willful denial of science and the strange paradox of simultaneously being popular and loved to death.

The park's chief scientist informed me in a personal phone call: "Originally, we were concerned the tidal wave of visitors setting new records and climate change were to blame. But after we conducted an aerial survey, we realized it wasn't just big things—and there are many—but innumerable small ones that were believed insignificant—and we took them for granted.

One ended up affecting another and, in turn, another. The Yellowstone region did not succumb to death soley by 1,000 cuts but death by 10,000 scratches. Many of those nicks were not inflicted inside the park but happened beyond Yellowstone's perimeter on nearby public and private land. You might say Yellowstone succumbed to an unstoppable convergence of cumulative effects. In short, we took Yellowstone for granted. I will keep you apprised of what we learn. Mourners are sending their condolences from around the world where the idea of Yellowstone has spread and grown large. I am sorry to say the Yellowstone you once knew is gone.

Sincerely yours,
The President of the United States

Why Yellowstone Matters More Now in the 2020s

O N SEPTEMBER 7, 1988, I was among a small group of reporters evacuated to the very edge of Old Faithful Geyser's blow hole. The open treeless ground of sinter dust rimming the famous gusher was considered one of the safest spots to be in the Upper Geyser Basin of Yellowstone. A park ranger frantically escorted us there where we waited in retreat from a giant wall of flames from an approaching wildfire as a roar of hurricane-force winds pushed it in our direction. We could hear the blaze's sonic approach long before the blinding smoke squall arrived followed by a blast of intense heat and accompanied by pelting raining embers that caused surrounding hillsides to erupt in conflagration on the other side of us.

Yes, it was surreal.

A fickle shift of only a few degrees in wind direction spared one of the most iconic rustic hotels in the West from encountering a direct hit and likely being reduced to ash. The human-built, historic Old Faithful Inn could easily have caught fire and burned down and we too might have perished. All the while, during the mayhem of human scrambling, Old Faithful Geyser continued to erupt and it was indeed otherworldly to see the fountain backdropped by what humans might describe as apocalyptic light.

No one or no part of Yellowstone died on that day.

Later, in the autumn of the same year, after a not very intense snowstorm had put out the massive fires that would not be suppressed with hundreds of millions of dollars spent by humans, I had a conversation with Yellowstone's chief scientist, John Varley, who offered a perspective I carry forward to you now.

"Nature," Varley said, "never *destroys* herself."

Quite the opposite, he noted. She is constantly creating, additatively or reductively, but not often in accordance with the desire of Homo sapiens to control her. We can harm Nature by simplifying her, even liquidating parts of our own life support system out of greed or ignorance.

Wildfire certainly didn't "kill" Yellowstone, as some politicians claimed in response to the historic blazes of 1988. With more than a third of the park's 2.2 million acres *touched* by fire, the ecologically uninformed pundits also wrongly asserted that Yellowstone had been rendered a lifeless "moonscape."

Yellowstone, like plant Earth, is a product of fire and other natural elements such as rainfall and snowpack affecting the landscape we associate with the hydro-geo-thermal panorama of the park, including its subterranean network of 10,000 wondrous geysers, hot springs, colorful pools and steam vents.

Not long ago, when scientists released the findings of the first-ever assessment on human-caused climate change for the Greater Yellowstone Ecosystem, they revealed that sometime around 800 years ago, maybe in the 14th century, extreme drought and high temperatures radically altered the flow of water as it moved across Yellowstone's surface and underground. It caused, for a time, Old Faithful, to stop erupting because they was not sufficient water moving through the natural underground plumbing system and allowing the gusher to spout. It could happen again, at any time, and likely it might if one of the thousands of tiny seismic events that occur every year in Yellowstone, atop of a giant magma plume known as Supervolcano, shake things up. Those are owed to natural forces.

Back then, Yellowstone and the parts of her had different names applied to exactly the same places by indigenous people but the appellation "Yellowstone" did not exist. The river that holds Yellowstone's name today, that begins in the mountains above Yellowstone Lake and which tumbles over two waterfalls through the Grand Canyon on a 700 mile journey as the longest undammed river in America, was called *E-chee-dick-karsh-ah-shay* (Elk River) by the Crow. Twenty six different tribes have some kind of connection the broader landscape on which Yellowstone sits and each one has a place-based lexicon.

But back now to Old Faithful. The legendary geyser, as it did in the 1300s could stop erupting again, later in this century, if temperatures rise another 10 degrees Fahrenheit, if humans keep burning fossil fuels and do lots of other things that load large amounts of carbon dioxide gas into Earth's atmosphere. We can't stop earthquakes but we are capable of changing the planet's thermostat and our influence in potentially shutting down Old Faithful is just one example of how our individual action—maybe driving a gas-burning vehicle—spews CO2 that then influences the atmosphere which then influences everything else. Would an individual shift to an electric vehicle or traveling less alter that trajectory? No. But when humans act at scale, in making changes, then challenges can be overcome.

It's we humans—a single prolific species that has done things often inadvertently harming natural systems—who have caused damage. We won't kill Yellowstone but we can destroy the very things that draw us to her, products of natural evolution that had little to do with us. The things we do inside and outside of Yellowstone can have ripple effects upon the natural things that exist without any adherence the park boundaries, and Yellowstone as a construct is a bellwether, a metaphor, a mirror for assessing whether we are willing to, with deliberateness, allow Nature to happen. Just as Yellowstone served as a counterpoint to the colonial destruction brought by Manifest Destiny, the Greater Yellowstone Ecosystem is an opportunity to not wholly surrender to the taming forces of the Anthropocene.

Yes, Yellowstone is a platform for pondering profound contractions.

My friend and writing colleague David Quammen, who authored a complete issue of *National Geographic* magazine devoted to Yellowstone (and which I modestly contributed to), referred to the park as "the paradox of the *cultivated* wild."

What does that mean? Yellowstone is one of the most studied nature preserves in the world and yet, in the 1960s, it adopted a policy of "management" that was hand's off compared to its earlier years in which its overseers, often people who were not very ecologically informed, choreographed how nature would be presented to the public. The "radical" new policy was called "natural regulation" or letting nature take her course, to have humans in many instances stand back, watch, listen and try to hear what nature was communicating. It was controversial and considered heresy by some trained in the hubristic traditions of academia that asserted humans had all the answers. Even though such ego-driven, human-centric ways of thinking had been proved naïve and full of folly.

The longtime Yellowstone science writer Paul Schullery who worked on staff and edited a number of reports prepared by researchers in Yellowstone, shared this observation in the journal *Yellowstone Science* when he retired: "At its most heartfelt level, the controversy over natural regulation exemplifies warring human value systems—the highest stakes going in our society. The extreme positions are the easiest to identify. There's the intensely agricultural versus the purely wilderness, or, put in another way, the zoo versus the wildland. From the beginning, even when natural regulation wasn't such a loaded term, a lot of people took the concept very personally. The very idea of natural regulation confronted us with hard questions. Was the park going to farm its elk, grizzly bears, and other charismatic features? If so, to what degree? *Or* was the park going to foster some larger and very hard-to-define resource called "wildness," and leave the details, like the size of each wildlife population, up to the wild community to sort out? How you answered that question depended a lot on how you perceived humanity's place on the planet. Underneath pretty much every controversy, no matter how grand or mundane, is the question of how wild Yellowstone should be—how far back are we willing to stand? Can we ever just let nature happen? It's ironic, really. I mean, here we are, probably the most nature-dominating culture in human history and yet we've created this institution that requires us to let nature make its own decisions."

Of course, climate change is forcing humans to make hard decisions.

Climate change *is* human-caused, and its effects are going to push some native plant and animal communities to the edge, some to the precipice of extinction. Should humans intervene? Should we try to bio-engineer landscapes and will we admit that we don't always know what we're doing? Should we genetically alter plants and animals to make them more resistant to exotic pathogens and resilient to better endure changing habitat conditions? Should we move plants and animals around, to places where they might not normally be considered "native" but where shifts in range, hastened by climate change, would make them native in the future?

The biggest immediate challenge facing us is whether we are willing to pause, after Covid-19 gave us an opportunity to reflect, on whether the relentless pursuit of economic growth, largely premised on the consumption of Nature, is worth the cost of depleting Nature's richness, strands of which might be crucial to our own life-support system and, at the very least, the joys of dwelling on a planet with more than just human and domesticated beings.

Why should you care about the Greater *Yellowstone* Ecosystem? You may choose not to. You may believe it doesn't have any relevance in your day-to-day life. That is your choice. But I will assert that such a decision is a grave mistake because how the mounting challenges facing Yellowstone are addressed by this society has existential consequences for the places where you live and the kind of world your loved ones and others will inherit after you are gone. Moreover, there is the ethical issue of responsibility; that is, if we're in a place to safeguard species from enduring harm, should we give them a voice by becoming their advocates?

You may be a curmudgeon who argues that we cannot peer altruistically into the future. At this very moment, we are living in a future shaped by others who came before us. We are dwelling in a future some of them ingeniously envisioned or dared to imagine. The Yellowstone *they* gave us, by act of Congress and the signature of President Ulysses S. Grant, again is not the same Yellowstone that belongs to you now. The park of today is better, wilder, and more profound because it's a recognized part of a larger ecosystem and because we are smarter. We are better informed and we are guided more by science than superstitions.

Not long ago, National Park Service scientist Dave Hallac, who oversaw the research division in Yellowstone, observed that in many ways, in response to earlier ill-informed human actions, Yellowstone and the encompassing Greater Yellowstone Ecosystem had become—prepare yourself for this bit of great news—*healthier*. That's right. Today, we may be living in the halcyon times in which a convergence has happened. We are not only less impetuously destructive and better able to care for other species; we are more willing to make room, co-exist more smartly, understanding that conservation is also good for the economy, and we possess the capability of exercising restraint in how much we consume by asserting our presence.

The function of this wildlife-rich region, unrivaled in the Lower 48 that stands apart, may be healthier than it's been since Yellowstone was founded even as the effects of climate change are beginning to deepen. Once upon a time, one of the reasons Yellowstone was born, every single large species that makes Greater Yellowstone the most complete native wildlife ecosystem left in the contiguous U.S. was nearly eliminated but conservation brought resuscitation. The ecosystem survived a bleak time in the past and it got through because humans were willing to reduce their appetite for taking.

But, Hallac and his scientific colleagues are asking, can this fragile moment of sublime wildness last? And, again, if not, what would be lost? In wildlife routes and passageways are the encoded memory of wild lands and indigenous knowledge, words and a language spoken for thousands of years but then suppressed. Wildlife leads us back to a kind of connectivity with nature we so desperately need and that indigenous inhabitants understood because it was essential to their survival and, in recognition of that, their spiritual being. Harm Nature, harm the gifts that the Creator offers, and you harm yourself.

We live in the human-dominated world; and a corollary is that we have begun to enter a time of species loss similar to five other major extinction events. None of those involved us, but this one is being caused by us.

Just as nature reminds of common chords, so too are there causes and effects. While nature cannot be "destroyed," she can be stripped down of her parts. We don't know what the total consequences will be, though we know that, in the health of people and other species, diversity matters.

A Meditation on "Wildness"

EVERY ONE OF US HAS OUR OWN NOTION of what *wildness* is. What's yours? Some humans believe that any living thing beyond themselves or their authority or the reach of a handrail is wild, or at least is a product of a cultivated manipulated wild; wildness that is only considered valuable to exist if it is there in service to us. Otherwise, what good is it?

Why care about wildness?

Because wildness is what makes us smarter is one answer. Wildness is the source of everything we "value," including the reason we exist. Like the primitive Western European edict that the rest of the cosmos revolves around the earth, the truth that led to its debunking was considered radical. Those who dared question it were subjected to prison or death. Of course, the idea that we stand above, apart from, or in opposition to Nature today is, well, fanciful.

You may not realize it but I just played a trick on you. You are still reading because you care. That was a test. Another test is asking you to reflect on how much more you wish to know? The fate of an extraordinary place—a region that is unlike any other, and that belongs to you in so many ways, as it belonged by law to your ancestors and will to your descendants or those who come after—depends on two things: how much you care now, and how much your mind, heart and soul wishes to know.

Wildness may or may not have anything to do with federal "Wilderness" lands as many people familiar with the cartography of America's public lands understand it. Indeed, there are some private lands that could be considered far wilder than a public land wilderness area or a national park saddled next to a city. In nearly four decades of being a journalist, having the opportunity to see wild places elsewhere in the world, I always delight in coming home to the Greater Yellowstone Ecosystem, located in the Northern Rocky Mountains at the intersection of three states: Wyoming, Montana and Idaho. It is a region unlike any other in the U.S. and it is exceedingly rare on the entire globe. I regard it as America's natural miracle.

Before we proceed any further, I invite you to read the following paragraph five times, because it's something you may not realize. Scientists tell us that repetition is the most important thing in cognitive memory retention and the following bit of trivia, which isn't trivial, is important. Here it is:

The Greater Yellowstone Ecosystem is the only bioregion left in the Lower 48 that is home to all of the original large mammals present in 1491, just prior to the arrival of Europeans on the North American continent. Animals that still exist at a population level, not as collections of individuals we see in zoos. Today, all of these big creatures—for fun, call them "charismatic megafauna"—are present and they move more freely—migrate—across the landscape. To and fro over vast distances. Everywhere else in the continental U.S., the kinds of wildlife still here—complete suites of predators and prey—have either been eliminated by humans, or fragmentation of habitat prevents them from moving unabated. That it yet happens here—wildlife migrations—in the third decade of the 21st century is remarkable. It happens nowhere else south of Canada. And it is up to us to make sure it survives.

Absorb the lines above, and now open your mind to why this expansive sweep of planet earth that belongs to you is worth a valiant rescue. Yes, *rescue*. The best way to avoid having an existential crises is to take preventative action and it is essential that we rescue Greater Yellowstone now from continuing to move headlong in a direction that led to inevitable outcome everywhere else. We've already done it once. That's the very reason Yellowstone exists.

I don't know what yours is, but I define true wild places as having wild non-human native creatures that can call them home. By that, I mean wild creatures that are probably inconvenient for humans to share the land with, animals like grizzly bears, wolves, wolverines, cougars, coyotes, foxes and the hooved creatures—elk, moose, pronghorn, mule and white-tailed deer, mountain goats, and the bighorn sheep they eat. They all need lots of space to survive at a population level. Greater Yellowstone has many of those. A common complaint is that large mammals get all the attention when smaller creatures hold just as much "existential" value and are just as important. So true.

Yet here's a fact: When you work to safeguard diversity for large animals that need lots of space you are insuring habitat protection for smaller creatures and the diversity they bring. Bison and prairie dogs, as keystone species, are habitat creators for hundreds of other animals. Wolves, by affecting how their prey species, like elk, use the landscape, have positive emanating influences. Beavers with their dam building, creates wetlands that benefit a lot of species. The interconnections go on and on.

These days, in order for landscapes to be—and remain—wild, people must consciously choose *not* to tame them. Wild landscapes can make our hearts palpitate, forcing us to be more sentiently aware and therefore feel more alive. Here in this province, you can be fatally mauled and eaten by a free-roaming grizzly. You can be gored by a bison and tossed through the air like a sock puppet if you venture too close. You can be impaled by the sharp antler of a bugling bull elk or stomped on by a moose mother protective of her calf. You can fall into a geothermal hot spring in Yellowstone, superheated by liquid magma miles below the surface of the ground, and literally dissolve due to the high pH level in the pool. You can hear the primordial howl of wolves at night. You can listen to the roar of a waterfall in "the Grand Canyon of the Yellowstone" that is 131 feet taller than the cascade at Niagara. You can stand in a wilderness, on a promenade of public land like Two Ocean Plateau, and you can vividly come to understand the rugged backbone of the American West: the Continental Divide. On Two Ocean, a single stream parts in two directions. Only feet apart, you can with your own eyes investigate how a melting snowflake creates a single droplet of water that joins others and ripples through the lives of animals, crops and tens of millions of people.

If that snowflake melts on the east side of Two Ocean Plateau, it will enter the rivulet of Atlantic Creek and begin a journey thousands of miles long before reaching the Gulf of Mexico south of New Orleans. If, perchance, the same frozen ice crystal liquifies a few strides away to the west, it enters the headwaters of the Snake-Columbia river system and twists toward an eventual meeting with the Pacific northwest of Portland, Oregon. Meanwhile, only a few dozen miles to the south, on the flanks of the Gros Ventre and Wind River mountains, creeks drain the headwaters of the Upper Green River Basin, sending the namesake river on a journey toward confluence with the Colorado River.

Without realizing it, a fairly large percentage of Americans have a watery physical connection to one of the remotest corners of the Greater Yellowstone Ecosystem. Where their water emanates from, grizzly bears, brought back from the brink of disappearing thanks to citizen-supported conservation, are leaving tracks in the mud. Now, is your imagination piqued with interest? Mystique relating the above is why many Americans over the course of their lives will have Yellowstone placed high on a bucket list.

But for as mind bending as the watery connection is, consider again the movements of Greater Yellowstone's wildlife. Pronghorn that spend summer in Grand Teton National Park beneath the Tetons will winter outside of Pinedale, Wyoming or the far side of the Red Desert 200 miles away. Once upon a time, some of those pronghorn might have mixed with others of their kind from present-day Colorado or Utah. Mule deer in Greater Yellowstone commute between the flanks of the Wind River Mountains in March and the outskirts of Island Park, Idaho, in June, through a winding gauntlet more than 200 miles, one way, and then back again. Elk, tens of thousands, spiral into Yellowstone from every direction, following "the green wave" of grass to the high slopes of Mount Washburn and then circumnavigate to lowlands maybe 150 miles away, outside the park, when the snow flies. Migrations represent tendrils of animation that function as a fluid life forces, like an electrical system of energy that flows between soil, grass and water to one-ton beasts like a bison, powering a grid of biodiversity. And it doesn't happen as magnificently anywhere else as it plays out here.

True wild places, I would argue, are those that make us feel humbled by truth, based on the humbling knowledge that for as smart as we are, as technologically savvy, we can never engineer all of the natural things going on inside a region like Greater Yellowstone—or equally as profoundly, re-engineer the same kinds of wonders that still hang on here but which have vanished from the rest of the Lower 48. Ironically, wild places are often those left alone, less heavily manipulated by our relentless desire to tinker. Those spots on Earth that still have healthy populations of certain wildlife species remain so because they *don't* have a lot of humans permanent inhabiting their environs or regularly moving through them in large numbers.

This is a fact tested over time and demonstrated by the irrefutable evidence that the kind of wildness present in Greater Yellowstone—as gauged by the web of species still present—has been treated as expendable elsewhere. This is as true for Yellowstone's 10,000 geothermal features, including Old Faithful Geyser. Elsewhere in the world where geothermal energy development has been allowed to proceed haphazardly, the kind of active wondrous phenomena in Yellowstone have vanished.

Greater Yellowstone is the region where black-footed ferrets, resurrected from assumed extinction and which depend upon healthy prairie dog populations, were rescued from biological oblivion. Trumpeter swans were rescued here. And wolves were restored after humans in the region deliberately killed them off—including the National Park Service inside Yellowstone. This region is the part of the Rockies where several of the most important wildlife protection conservation stories in the history of this country happened. Along with the first national park in the world, Yellowstone, and one of America's most majestic, Grand Teton, it is a realm that augured forth national forests and national wildlife refuges, based on a harrowing rescue of decimated elk, and represents today the most robust nature-tourism economy. And, to return to the topic of wildlife migrations, it holds three of the longest known terrestrial wildlife migrations in the Western Hemisphere, involving elk, mule deer, and pronghorn. In fact, all the animals of Greater Yellowstone move in some way.

Ask yourself: are the things above worth inconveniencing yourself in your busy life and doing something to keep them viable—to prevent a metaphorical death of Yellowstone?

On a finite globe with expanding numbers of *Homo sapiens* and some of us possessing big appetites for greed and consumption, wildness is ever shrinking and becoming exceedingly scarce. This is what the so-called Anthropocene—the new unprecedented age in which human activity has become *the* dominant influence in shaping the environment and climate—means for the twenty-first century. Literally, the presence, abundance, and survival of many species will come down to decisions made by people, communities and decisionmakers in pondering how much they choose to impact the last wild places.

Ripple Effects is not a book that employs doomsday scare tactics. It doesn't need to be. The future, just as what much of the rest of the world has become, is racing toward us faster than it ever has.

I finished writing this book *before* the unanticipated Covid-19 pandemic arrived and before the release of new startling reports on climate change and the new 2021 U.S. Census Bureau statistics on the population of America and where her citizens are living. I had to do a rewrite, a dramatic revision. People fleeing crowded cities because of the pandemic resulted in an unprecedented wave of us from outside the region moving and visiting. It was as if a future many believed would not happen until decades into the future had arrived in fast-forward, catching those who manage public lands and are in charge of planning development were caught by surprise. On top of it, the West found itself in the midst of a megadrought and record heat and shortages of fresh water and outbreaks of wildfires but most strikingly, was the added accelerant of people resettling in the Greater Yellowstone region.

Bozeman, Montana has become one of this country's small "it" cities, a place where people are moving to. Because of its geographic position, it has also been viewed, more or less, as the capital of Greater Yellowstone located north of Yellowstone Park in the northern reaches of the ecosystem. Since it was founded in 1864, Bozeman was largely considered an out of the way destination and since the arrival of airplane travel, as a flyover place in the Western interior. That is changing fast and what happens here has huge implications for Greater Yellowstone.

The most recent census figures say that Bozeman and Gallatin County have around 120,00 full-time residents. A prominent local demographer says that within a decade, by the early 2030s, the area will add 40,000 new residents and within 20 years at current conservative growth estimates 90,000 people. That's the equivalent of adding a Billings—Montana's largest city—on top of what is here today. What does it mean for wildlife habitat, for water, for sense of place and what will its spillover effects be on nearby valleys.

If current trends continue unabated, a one-of-a-kind surviving remnant of wildness, truly worthy of being dubbed "America's Serengeti" and one the last wild intact ecosystems in the temperate zones of the Earth, will be just like most other places. And that will be the death of Yellowstone. The intent of the following pages is to spur hard conversations about issues that we do not normally wish to discuss. Why? Because they make us feel uneasy. We don't want to talk about, for instance, the impacts of growth and development. We don't want to call attention to the downsides of boomtimes, particularly what this boom in the Northern Rockies is already foreboding for wild landscapes. We don't want to mention that the better protected Greater Yellowstone becomes, thus making it more desirable as a destination, the less likely it is for working class people to live here. And we don't really want to accept blame for how our personal actions and inactions now are creating the climate-changed world our kids will live in.

The bottom line: we don't want to inconvenience ourselves and change our thinking and behavior but, like a patient who has just had a vigorous health examination and been told by a doctor to alter lifestyle, diet and reduce stress—or perish—we gaze into the beauty of Greater Yellowstone and we are cast into a spell of denial.

Some might refer to the following topics as the "elephants in the room," the doctor's dire diagnosis of trouble: the prescription advising us is that we need to dramatically alter the (blind, unflective) path that brought us here because the same navigational instincts will not get us to safety.

These years of the 2020s coinciding with the 150th anniversary of Yellowstone's creation as a national park, provide an opportunity for celebration and congratulations of momentous conservation accomplishments, yes, of course, but also reflection and a reinterpretation of what wildness *is* and how it must be protected. There is a precedent for this: Yellowstone herself. Amid a tidal wave of colonial Manifest Destiny sweeping across indigenous and wildlife homelands in the West, fomenting genocide and ecocide, Yellowstone was put off limits to the kind of resource consumption emptying the West of its essence.

It is the rage today to focus on Yellowstone almost singularly as a place where wildland conservation should be put on trial, having to answer to charges of racism, because native peoples were extirpated as part of the park's creation.

Such thinking, focused on Yellowstone alone, is myopic because the same colonial forces that produced Yellowstone happened *continentwide*; to fixate on Yellowstone in isolation of that fact serves as a distraction to the larger vital reckoning involving human justice, diversity, equity and inclusion that must happen, but, moreover, it ignores the radical role that Yellowstone plays in the preservation of biodiversity now. A fragile rare remnant in the here and now that can still exist for the new America fast evolving.

The very same attitudes inherent to racism are present in speciesism. The causes of championing human diversity and biodiversity are not mutually exclusive. Both are linked to healthy societies, natural life support systems and, yes, healthy sustainable economies.

The role that Yellowstone plays today, as being the beating heart of a wild ecosystem, is not the same as existed in its moment of invention, which was, essentially, as a nature-related amusement park, a 19th-century equivalent of Disneyland that catered to white elites.

Today the park is a bold, you could call it, *defiant*, counterpoint to the urban-suburbanization of America where non-human beings still have a remnant place of refuge. How can the cause of wildlife conservation become a catalyst for all humans to broaden our thinking about nature and give a voice, too, to other species? Or, perhaps a better way to ponder the opportunity and challenge before us now is to ask the question:

Will a noble victory in human justice, equity, diversity and inclusion be achieved if humans, as a species, cannot rally in common cause to save a rare and fragile wonder of our shared natural heritage, as that which exists in Greater Yellowstone? How is a human movement that is not devoted to guaranteeing the rights of other species to exist not an extension of Manifest Destiny?

Why do other beings matter? How can concern for wildlife unite a divided nation? Consider this: Go to a zoo where toddlers of all nationalities and genders are gathered in front of non-human species. There you will find an equality of love, a shared undeniable expression of biophilia. Another place where this persists but with wild free-ranging non-human animals, is in Greater Yellowstone.

Ripple Effects

AT 15 MILES ACROSS in its widest point and covering a surface area of 136 square miles (all five boroughs of New York City combined encompass 302 square miles), Yellowstone Lake can convey the appearance of being a blank spot on the map of our first national park. Compared to the dramatic theater involving wildlife that plays out conspicuously in the geyser basins, river corridors, and broad valleys, this large tarn, like an inland freshwater sea, is akin to negative space set as a design element into a romantic landscape painting.

But reflected in Yellowstone Lake's tranquil and sometimes stormy waters is perhaps the most profound lesson of Yellowstone and the Greater Yellowstone Ecosystem: the revelation that superficial appearances based upon what we see through our vehicle windshield are often deceiving, that there is always more than meets the eye. Beneath the surface, largely out of sight, the presence of a hidden species symbolizes the very essence of a ripple effect.

Six years after my conversation with John Varley and him saying "nature doesn't destroy herself," there were rumblings emanating from Yellowstone, whisper talk about a shocking unwanted discovery. I'll never forget the day in 1994 when the superintendent's office confirmed that lake trout had been found in Yellowstone Lake. An angler landed a big fish that didn't look like a namesake Yellowstone cutthroat trout. The catch was examined and fisheries biologists were shocked by the implication of dealing with an unwanted intruder that couldn't have gotten there on its own.

Subsequent investigation revealed that lake trout were, in fact, prolific in Yellowstone Lake and they were probably illegally put there years earlier by a human, thus enabling their numbers to grow unchecked. With successful reproduction, they were expanding exponentially. Once scientists stopped scratching their heads, they realized with alarm the implications. Some considered it an act of eco-terrorism, of idiotic vandalism to the dark liquid ruby embedded in the center of our crown jewel national park. A few concluded it was the work of a bubba merely practicing bucket biology.

Many additional theories circulated to explain how lake trout got there. A few reasoned that it might have happened during the 1988 forest fires when helicopters refilled their water buckets at nearby Lewis Lake and then dumped the load on the blaze burning at the edge of Yellowstone Lake, accidentally scooping up lakers and depositing them there. Others speculated that a white pelican or bad eagle or osprey might have snatched a fish from Lewis or Shoshone Lake and fumbled it into Yellowstone Lake. A few claimed that an enterprising laker had swum out of Jackson Lake dozens of miles to the south, up small tributary streams and leaped into a descending stream.

Whatever, though a source for intrigue, it didn't really matter. A stone had been tossed into the lake and it was rippling. Disaster was already lurking in the liquid middle of Yellowstone before 1994 and lying in the balance was the survival of the largest cutthroat trout population in the American interior.

Please stay with me here as I offer an invitation to navigate an aside. Once upon a time, I cast a crude nymph into a body of water and pulled out a trout. I was ten years old.

The place where I caught my first-ever rainbow was a fake pond in a crowded indoor convention center in Minneapolis hosting the annual "outdoors" show: the Lalapalooza of hook and bullet events in a state blessed with lakes and a rabid Nature-loving populace.

The "rod" I used was a jerry-rigged cane pole, the equivalent of today's Tenkara and it had no reel. Pushed onto the barbed size-eight hook was a kernel of corn. In front of me was a circular marine-blue trough that looked like a swimming pool filled with hatchery-raised rainbows of various sizes. Other anglers were bunched shoulder to shoulder beside me on the rounded perimeter platform and each of us tried to entice a member of Ocorhynchus mykiss.

When it comes to angling, some seem to believe, a fish is a fish is a fish; it doesn't matter what species is in a lake, ocean or river; any will do, as long as there are lots of piscatorial creatures to catch, play, fight, and possibly to eat. Fish, they say, exist foremost to serve our desire to have fun or pay the bills. To people who only regard a fish for human utilitarian purposes, waters are considered healthy enough if they can support catchable fish.

Now as I write these words from the West, I am surrounded by similar folk who say journalists like me are making too much about the importance of native species, that trying to rally respect for them is too idealistic and that I am a purist living in denial with the age of the Anthropocene—a code word which means we ought to tinker with Nature to our heart's content—upon us. They say we ought to just get used to having altered broken Humpty Dumpty ecosystems with exotics replacing indigenous flora and fauna. They ask: what does it matter if a trout lake becomes dominated by walleyes, northern pike, bass, suckers, carp or, in the case of Yellowstone Lake, lake trout instead of world-famous endemic Yellowstone cutthroats?

A fish is a fish is a fish, they say; just get over it.

The feeling I had that evening long ago in Minneapolis when I lifted a two-pound rainbow out of the artificial fishing hole still haunts me. It wasn't enough to just hold it in my hands and carry it home to consume. I remember the existential disappointment of this crude exercise in put and take and wondering then: "Isn't there more to catching a trout than this?" Like a lot of us, I had a good grandfather (who taught me to fish) and a dad who enjoyed getting out when he wasn't running a restaurant. There is wisdom to the notion that fishing isn't about the catch; it's about everything else happening around the experience. In my case, it led to an ongoing quest to better understand a fish's relationship to its native home, the place where it evolved and how it is a strand of a place connected to species that also evolved there.

Everywhere in the world today, exotic non-native species are on the move, disrupting ecosystems, transforming them, re-ordering them, and in some cases destroying a web of life that evolution had created. In the decades to come, climate change is going to accelerate that disorganization. Right now, exotic South Asian Burmese pythons are wreaking havoc on the Florida Everglades. They are a new apex predator haphazardly released into the ecosystem by people who were tired of caring for them as pets. They were dumped into the Everglades and Burmese pythons have no natural enemy in south Florida. What's the big deal, you ask?

Burmese pythons proliferate fast and they consume anything that will fit inside their mouths and be able to be digested while sliding through their stretchy GI tract. One survey suggested that these constricting snakes are linked to a 99 percent decrease in opossum observations, an 87.5 percent decrease in bobcat sightings, and a 99.3 percent drop in raccoon and 100 percent drop in rabbit viewings. Birds have become rarer. Pythons have even eaten American alligators. They have devastated what was one of the richest wetlands in the world.

Aquatic and terrestrial invaders, like plants, are equally worrisome, causing ecological and economic damage. On Yellowstone's front doorstep, non-native cheatgrass—originally planted by ranchers in the West to provide early forage to exotic cattle—is among plant invaders moving up toward the vaunted Northern Range where large numbers of grazing animals gather.

"Noxious weeds are spreading at an alarming rate in Yellowstone, where approximately 200 nonnative plant species have been identified. Others that present the most serious threat to the park include aggressive invaders such as spotted knapweed, oxeye daisy, yellow and dalmatian toadflax, St. Johnswort and leafy spurge," the park stated in a report. "Invading, nonnative plants spread quickly, often displacing native species and disrupting local plant and animal communities. Many of these plants are not edible to native wildlife such as elk, bison, bighorn sheep, mule deer, and pronghorn antelope, and they can suffer a loss of feed. In some areas, rare plants could be lost."

Similar things are happening with aquatic invaders in Yellowstone and across the country.

Clint Sestrich, a fisheries biologist with the Custer Gallatin National Forest—which has partnered with Yellowstone in trying to preserve and restore native fish, wrote in the journal *Yellowstone Science* that no greater threat exists to public recreation, infrastructure, and aquatic resources in the Greater Yellowstone Ecosystem than that from aquatic invasive species.

"The Greater Yellowstone Ecosystem is a nationally important hydrologic resource with over 27,000 miles of streams. Species considered by managers to pose the greatest risk to ecologic, recreational, and economic values include zebra and quagga mussels, Asian clams, Asian carp species, Eurasian watermilfoil, hydrilla, flowering rush, whirling disease, and viral hemorrhagic septicemia. Zebra and quagga mussels, collectively called dreissenids, are of particular concern given their ability to attach to watercraft, survive many days out of water, and cause irreparable harm. Once established, these efficient filter feeders can significantly reduce the biomass of phytoplankton, the foundation of aquatic food webs. Dreissenid mussels have the ability to rapidly colonize hard surfaces thus blocking water supply pipes of power and water treatment plants, irrigation systems, and industrial facilities. In addition, mussels can impact recreation activities and associated economies by covering docks, boats, and beaches." The Idaho Aquatic Nuisance Species Task Force estimated the potential economic impacts to infrastructure and recreation from a dreissenid introduction would be in excess of $94 million. "Fortunately, dreissenid mussels are not yet present in the Greater Yellowstone Ecosystem due to proactive watercraft inspection and decontamination programs," he and his coauthors wrote.

Yellowstone, touted as a beacon of preservation, is at the forefront of a Sisyphean struggle to hold the line on its native flora and fauna. Is it merely a desperate attempt to delay the inevitable? The biggest battle of the moment involves fish.

In his book, *The Imperiled Cutthroat: Tracing the Fate of Yellowstone's Native Trout*, Australian angler and author Greg French expressed skepticism about Yellowstone's campaign to retain as many of its native species parts as possible. French offers this thought: "What I am suggesting is that, just as there is no way to define species, there is no way to define natural or unnatural, native or nonnative, and worse, the aims of preserving biodiversity are often at odds with our ideals for animal welfare. We have a quandary: conservation is more complex than most of us are able to comprehend, certainly more complex than most of us want to comprehend."

By the point at which French offers the above rumination, page 244 in his 254-page book, he has struck the pose of the classic effete fly-fisherman, and implies that the purpose of having a healthy trout population is paramount to serve the interests of people. He establishes himself as being squarely in the camp of a fish is a fish is a fish. And he argues that people in the Greater Yellowstone Ecosystem are making rather much ado about nothing for their tenacious efforts to maintain and restore cold water fisheries where exotic trout have supplanted or threaten to invade and replace native "wild" species. Staking out that perspective makes sense, since Mr. French's home waters are the make-believe streams of New Zealand where the river stretches, while full of exotic salmonids, are an artificial construction; they are in many ways parallel to that swimming pool I encountered at the outdoors show in Minneapolis.

Why does having native wild fish matter in the Greater Yellowstone Ecosystem? Why does it matter that we have a beating heart in our chest and an organ located between our ears that allows you to visualize wildness right now without actually sitting in it?

For me it has to do with that oft-quoted observation made by John Muir, "When we try to pick out anything by itself, we find it hitched to everything else in the Universe." And to Aldo Leopold's eternal wisdom in A Sand County Almanac and his humbling acknowledgment of how little we know about the innerworkings of ecosystems from predator-prey trophic cascades down to the microscopic level of thermophiles living in Yellowstone's extreme super-heated environs. "To save every cog and wheel is the first precaution of the intelligent tinkerer," he wrote.

Some, let's use Greg French as an example, might view fish as interchangeable pieces in a river system. Lose one species, no worries; simply replace it with another. Have "vacant habitat"? Plant one. Lose a wild population, just refill the waters with captive-reared hatchery fish. That, after all, has been part of the put-and-take hatchery mindset that dominated recreation fishing management for the 20th century. And in Yellowstone what happened there exposes just how uninformed early wildlife managers were about potential causes and effects.

Dr. Todd M. Koel, Yellowstone's chief fisheries biologist, has been on the front lines of dealing with the consequences of the proliferation of lake trout. Koel is an adherent of Leopold and invokes the quote: "A thing is right when it tends to preserve the integrity, stability, and beauty of the biotic community. It is wrong when it tends otherwise." What his predecessors did in Yellowstone in head-spinning. At first, rangers in 1881 put Yellowstone cutthroat trout into "fishless waters"—creeks where waterfalls had served as barriers, preventing fish from naturally reaching them. Then, in 1889, non-native fish—lake trout, brook trout, brown trout, and rainbow trout—were brought in. It took about 40 years before managers realized those introductions had caused loss of native fish and stocking efforts were discontinued.

But not halted was the practice of taking cutthroat trout out of Yellowstone Lake and transplanting them elsewhere, including places where they had never occurred. "More than 818 million cutthroat eggs were shipped by rail to locations across North America. They were also stocked extensively across the park, including waters that already supported native cutthroat trout with unique genetics (e.g., Slough, Soda Butte, Grayling, and Specimen creeks). Overall, from the early 1880s to the mid-1950s, more than 300 million fish were stocked throughout Yellowstone. As a result, non-native species became firmly established in most lakes and in larger rivers and streams; exceptions were Yellowstone Lake, the upper Yellowstone River, the upper Lamar River, the upper Snake River, and tributaries to these watersheds," Koel and co-authors write.

"Constrained by waterfalls, watershed divides, or other landscape features, the native fish within these stocked waters were forced to live together with the non-natives, be displaced to downstream habitats, or die," they added. "Non-native lake trout, brook trout, and brown trout consume native fish and compete for resources, thereby reducing native abundance and, as occurred in the Madison, lower Gibbon, and lower Firehole rivers, completely eliminating natives (Arctic grayling and west-slope cutthroat trout) from large pristine habitats in the park. Native fish losses also occur through interbreeding. Because Yellowstone cutthroat trout, westslope cutthroat trout, and rainbow trout are closely related, they can hybridize when living in the same areas. Hybrid individuals can also be capable of reproduction, further exacerbating the problem. In only a few generations, hybrids proliferated in many rivers and streams. Large areas of the park where significant hybridization has occurred include the Bechler, Gallatin, lower Lamar, and lower Yellowstone rivers, and their tributaries."

The legacy of "bucket biology" in which anglers and scientists of yore hauled their favorite exotic fish into waterways and dumped them in to create new fishing opportunity is widely documented. "Critical and at-risk populations of wild fish are shrinking all the time," my friend Marshall Cutchin, a former professional fishing guide who worked in Key West, Florida told me.

Cutchin today lives in the Colorado Rockies, is the founder of one of the most widely read recreational fishing sites online, *MidCurrent*, and he is an outspoken conservationist who still carries on a lifelong passion of fighting to save the Florida Everglades. "If you think only about wild fish, which none of the commercial fishing groups do, and if you think about native species, they are the most threatened of the threatened. The most common fish are hatchery-raised stock fish. More imperiled are naturally-producing wild fish and most endangered are native fish that remain in the waters where they evolved."

He goes down a list of salmonids, citing native wild brook trout in the Eastern U.S., cutthroat trout in the West, steelhead and salmon on the West Coast, and Atlantic salmon along the Atlantic. "They are signposts, signals that we completely fucked up everything. But there are others who only view Nature simply. They say as long as we got fish to catch then they are worth protecting. The thing that makes them worth protecting is we can catch them, and if that's true then they want to make sure we have healthy populations. But that has nothing to do with biodiversity or habitat protection or acknowledging how native and wild fish are a remarkable expression of the place where they evolved. And the rare genetics they carry that speak to it. And to the role they play within the intricate fabric of the food web."

Wild native fish, especially colder-water species, are in trouble everywhere. Trout and salmon are joined by sturgeon, paddlefish and dozens of oceanic species that have been overfished, become casualties of habitat destruction, and now are facing warming, more acidic waters caused by higher concentrations of absorbed carbon dioxide. Cutchin often hears from friends and colleagues who say safeguarding the last bastions of wild fish is a lost cause, that the changes coming will be overwhelming and absolute. He doesn't accept surrender. "I think not accepting that as an inevitability is the most important thing worth fighting for," he says, but it requires humans slowing their consumption of nature. Recreation doesn't equal and isn't automatically synonymous with conservation, he says. Using a resource isn't tantamount to being an advocate for its protection.

The true test of a conservationist, Cutchin says, is a user who is willing to consciously not consume the very thing that gives her/him pleasure.

Yes, it was a mess that current biologists are trying to clean up and their strategy is an outgrowth of a landmark document, the Native Fish Conservation Plan, crafted in 2010. It's an all-out attempt to eradicate non-native fish so that natives can be restored without hybridizing and foremost to establish new strongholds that might be able to withstand coming changes. They will function as a living genetic storehouse.

So let us return to lake trout. Using a variety of forensic techniques, investigators determined that lake trout had been deliberately and illegally put into the lake. Scientists, knowing what had happened elsewhere with elicit laker transplants, evinced alarm and despair. At stake was the world's biological stronghold for a native salmonid, Yellowstone cutthroat trout. The occurrence became a poster child for what can go wrong when "exotic, invasive" species enter "natural" systems.

In 1995, the National Park Service convened an emergency panel of experts to craft an action plan to confront the interlopers. For myriad reasons, they couldn't poison the water nor logistically would it work because of the lake's vastness. They had no silver bullet. What they shared was a conviction that they wouldn't allow the usurping predator to wipe out Yellowstone's most emblematic fish.

Lake trout, largest of the freshwater char, are deep-dwelling fish. They spawn in the lakes they inhabit. They live out their entire lives many fathoms beneath the surface. Cutthroat trout spawn in small, shallow creeks and rivers; they rise to eat bugs on the water surface. Their habits make them accessible to be eaten by other non-fish species; Yellowstone grizzly bears, for instance, congregated in the tributaries to Yellowstone Lake every spring when cutthroat trout moved into them to lay their eggs. Lake trout are less or non-accessible to the creatures that cutthroats are.

One more thing about the differences between the two species: cutthroat trout are smaller, easy prey for hulking, piscivorous (fish-eating) lake trout and lake trout have few effective predators, save for people. A mature lake trout, which can grow to weigh dozens of pounds, eats 40-plus cutthroats a year. The cutthroat population tumbled precipitously and reached five percent of its historic high.

The need to muster a swift response brought another kind of devastating blow to park managers. Millions of dollars would be necessary to launch a gill-netting campaign and research program to identify other strategies and it meant that Yellowstone had to divert millions of dollars away from other operational priorities. Even then it wouldn't be enough. That's why it pays to have good friends. Created to serve as an ally in helping Yellowstone confront critical needs that aren't covered in the normal Congressional appropriations process, the Yellowstone Park Foundation (today Yellowstone Forever) stepped forward and pledged to contribute millions of dollars annually, on top of what Yellowstone had, to get the unprecedented lake-trout control program set in motion. "This is why we exist and the need was urgent and obvious," says JD Davis of Yellowstone Forever. "There was no time to sit back. The consequences of inaction would be losing the very fish species that is synonymous with Yellowstone. You're investing money not to build a new visitor center. You're doing it to prevent a very bad thing from happening."

Another major ally was the Wyoming state chapter of Trout Unlimited, along with other allies such as the Storer Foundation and Greater Yellowstone Coalition as well as individuals who love the park and recognized the gravity of the moment.

The most obvious option was plotting how to attack and deplete the lake trout population as quickly as possible. The park and tactical fishing experts unleashed a gauntlet of gill nets and trap nets but struggled to identify where lake trout were feeding and clustering. Nets were deployed as soon as the ice cleared in late spring and weren't pulled until October. Each year, somewhat alarmingly, the number of lake trout removed and pounds extracted continued to climb, meaning they hadn't put a dent in the population.

"We were taking out a lot of lake trout and it meant that a lot of cut-throat trout were being consumed and we didn't know how to proceed because we weren't knocking down the lake trout numbers fast enough," said Pat Bigelow, who has worked in fisheries for four decades and has been on the front lines of lake trout suppression.

Desperate for answers, the Park Service convened two scientific panels drawing upon insights gleaned from other lakes where battles with lake trout were being waged. In 2009, Yellowstone then enlisted the services of a family-run fishing business that possessed special credentials. The commercial company, Hickey Brothers Fisheries, based in Baileys Harbor, Wisconsin, knew how to intensely target fish populations in the Great Lakes. They erected arrays of gill nets and traps that proved to be remarkably effective in catching big lake trout, which had pushed the native cutthroat population to the edge of piscatorial annihilation.

An article appearing in the journal *Yellowstone Science* speaks to the enormity of the undertaking. "Estimated abundance of age two and older lake trout increased from 125,000 fish in 1998 to 790,000 fish in 2012, despite the removal of over 800,000 fish during this period. The Park Service suppression netting effort was then greatly increased, resulting in more than 1.5 million lake trout removed from 2012 to 2016. Lake trout abundance remained at more than 700,000 fish in 2015."

On a snowy afternoon at Big Sky, Montana, Tom Spruance and his son and daughter were relaxing after a morning of downhill skiing. They were meeting with JD Davis, whom Spruance has supported on a number of fronts. He told the story of how his son fell in love with fishing and how Yellowstone Forever's campaign to address lake trout served as fodder for a number of father-son discussions about nature, the challenges facing it, and the empowering actions individuals can take to be part of solutions.

Spruance had also supported the work of the Scripps Oceanography Institute in San Diego, which has been a global leader in trying to address the loss of coral reefs. Anchors of biological diversity in marine ecosystems, corral has been dying or disappearing at an astonishing rate, caused by pollution, overfishing, ocean floor trawling, and bleaching linked to climate change. "I see my philanthropy as a way of investing in the future, of the world my kids will know after I'm gone," he said. "When you have a finite amount of resources you want to make a difference and I see these two areas as having impact." The genesis of this book grew out of conversations with Davis and Spruance.

Two decades after lake trout were identified, I ventured out into the waters of Yellowstone Lake, on three successive summers, joining park aquatic specialists and some hired guns as they were mounting a counterattack. Population models that also produced distribution maps of lake trout locations and densities in the lake led researchers to conclude that in 2012 the lake trout population was no longer growing. Still, a mark and capture study of lake trout coordinated by the Park Service and Montana State University resulted in a population estimate in 2013, of there being 367,650 lake trout eight inches or larger. Meaning, larger reproducing fish were being depleted by suppression efforts.

A number of search and destroy techniques have been put into practice. Besides gill netting, radio transceivers were attached to thousands of fish, dubbed "Judas fish," that have led human eradicators to the places where lake trout gather and spawn. Researchers have tried electroshock techniques and they've dumped the rotting carcasses of dead fish on spawning beds to smother eggs. The assault eventually started paying small dividends and then, in 2019, Yellowstone officials announced they believed they had turned a corner in not only halting the lake trout proliferation but suppressing lake numbers enough so that enough mature cutthroats could spawn and produce enough surviving fry to perpetuate the population.

Eradication efforts have resulted in a 71 percent decrease of older fish, a decrease in fish three to five years old and holding the line on young lakers. This isn't, however, just a battle between a voracious exotic fish and a vulnerable native one. It's about going under the hood of a system and now we arrive at the punch line, the one that made Tom Spruance and other citizens want to step up to the plate. They too don't accept the rationale that a fish is just a fish.

The quarrel that people have with Greg French is not directed at this self-interested angler himself; it is with his mindset. It is true that changes are coming, fast, and that at the current rate of warming, the cold-water fisheries we know today could be in big trouble by the middle of this century. But it's not just the presence of a suite of native wild trout. They are indicators of dramatic changes in the systems and some liken their falling to that of dominos. No, this isn't a Jeremiad or prattle of Chicken Little: it is a concern being expressed for the equivalent of an intricate Swiss watch.

Still, if you are a disciple of fish only being valuable if people can catch them, consider the sticker that adorns the bumper of the truck I drive and was given to me by an ecologist I respect. It reads: "Lake trout kill elk."

Wild fish exhibit special adaptations that come from evolving in specific locales. Their lifeway routines have a synergy of interdependence with those of other species. Since the year of their discovery in Yellowstone Lake, upwards of four million lake trout have been eliminated and 300,000 fish are still being removed annually. Stopping the costly removal is not an option. In just one year, 1998, as the lake trout population was ramping up, researchers estimated that between three and four million cutthroat trout were eaten. The difference of having one fish over another means that tons of cutthroat trout biomass that would ordinarily benefit other species did not cycle through the Yellowstone food chain. The impacts reached all the way down to phyto- and zoo-plankton levels of the food chain, affecting water quality and nutrient levels. But the biggest visible ripple effects were apparent in 20 different species that included cutthroat trout in their diet.

How can the presence or absence of one species ripple? What's the difference between having a species that evolved in a system versus one that is introduced thereby becoming an interloper? This is the quintessence of ripple effects.

For the last decade, Yellowstone, along with crucial funding provided by the park's non-profit partner, Yellowstone Forever, Trout Unlimited and other conservation groups, have poured millions of dollars into gill-netting lake trout to reduce their numbers and allow cutthroat trout to recover. Why? Because other species teeter on fish.

Lake trout, being voracious, deep-water-dwelling fish eaters, reduced cutthroat trout numbers by 90 percent. That represented the first of several dominos to fall. With cutthroats no longer spawning in several dozen tributary streams, their absence, in turn, affected different species that relied on them for sustenance, including grizzly bears.

During the late 1980s, bears were active on 93 percent of the lake's cutthroat spawning tributaries with evidence of fish consumption on 61 percent or more than 60 different streams. At least 44 different bears congregated and the number grew to include upwards of one of every five grizzlies in the entire Greater Yellowstone Ecosystem. But as lake trout took hold, bear presence declined and in a three-year span from 2008 to 2011, no bear activity was documented. In parallel, the number of black bears feeding on trout declined by 64 to 84 percent, depending on the year, reaching the latter as the estimated amount of normally available cutthroat biomass plunged 90 percent. In actual fish numbers, the estimate was that 21,000 cutthroats were consumed by grizzlies in the late 1980s, just 2200 in the 1990s and only 302 in the late 2000s.

In response, bears had to find an alternative food and they found it, researchers say, in young elk calves. It just so happens that the window when cutthroat trout spawn coincides with the time of elk calving. At one point, preliminary evidence showed that bears were killing about 41 percent of elk calves—more than wolves killed. A study found that grizzlies on average killed between one and six ungulates a year, 13 percent of which were elk calves. Yet more extensive investigation suggests that grizzlies on the park's Northern Range kill 19 calves each year and within the Yellowstone Lake watershed, 7 calves. Whereas in the 1980s meat from ungulates comprised 5 percent of a grizzly's diet at peak elk-calving time, since the crash of cutthroat trout it has soared above 50 percent. Thus, lake trout kill elk, ergo ripple effects expanding far beyond the shore of Yellowstone Lake.

An added wrinkle is that it's dangerous for some bears to be a meat eater. Female mother bears in recent years, linked to a decline in cutthroat trout and possibly to the startling disappearance of the whitepark forest, which yields cone crops filled with nutritious seeds that bears gorge upon to fatten up, have more meat in their diet. Male bears will kill the cubs of female bears because when cubs die and females stop lactating, they can go back into estrus and males will breed with them.

Meanwhile, hunters and outfitters and guides in Montana had blamed the reintroduction of wolves on a dramatic decline in Yellowstone elk stretching from the late 1990s to around 2010, notes Yellowstone's chief wolf biologist Doug Smith. In addition to pressure from lobos, and drought, and years of winter hunts, and competition for grass on the Northern Range from bison, grizzlies were a huge culprit, as well as cougars.

Smith wears two hats in Yellowstone. He's both the park's lead wolf researcher and he double-duties as the overseer of avian (bird) conservation. He doesn't remember the moment he realized that a serious ecological crisis was under way in Yellowstone. A key piece in the puzzle, for what he now calls "an expanding picture of avian collapse," presented itself on the normally tranquil tarn of Riddle Lake.

There, floating upside down, dead in the water, was a young trumpeter swan killed by a predatory bald eagle. The cygnet was the only one born in the park that year. Not long afterward, Smith received another grim clue while paddling a canoe across the southern reaches of Yellowstone Lake. Littering the glassy surface were vast patches of feathers from ducks, California gulls, white pelicans, double-crested cormorants and Caspian terns torn apart and eaten.

"For all of the attention that gets paid to this park's geothermal features and its famous large mammals, what we're seeing with birds is as dramatic as anything making headlines with wolves, grizzlies, and bison," he told me for a story I wrote that appeared in *National Geographic*.

"We could be witnessing the complete elimination of some nesting bird species in Yellowstone."

Along with the species mentioned above he adds common loons to the list of casualties that could soon vanish from the nation's most iconic nature preserve hailed for its wildlife. Three converging forces set off a lethal chain reaction: the rippling impacts of an exotic fish, lake trout, which have decimated what used to be the last major stronghold for native Yellowstone cutthroat trout; climate change altering habitat; and humans haphazardly displacing sensitive species.

It's a jarring glimpse, Smith says, into the challenges facing natural systems once thought stable. Native species that evolved with certain places are getting interrupted, pushed around and sometimes eliminated. "The world as we've known it is being transformed. And, if it's happening in Yellowstone, it is happening everywhere," Smith says.

Since wolves were restored to Yellowstone in the mid-1990s, the park has been touted as the vanguard for an intact, fully functioning ecosystem with every major species present that was there when Europeans arrived on the continent half a millennium ago. Smith says that vaunted status is in jeopardy.

Most startling is the broad pattern of "ecological mayhem" playing out at Yellowstone Lake, one of the largest high-elevation freshwater lakes in the world and the liquid centerpiece of the park. River otters, too, were seriously affected by having fewer cutthroat trout.

Yet Smith says the biggest cause-and-effect correlation has involved fish-eating birds. In the early 1990s there were 62 osprey nests documented on Yellowstone Lake with 67 fledglings in the summer of 1994. In 2017, there were just three osprey nests and one fledgling produced. Osprey are exclusively fish eaters so they went elsewhere. Bald eagles, meanwhile, are formidable opportunistic generalists.

After cutthroat trout numbers fell, eagles turned their hunting from fish to other birds. Yellowstone Lake has small colonies of California gulls, American white pelicans, double-crested cormorants and Caspian terns on nubs of sand and rock like the Molly Islands in Yellowstone Lake.

Eagle predation and unusual weather in late spring have pushed those to the brink of elimination, Smith says. Caspian terns have vanished and there's been no reproduction of California gulls. Eagles also have keyed in on loons and, in addition, have begun targeting young swans at Riddle Lake: one of just two locations where breeding pairs of trumpeters have successfully nested.

On top of that, there is another complication. In recent years, Canada geese have proliferated in the park and high numbers of goslings have provided a bounty for eagles, maintaining eagle numbers that have brought more predation on other vulnerable birds. Geese, being aggressively territorial, also drive birds from their nests.

The last thing Yellowstone managers are going to do is lethally control numbers of geese and bald eagles, the latter being America's national avian symbol and ironically a bird that not long ago nationwide was on the federal Endangered Species list.

Meanwhile, the Greater Yellowstone loon population represents the southernmost enclave in the Lower 48 and it is one of the most geographically isolated. Just 18 breeding pairs remain in Wyoming, 70 percent of those in Yellowstone. Loons have been beset by eagles taking young birds and by abnormally high water levels, due to precipitous snowmelt in the spring, swamping under their nests.

Trumpeter swans and loons contribute much to the wild ambiance of Yellowstone, Smith says. Snow-white trumpeters have the largest wing span of any bird in North America and are known for their gracefulness in flight and on the water. With loons, their haunting crepuscular trills are as primordial as any howling lobo.

Swans are long-lived and the number of permanent residents in the park can be counted on one hand. For a few consecutive years, Smith said, following an aerial survey, no new cygnets were being produced. In 2011, when just five swans remained, Yellowstone convened a meeting of national experts to advance recommendations for how to save the resident population, warning that extirpation appeared to be imminent.

"If all of these problems were linear, solving them might be easier but with declines of species it's never just one thing. It's usually a combination of all of the above," Smith says.

One of the experts summoned to the 2011 meeting was Ruth Shea. As director of a research effort called Northern Rockies Trumpeter Swan Stewards, Shea is recognized as "the grand dame" of swan conservation in the Greater Yellowstone Ecosystem, having begun her conservation work in 1976.

"If the present trend continues, I don't think there's a snowball's chance you can save the resident breeding swan population in Yellowstone," she told me. Historically, when trumpeter swans continent-wide were pushed to the precipice of extinction caused by market hunters who killed them for their meat and feather plumes, Yellowstone was a last refuge and the early research by George Wright paved the way for creating Red Rock Lakes National Wildlife Refuge west of the park.

"If it weren't for Yellowstone being central to rescue efforts, we might not have trumpeter swans today," Shea says. "It's a sad day to think the place that saved them can't keep them alive. It's not devastating biologically because swan numbers outside the park are increasing but symbolically it reveals the challenges our most iconic parks are under."

Yellowstone, she notes, is confronting a constant onslaught of pressure brought by groups and individuals that want more recreational access, not less.

Should backcountry areas that harbor fragile species that need solitude to survive be put off limits to human intrusion? Shea points to a paradox at Riddle Lake. After Yellowstone managers delayed the opening of hiking trails to the lake in order to safeguard mother grizzly bears raising new cubs more than a decade ago, swans "became wilder" and more skittish around people. That had a downside, too.

When trails were re-opened, young swan cygnets and their parents would flee nesting areas along the shore and head out to the middle of the lake where they were vulnerable and immediately got preyed upon by eagles. Shea notes that a field report from as far back as the 1930s documented that human presence can drive sensitive swans from nests.

Between 1930 and 2010, a total of 486 cygnets fledged in Yellowstone, and 388 (80 percent) of them were produced from 12 lakes, Shea noted. By 1984 nesting pairs had decreased to six. During that time, the clutch size was the lowest of any population studied in North America.

To try improving the chances of nesting success, Yellowstone has installed artificial nesting platforms for both swans and loons. To little avail, researchers have also tried "grafting," hatching swan cygnets at a lab and putting them in wild nests with the hope they'll be adopted.

As difficult as natural swan and loon reproduction has become in Yellowstone, pressure from eagles makes their survival more dire. "When your population is reduced to handfuls of birds and even a smaller number of breeding pairs, it doesn't take the loss of many before death outpaces reproduction and eventually they just wink out," Smith said.

When a species disappears from its homeland, the loss goes far beyond visuals. All of the bird species Smith and his team are chronicling exist in relatively small numbers and on the edge, yet in Yellowstone they've persisted.

"We know that climate change has a potential to profoundly affect wildlife by itself, but you add in other factors and the complicated natural systems that exist in places like Yellowstone could become simplified with less biological diversity," Smith explains. "Every species makes its contribution to a richness whose worth cannot be calculated."

The birds of Yellowstone provide more than photo opportunities. They carry knowledge that has been passed along, over millennia, from one generation to the next. It includes fine-tuned courses of migration that enable them to travel thousands of miles between their summer breeding grounds in Yellowstone and winter habitat around Baja Mexico or the Gulf; the accrued, hard-learned lessons of where to feed and successfully nest; and how to outwit predators.

"Once its lost, it's incredibly hard to bring it back again, if you ever can," Smith says.

He referenced the observations by Muir and Leopold. The point of their ruminations, he said, is that, in nature, everything is interconnected. He says the irony is that Yellowstone has been an exemplar of that ideal and the notion of dynamic equilibrium in wildlife populations but it might also become a case study in how things with exotic species can cause systems to fall apart.

The conundrum now before Yellowstone is deciding when to intervene versus being hands off, Smith says. "The rule of thumb we use is if impacts are natural, then we leave things alone but if something is human caused then we will take action to provide remedies to problems," Smith says. "Introduction of an exotic species is an example of that, so is human use and climate change."

Yellowstone's mission is to protect park wonders but if climate change has a deleterious effect on species, it could result in managers constantly trying to mitigate harmful impacts: a radical departure from current protocol that favors "letting nature take its course."

Eradicating lake trout entirely isn't possible but millions of the hulking fish have been taken. Dr. Koel stated that cutthroat losses have stabilized, though it could take many years—if ever—before they support other species like they did previously.

"The magnitude of the lake trout problem in Yellowstone Lake remains enormous. Lake trout have had several decades to expand throughout the lake and pioneer several spawning areas. Yellowstone Lake provides near-perfect spawning and rearing habitat for lake trout with few natural predators present. Lake trout are long-lived, and one individual female can produce thousands of eggs each year. The survival of young lake trout in the lake is estimated to be 2.5 times higher than in its native range. Even without cutthroat trout, other foods in Yellowstone Lake would support a large lake trout population. Reducing the lake trout population to a level that will have only minor impacts to the cutthroat trout population is predicted to take until at least 2025, provided we maintain current high levels of suppression effort." That year has been extended.

Welcome to conservation in the Anthropocene. If you want to stand for something, if you want to defend an assemblance of wild nature and pass it on in as fine of condition as you found it, it requires a vigilant endless attempt to hold the line. The great conservationist Thomas Lovejoy dismissed the long-held Manichean perspective that safeguarding the Natural world comes at a cost to humans, society and the world, "…the choice is not between wild places or people, it is between a rich or an impoverished existence for Man."

Smith and Koel say that the motive is not about preserving natural function the way one would a museum specimen and hold it in place forever. Just like with restoring wolves it's about having important parts in place and allowing the system to be a teacher. "Native fish cannot fulfill their ecological role in Yellowstone if their populations are extirpated or remain decimated, hybridized, and isolated," Koel says.

In 1977, resource economists made a rough calculation, speculating that the value of naturally-functioning ecosystems was $33 trillion annually or twice the value of all the goods and services produced by humans. That was half a century ago. It goes beyond assessing the value of ecosystem services. What is the intrinsic value of an incomparable place?

The superintendent of Yellowstone, Cam Sholly, who is a military veteran, says: "There will never be a point where we can lower our guard because if we do, lake trout numbers will bounce back. The upshot is that through action the seemingly impossible turned out to be achievable. He sees that anti-lake trout campaign as a metaphor that applies to holding the line on other exotics and gleaning as much information as possible to help guide strategies for slowing the impact of climate change. To do nothing, in his mind, is unconscionable. Nobody wants to be the person helping to write Yellowstone's obituary.

Great Migrations
(America's Own Version of the Serengeti)

T HROUGH THE FIRST HALF of the 19th century, it was still possible to be positioned in the middle of the untilled, unbroken American prairie and see bison in all directions, as far as your vision could reach. Passing through the great massings of subherds, mile upon mile, could take days. The biomass, i.e. the physical bodies of 30 million bison, is a lot of energy flowing through the ecosystem. Billions of prairie dogs would've been at their feet in cities of burrows. Together, big ungulate and little rodent, each a keystone species, formed an engine of habitat creation that lasted a while longer and then disappeared. The short- and mixed-grass prairie was home to every major mammal species, save for mountain goats, that you see in Yellowstone today.

The bison and prairie dog ecosystem supported hundreds of other species intertwined in dynamic synergy. The movements of bison, with their grazing, defecation and corporeal decomposition part of a continual positive feedback loop of nutrient recycling, produced rich soils and an interwoven tableau of plantlife.

When you think of the things that "hold natural landscapes together," what comes to mind? Mention the word *Serengeti* to a room full of informed enthusiastic lovers of nature and, to a person, there is no question what you are referencing. The same kind of instant "place recognition" exists when one says "Yellowstone National Park."

Now meld those two geographical icons together into this: "*American Serengeti.*" Although the allusion may initially elicit head scratching for some, it is this conjunction that represents one of the most exciting emerging frontiers for pondering 21st century landscape-level conservation. Yes, there's a parallel to be drawn between the heralded mass movement of millions of large mammals (wildebeest and zebra, lions and cheetahs, antelopes and elephants) across the famous plain in eastern Africa and the ironically lesser-known marvel happening right in the middle of the American West.

The movement of two million wildebeest is considered epic in our time; imagine ten times as many bison constantly on the move across the plains and prairie stretching from southern Canada to Texas and into Mexico. Some literalists today assert that it's wrong to draw a comparison between Greater Yellowstone and the African Serengeti in the 2020s with the latter having 70 large mammal and 500 bird species. Yellowstone Park and its surrounding environs have 67 mammal species and about a dozen large ones. While the Great Migration that occurs across the Serengeti in Kenya and Tanzania is massive and conspicuous and the flow of mammals in Greater Yellowstone far more discreet and inconspicuous, it is perhaps the only location that serves as an adequate reference point.

Yellowstone represents a central hub not only for tourists; it's a nexus to some of the greatest wildlife migrations still occurring on the North American continent. Together with the park and the mosaic of public wildlands and private property surrounding it, the larger ecosystem is home today to the *longest* migrations for elk, mule deer, and pronghorn known to exist.

While the phenomenon has been happening for millennia, and active use of the pathways stretch back 8,000 years predating construction of the Egyptian pyramids on the other side of the world, these unparalleled treks of "charismatic megafauna" in Greater Yellowstone have, in fact, only recently been "discovered" and mapped. Thanks to GPS technology and other sophisticated tracking devices, the journeys are only now being understood.

"All along, these migrations were right under our noses and though generally we knew wildlife moved seasonally between high elevations and lower terrain, we didn't understand fully the whys and wheres," says Matthew Kauffman, a wildlife biologist with the U.S. Geological Survey who is a leader of the Wyoming Migration Initiative, today an internationally recognized multi-agency research outfit pioneering the study of migrations.

Kauffman likens the giant leap forward to scientists, upon invention of electron microscopes, having their eyes opened to a mind-blowing, previously unknown world of super-minute life forms, such as viruses and structures within single-celled organisms. It existed nearly invisibly just beyond the grasps of human comprehension.

Now, at the opposite end of the spectrum, on a macro-scale, satellite technology has brought illumination to the routes of hundreds of thousands of wild, hooved animals, wonders of nature that command as much awe as the movements of neotropical songbirds flying thousands of miles twice a year between the northern and southern hemispheres, the remarkable life histories of sea turtles and spawning salmon.

That's the inspiring, tantalizing part of "the American Serengeti." Yet accompanying the emerging revelations is a daunting reality. Without action taken to secure landscape protection in the next few decades, these ancient animal movements and the integrity of the corridors where they occur could be lost forever. It's amazing how an understanding of what scientists call "the Great Migration" has evolved. I remember when it was just in its nascency.

In 2005, Steve Belinda and I were standing in the middle of a panorama of federal public land known as the Pinedale Anticline whose oversight belongs to the Bureau of Land Management. He was a wildlife biologist with the BLM stationed in Pinedale, Wyoming.

To the uninitiated, Pinedale is located in the middle of nowhere and yet this quaint, sweet little town factors into the center of thinking about some of the greatest wildlife migrations remaining on the face of the earth. Pinedale has, for many years, been a crossroad where natural history converges with both the Old and New Wests. It was here, at "Trapper's Point," where between 1825 and 1840 "mountain men" of European ancestry gathered with members of indigenous tribes at events known as rendezvous, exchanging goods, fur pelts, and parlay related to the short-lived global fur trade in beaver.

Belinda handed me a map and explained the kind of intense industrial strength infrastructure that would pepper the Anticline in the next few years; his description was hard to imagine. But he was adamant. He had seen his BLM colleagues laying out a plan where gas drilling was going to occur. Having earlier worked as a biologist in the Permian Basin of New Mexico and West Texas, he knew what was coming; but the public didn't.

During these years, a predecessor to the Anticline, the Jonah Gas Field, had roared into full production. Then Wyoming Governor Dave Freudenthal, who was always a fan of Wyoming's views, saw the industrial footprint and was aghast. He referred to gas development occurring there as a sacrifice zone, "an example of what not to do" with energy production, and which industry officials claimed would be done in ways that were compatible with nature.

For Wyoming, the prospect of the money was just too good to pass up. And so the gas boom went super nova, with oil and gas executives, and politicians favorable to their activities strutting with a rhetorical swagger, dismissing the protests of environmentalists and government and independent scientists like Belinda. What was at stake?

Like the famous migration in Alaska involving thousands of members of the Porcupine caribou herd across the Arctic National Wildlife Refuge, this part of Wyoming too is a wildlife superhighway, he said, then noting something that caught my attention. "And a big part of it is going to get wrecked." My trip to Pinedale was part of reporting assignments for *The Christian Science Monitor* and *U.S. News & World Report*.

At the time, a renowned conservation biologist with the Wildlife Conservation Society, who on several occasions has been nominated for a prestigious Indianapolis Prize given to the top conservationists in the world, was studying the movement of pronghorn hundreds of miles between Grand Teton National Park in the heart of Jackson Hole and these lands, which are part of the Upper Green River Valley that begins in the Wind River Mountains and straddles the Red Desert. Between 40,000 and 50,000 pronghorn moved in and across the treeless peneplain. Also, a few hundred made a seasonal commute between the outskirts of Pinedale and Grand Teton Park, hewing to a corridor that had likely been used for thousands upon thousands of years.

That scientist, Joel Berger, would work with a scientist in Grand Teton National Park named Steve Cain and with colleagues at the U.S. Forest Service and BLM to identify and declare a route—Path of the Pronghorn—to protect those movements from a rapid convergence of threats ranging from energy development to residential subdivisions, from highways where animal-human vehicle collisions was high, to simple things like barbed wire. Another researcher, working independently, was Hall Sawyer who had, like Berger had accomplished with pronghorn, put radio collars on mule deer moving between the Red Desert and Hoback Junction located to the north. They were on the leading edge of a game-changing epiphany that changed the way many people think about the organic ingredients of ecosystems and the things that can unravel them.

For years, the Greater Yellowstone Ecosystem was described mostly in terms of its topographical characteristics: by the names of towering mountain ranges, picturesque valleys, and rivers that transcended the artificial boundary lines of public and private lands, be they three different states, national parks and forests, BLM lands and federal wildlife refuges, or cattle ranches, farms, and city limits.

Lacking, however, was a unifying sense of cohesion that connected human communities in Greater Yellowstone and called them together in common cause. Less than a human generation ago—i.e., very recently— the concept of what makes Greater Yellowstone tick took a giant leap forward; it wasn't about discovering something "new" but rather confirming an ancient phenomenon that was already present, stretching back to the retreat of glaciers more than 10,000 years ago. It was happening before the Egyptians constructed their pyramids, before the Chinese built their dynasties, and prior to the civilizations known Great Zimbabwe, the Mayans, Incas, and Greco-Roman empires.

The tendrils of migration connectivity extend to every community in Greater Yellowstone: Green River, Wyoming at the far southern edge of the ecosystem with the Crazy Mountains in Montana; Lima, Montana and Idaho Falls, Idaho on the west with Greybull, Worland, Thermopolis and Lander, Wyoming. They connect the Arapahoe (*Hinono'eino*) and the Shoshones (*Newe*) with the Crow and Northern Cheyenne (*Tsêhéstáno*). They remain touchstones of remembrance for the Blackfeet (*Ampskapi Piikani*), Nez Perce (*Niimíipuu*), Salish-Kootenais (*Séliš-Ksupawičq̓nuk*) and the Lakotas.

They fuel a common regional identity and pride. They should give businesses on Main Street, which benefit mightily from nature tourism, an appreciation for pastoral ranchers and farmers who share their land as habitat and know that cows are better than condos. Our migrations, this bastion of free-ranging animals, is beyond the daily ken of modern life for Europeans, hinted at only in the haunting cave paintings of Lascaux: the "prehistoric Sistine Chapel."

No other bioregion has this kind of still-living linage between people and landscape. It is what most sets Greater Yellowstone apart and it is also a remarkable expression of our shared national natural heritage involving that tangible, elusive concept, wildness. Yet so often we don't treat it as a marvel. To lose even a single large mammal migration corridor is no different than losing a wild river to a dam or an historic human neighborhood to a freeway punched through it. Some resource extraction industries that operate under a cut and run mindset act as if they look upon corridor protection as a liability to their profit motive or with callous disregard.

The avian migrations of songbirds, waterfowl, and sandhill cranes that happen every year are miracles; so is the roundabout pilgrimages of salmon and sea turtles returning to the places where they were born.

The indigenous peoples dwelling in Greater Yellowstone were intimately in tune with wildlife animation, their movements harmonically matched. In a generic sense, scientists as well as hunters and later-arriving Euro-landowners knew that the great ungulate quadrupeds of Greater Yellowstone (elk, mule deer, pronghorn, bison, moose, and bighorn sheep) migrated; they knew the animals moved seasonally between summer high ground and more hospitable habitat, during winter, at lower elevations. They knew they showed up in certain places at certain times of the year.

But they didn't really understand the full mechanics of these commutes of survival or possess a sophisticated grasp of their nuances and fragilities. And then everything started to change. With the advancement of technology such as GPS tracking devices, remote "camera traps" set up along game trails, and adopting better ways of "seeing," researchers have brought to light something that was, from a practical point, right under their noses and yet nearly invisible. It was as if mitochondria were being viewed through an electron microscope.

When things are invisible, they are not factored into public- and private-land use planning, or even the awareness of millions of people moving through the landscapes of Greater Yellowstone, via highways, where they place their development and residential subdivisions, where they allow the siting of oil and gas fields.

Literally, if you count up all of the ungulates set in motion, circuiting through Greater Yellowstone—elk, bison, mule deer, pronghorn, moose, bighorn sheep, mountain goats, and white-tailed deer—we are talking well in excess of a million animals whose health is supporting and serving as a banquet table for wolves, cougars, bears, coyotes, foxes, wolverines, lynx and bobcats, badgers, eagles, falcons, hawks, ravens and other corvids, and rodents. This represents a fully-integrated network of pulsing, sparking energy, happening all at once both vertically and horizontally, which in most other places has had parts stripped away that may never be restored. The movement of ungulates via corridors is a conveyor belt of biomass— calories on the hoof—that fuel a terrestrial food chain unsurpassed. The body of a one-ton wild bison is formed by grass, water, sunlight, and soil; when the animal dies it feeds a wide range of other creatures and when they die others eat them, and when all die their decomposition adds nutrients back into the soil. The migrations of Greater Yellowstone distribute a sense of place far and wide. They fuel a hunting industry and wildlife watching economy. They re-bind indigenous people with lost or stored transcendental memory that has lain dormant.

Kauffman and Middleton are pioneering an epic monitoring effort that has attracted attention from around the world. People are paying attention to it from their rural outposts on the Serengeti Plain of Tanzania, the steppes of Mongolia and the tundra in the high Alaskan Arctic. For apart from these places, the kind of terrestrial journeys Kauffman and colleagues are chronicling can be described as nothing less than 21st century miracles.

The maps offering a cartographic and geographic representation of the corridors are wowing, though there is a race against time to get them identified on paper and distributed, suggests Robert Keiter, legal policy expert who has held the Wallace Stegner Chair at the University of Utah Law School. Ongoing research has revealed the importance of these annual migration rituals and is helping to coalesce support for the conservation measures necessary to safeguard the routes.

"Elk habitat in the GYE has declined noticeably since the 1970s, with estimates that 75 percent of elk and other ungulate migration routes in the GYE have been lost. According to one respected biologist who has extensively studied GYE migration patterns, the 'flow of elk in and out of Yellowstone sustains the entire ecosystem.'" The implication is that new housing subdivisions are being platted and approved by county commissions in Greater Yellowstone right now without any understanding of what their consequences are.

Here's a profound irony, however. In Montana, for example, today, there are an estimated 140,000 elk—some 50,000 elk over the desired population objective set by wildlife managers with the Montana Fish Wildlife and Parks Department. There is an abundance of elk in Wyoming and Idaho too. Most hunting units in those states have elk populations that are at, or above, desired levels. There are more elk today in the Northern Rockies that there has been in 120 years. And, as we will discover, wolves have hardly decimated elk as some predicted when lobos were reintroduced to Yellowstone and central Idaho in the mid 1990s. What's important to understand is that, in the Greater Yellowstone Ecosystem, the vanguard for wildlife migrations, ancient pathways used by elk going back thousands of years leading to Yellowstone Park in summer and back out again, are being plugged, disrupted, blocked, fragmented, by human development and other kinds of human pressure, including outdoor recreation on public lands.

As indigenous people know well, when migrations are lost in wildlife, so too are many other things, including a kind of biological memory that functions as a window into landscape health and knowledge and learned behavior. Knowledge and behavior central to the culture, language and lifeways of indigenous people and that, as long as wildlife migrations still exist, there is hope that the rich, deep lifeways of indigenous people can flourish again. It isn't just a matter of having "more elk;" vital is keeping their movements intact because after all the health of their movements positively ripples with other native species that share the landscape with them.

The Wyoming Migration Initiative, a collaborative effort housed at the University of Wyoming, is devoted to studying an ecological process involving major mammal species—pronghorn, mule deer, elk, bighorn sheep, and moose—that sets the Greater Yellowstone region apart from almost anywhere else in North America.

Upon closer inspection, migrations function as a living, breathing encyclopedia of insights, the volumes of which are only starting to be cracked open. Founded in 2012, the Wyoming Migration Initiative started searching for answers to two questions: where are the corridors and how are they threatened? "We were concerned especially with energy development because it was happening quickly and changing landscapes so rapidly," Kauffman said. "But obviously our scope has expanded."

Across America, it's not just wildlife that isn't found in the same diverse abundance where it used to be; the traditions and ecological knowledge forged by those animals is gone, too. Left behind are no longer "discreet" species fine-tuned to their surroundings, but "weedy" species:

highly-adaptive generalists, such as white-tailed deer, coyotes, raccoons, skunks, catbirds, and starlings that have shown their ability to thrive almost anywhere.

Kauffman grew up in southern Oregon, the son of a horse logger. He spent a lot of time in the woods. He went on to get undergraduate degrees in ecology and biology, earning a PhD in conservation biology from the University of California at Santa Cruz, doing post-doc work at the University of Montana in Missoula and then landing at the University of Wyoming in 2006.

"When I started, the plan was never to specialize in migration but the GPS collars on a lot of our animal collars just kept bringing in a deluge of data. When we put it together on maps, it would surprise us what the animals appeared to be doing," he said. "You see all of this movements and you can't help but wonder why."

Over the years, Greater Yellowstone has boasted a roster of extraordinary researchers contributing to major scientific advancement, from Jackson Hole's own Olaus and Adolph Murie writing on elk, bears, wolves, and coyotes, to Frank and John Craighead's seminal work with grizzlies and radio telemetry, to geophysicist Bob Smith's insights into Supervolcano; plus there's the Yellowstone Interagency Grizzly Bear Study Team, a groundbreaking study on trumpeter swans, lobos, fire ecology, and microbes in Yellowstone linked to the innovation of DNA fingerprinting.

The work of the Wyoming Migration Initiative is the latest contribution to that incredible resume. In fact, because of it, we now know the 22.5 million-acre tri-state region of Wyoming, Montana and Idaho contains some of the longest-known pathways for mule deer and pronghorn ever documented; overland routes that rival, in distance, the movement of wildebeest on the Serengeti and caribou herds in the Arctic.

An array of metaphors has been invoked to describe the significance of wildlife migrations. Middleton, who is a regarded as a leader in 21st century landscape conservation, has helped make the concept understandable to the masses. After doing doctoral work at Yale and working closely with federal and state researchers in Wyoming, Middleton has been based at the University of California-Berkeley trying to spearhead ways in which sound science can result in better protection.

He draws a comparison between Greater Yellowstone's mammal

migrations and the circulatory/pulmonary systems of the human body, a flowing of blood and oxygen vital to the health of our internal organs and the function of external appendages.

At least nine elk herds converge upon the mountain slopes of Yellowstone in summer and then funnel back out again to distant winter range. And there's the pronghorn migration. Then, just to the south, a mule deer population that is 500 animals strong in the Hoback River Basin embarks seasonally on a 300-mile roundtrip trek to the Red Desert. They have caused ecologists to rethink how the boundaries of Greater Yellowstone are drawn, contributing to a more expansive view of how the region is tied together across man-made lines scrawled on a map.

"Rivers run in only one direction: downward, carried by gravity," he tells. "But large megafauna using their ancient corridors flow back and forth, up and down mountains, between winter and summer range. They pulse through the landscape like heartbeats, pumping and recycling caloric energy. In another way, they function like lungs breathing in and out. In the late spring, higher elevations of the Yellowstone Plateau green-up with grass and pull them in and in the fall, there is an exhalation as they head to lower elevations."

Again, migrations are more than merely seasonal events involving animal travel. They have a symbiotic relationship with ecological well-being and in some ways represent the bottom tip of an inverted pyramid. When animals move across the landscape, it is about more than them simply traveling between two seasonal home ranges. They are like the sparks that flow through the circuitry: transporters of energy. They convert light from the sun, which triggers photosynthesis in plants that grow and are eaten, into calories that not only sustain the animal but build body mass.

Migrations facilitate the movement of biomass, not only in transforming grass to meat, which in turn becomes available to human hunters, wildlife predators such as grizzlies and wolves, and dozens of species of mammalian and avian scavengers, but it reaches down to the microbial level in the soil through hoof action by hundreds of thousands of animals and decomposition of ungulates that die in transit, according to Middleton. As they travel, living and then dying, their carcasses support the survival of an array of other species, from grizzly bears to wolves and mountain lions, to an array of scavengers, from coyotes and foxes to eagles, ravens, rodents, and beetles that aid in decomposition and thus producing healthy soils. The grasslands of Greater Yellowstone evolved to be eaten by ungulates; healthy plants and healthy soils absorb carbon and, in turn, also nourish other life forms. It is a major foundation for Greater Yellowstone's biological diversity.

And far from just being linear pilgrimages, migrations do not always adhere to straight routes between points A and B, but involve meanderings attuned to "riding the green wave of grass": snowfall, temperature, climate, and other factors that shape highly nuanced timing in travel across landscapes.

The good nutrition they find along the way is what drives individual animal and herd health, including fecundity (successful reproduction). Animal physiology has been perfectly timed to being at the right place at the right time when food is available to propel animals forward.

Just to the south of Yellowstone, a pronghorn population that has a summer home in Grand Teton National Park and roams the floor of Jackson Hole, Wyoming departs in the fall on a pilgrimage of more than 150 miles through national forest, BLM land, and cattle ranches southward to the flanks of the Wind River Mountains and Wyoming's Red Desert.

Certainly the most praise, at least what's been uncovered so far, goes to mule deer. One famous mulie doe, research animal # 255, was shown to move more than 500 miles in a roundtrip course between the Red Desert on the southern tier of Greater Yellowstone and Island Park, Idaho—*and then, astoundingly, back again.*

Distance wise, that's like a deer summering in New York City and wintering in Washington D.C. More extraordinary is that 255's one-way trek involved crossing two different national forests, a national park, the Continental Divide, to and fro across busy highways, rivers, over fences, through a gauntlet of predators (wolves, bears, cougars, domestic dogs, and human hunters), circumnavigating Jackson Hole, the north side of the Tetons, other mountains, towns and farmland. She did all of this, *and then* turned around and went in the opposite direction, completing the journey a couple of times before perishing.

Scientists are now in the early stages of understanding the migrations' ecological function. The groundbreaking research commenced by the Wyoming Migration Initiative and the Wyoming Game and Fish Department is being expanded to neighboring Montana and Idaho.

Wyoming, too, is a national leader in engineering wildlife overpasses and underpasses across busy highways to enable continued movement through landscapes and reduce high rates of roadkill caused by vehicle collisions All of Greater Yellowstone's major wild hooved animals: elk, deer, pronghorn, moose, bison, bighorn sheep, and mountain goats move as part of their evolutionarily-engrained behavior; they are part of matrilineal learning passed down in herds from mothers to young over hundreds of generations. Migrations happen wherever there are large wild mammals on the move.

Why it still happens so epically in Greater Yellowstone is simple. Epic wildlife migrations used to exist across most of America but various kinds of habitat fragmentation have created impassable barriers causing the migrations to die out. Greater Yellowstone has corridors of open space through which animals can still pass.

To return to Middleton's metaphor: "Just like a pulmonary or circulatory system in the human body, if you have a blocked or clogged artery or obstructed breathing passage, you're in real trouble. It's like having a stroke or heart attack. One major blockage can kill a corridor," he explained. "If these migration routes are going to persist, then protecting the pathways where they happen is essential."

The equivalent of a coronary could be something as seemingly insignificant as a few houses built in the middle of a narrow corridor, a traditional ranch converted into a subdivision that peppers a wide migration route, or a major oil and natural gas field with dozens or hundreds of wells, access roads, and pipeline carving up winter range. Impacts can be overt or insidious. Animals might be halted entirely from passing, or a highway might cause enough roadkill disruption that animal numbers fall. Displacement can result in animals being forced to move into less desirable habitat and it negatively impacts reproduction over time until a formerly robust herd almost disappears.

The Greater Yellowstone region encompasses more than 22.5 million acres across three different states and 20 counties. Most of it consists of federal public lands managed by the National Park Service, U.S. Forest Service, Bureau of Land Management, and U.S. Fish and Wildlife Service, plus some state-owned tracts in Wyoming, Montana, and Idaho.

"It's stretching our thinking about how to best manage wildlife cooperatively in a way that transcends boundaries and yet respects them. You can't protect what you don't know exists so documenting what happens in a spatial and temporal sense is really important," observed Yellowstone Park Superintendent, Cam Sholly, who served as chairman of the Greater Yellowstone Coordinating Committee. The GYCC, as it's called, comprises senior land managers from all of the federal and state agencies and is supposed to oversee Greater Yellowstone. It has made corridor protection a priority and it has support from both the U.S. Interior and Agriculture departments.

Were it simply a matter of developing a corridor migration strategy for public lands, the challenge would be much simpler. However, interspersed among public lands are between four and five million acres of private property, taking the form of towns and agricultural lands that experts say represent the most important pieces of the puzzle.

How wildlife moves and when and where it goes also affects lots of other things: abundance of both prey and predators, the potential spread of diseases, hunting opportunities, tourist economies, and decisions regarding the potential location of natural resource extraction, highways, and human development. Elsewhere in the Lower 48, where migration routes were unrecognized and became fragmented by human settlement, they often vanished and along with them animal homing instincts that evolved over ages.

While Middleton and his colleagues believe the still-intact migrations rank among Greater Yellowstone's profoundest wonders, equally jaw-dropping is that the full extent of these wildlife highways were only recently discovered.

Shortly after the new millennium began, around the time I was meeting with Belinda on the Pinedale Anticline, wildlife biologist Hall Sawyer opened eyes when he began studying mule deer and the potential impacts of oil and gas drilling in western Wyoming. What biologists with Game and Fish knew is that some mule deer herds were in steep decline.

Sawyer is credited with discovering the Red Desert to Hoback migration and today he is part of the Wyoming Wildlife Initiative's distinguished extended nexus of field scientists. "Mule deer are creatures who express incredible fidelity to their migration routes based upon behavior passed down from mothers to offspring over generations," Kauffman tells me. "Unlike mule deer, pronghorn are more flexible in their migratory strategies on where they go and need to go. Elk are more toward the mule deer side of the spectrum in terms of their fidelity."

Too often, the way science works is that data is collected, published in a peer-reviewed article, circulated narrowly in a journal, and then put on the shelf, seldom to find its way into applied science. Information gathered by this initiative, however, is readily disseminated to government land management agencies and the public. In fact, the organization has an excellent website where even school children have gone to trace the journeys of critters.

Under Kauffman's leadership, the Wyoming Migration Initiative (migrationinitiative.org) is currently assembling a comprehensive atlas of maps to document where the wildlife routes are. Noteworthy is that for all the public land that migrations cross, the persistence of elk, mule deer, and pronghorn herds also comes down to how just three or four million acres are stewarded on private ranchland.

As a result of better information unearthed by Sawyer, a key stretch in the mule deer corridor was identified as being vulnerable to development. The late Luke Lynch of the Conservation Fund, after whom a new wildlife area is named, led an effort to buy 364 acres for $2 million, nearly half paid for by the Knobloch Family Foundation in Jackson Hole. The other contributors are the Wyoming Game and Fish Department and the Wyoming Wildlife, Natural Resources Trust Fund, and the National Fish and Wildlife Foundation.

Fundamentally, the greatest epiphany is recognizing corridors as their own rich subsets of habitat. Most of these migrations do not involve animals zipping between winter and summer ranges like commuters racing on the interstate, Kauffman tells us. "They are stopping over along the way. Upwards of 90 percent of the time they are not making forward progress," he explains. "Migrations can be two months in spring and two months in the fall so for a whole third of the year they are lolling and feeding along the way."

Kaufman reports that on their way to green-up in the mountains, the animals are getting the best groceries available all year around, young plants high in protein and low in fiber. It affects how fat, healthy, and resilient they'll be through summer and into fall and winter.

For Middleton, his "a-ha" moment in understanding the importance of migrations occurred a few years ago when he was investigating declines of calf elk in the Clark's Fork Herd north of Cody. Fewer numbers of young elk on their winter range were immediately blamed on wolves.

But by trailing the herd on the full extent of its annual migration, he discovered that the effects of an extended drought, impairing the abundance of summer grasses in the mountains, affected elk survival and fecundity, resulting in fewer healthy offspring. Young elk also were dying from grizzly bear predation.

"You can't make broad extrapolations about what is going on based upon one data point," he cautioned. "I realized I had to go where the elk went to understand the full story and that meant seeing what happened at every leg of their migration."

That, in turn, led him to wonder about the movements of the rest of the elk in the heart of the ecosystem. "Elk are the ultimate trans-boundary species in terms of entering and exiting Yellowstone Park," Middleton says. "Their journeys and those of other migrating animals form the essence of why Greater Yellowstone needs to be viewed across the individual borders of the different land management jurisdictions that comprise it."

A key portal that opened the eyes of researchers has been the dazzling imagery of *National Geographic* photographer and UW graduate Joe Riis. Using camera traps, he has chronicled elk passing through the Thorofore in the southwest corner of Yellowstone: the most remote roadless area in the Lower 48; he saw them climbing steep mountains and fording raging rivers. Riis has also documented antelope wending their way along the so-called "Path of the Pronghorn" through Trapper's Point, crossing national forest, federal Bureau of Land Management tracts, and private land.

"What's rare about Greater Yellowstone is the diversity and the comprehensiveness of these migrations radiating around multiple populations of six different species. Around the world, the number of places that have epic migrations of wildlife is in fast decline," Middleton states. "What I hope our research does is inspire people in other areas of the country to look closer at wildlands in their own backyards. My hunch is that migrations are more common than people think. They are right under their noses."

"Losing wildlife migration is like destroying a human language," says Joel Berger with the Wildlife Conservation Society. Indeed, migrations reflect more than physical navigation. They serve as windows into the cultures of wildlife, including the learning passed down from mothers to offspring, instincts which have ensured survival from one generation to the next.

Kauffman and Middleton hope that migration routes, once invisible to the human eye and now catching us in marvel, don't suffer their own versions of a coronary episode. "A person who suffers a heart attack has done incremental things over time that leads to poor health. The same thing could affect the circulatory system of Greater Yellowstone," Middleton observes. "With these magnificent migrations and the corridors they depend upon, it won't be a single clog in the arteries but many slowly encroaching over time. Then one day, the heart just stops beating and they're over. We have to make sure that never happens."

What will be the effect of climate change? Answer: Kauffman says no one knows, yet. One thing that hasn't been a surprise is how animals respond to human-caused disturbance of habitat, because a lot already is known pertaining to residential development, the impacts of roads, and more recently, outdoor recreation. "The effect is always the same. Animals don't like to be near humans but they alter their behavior in response to human disturbance."

Recreation pressure can impact corridors, too. "I am an avid mountain biker and I bike in animal range near where I live in Laramie," Kauffman adds. "I frequent areas where there are a lot of moose but I've only seen moose two or three times. That doesn't mean the moose aren't there, but that they've moved. Human activity displaces animals. The question we must ask is what are the costs of that displacement. If an animal is fleeing habitat that offers superior forage or escape cover from predators or deep snowpack for less optimal areas, that is a concern."

The Wyoming Migration Initiative is all about building partnerships and one of its newest allies is the Western Landowners Alliance, whose members have begun discussions with ranchers in Greater Yellowstone in a position to make a profound difference with protecting corridors, especially elk winter range. Tweaking little things can yield huge dividends in preventing conflicts or eliminating them.

The Western Landowners Alliance is led by executive director Lesli Allison and has fostered discussions with some of the largest ranch owners in the West who cumulatively preside over more than 12 million acres of private land, including some of the best underdeveloped wildlife habitat and open space. The Alliance has worked closely with ecologists like Middleton, who spends a lot of time in Cody, Wyoming when he isn't teaching students at prestigious universities. The valley formed by the South Fork of the Shoshone River south of Cody represents a crucial spoke in elk and deer migration.

"If we want to change the dynamic that results in resistance to conservation, we need to flip the whole approach upside down. Instead of looking first for threats, start by looking at what is working. Why are wildlife using that piece of land? What is going right there? Then figure out how to support what is working," Allison explains, pointing to conservation easements that have been secured on ranches in the South Fork, and notably in the Madison and Paradise valleys, of Montana.

Little known even to many residents of Greater Yellowstone is that the Madison Valley is home to an elk migration involving, in most years, well more than 10,000 wapiti moving between Yellowstone National Park westward through the Madison mountains, and across the Madison Valley and Madison River to a number of state game preserves and points distant, as far away as the Centennial Valley. Every single animal crosses various private ranches. In fact, it's one of the most spectacular migrations in Greater Yellowstone; but because it doesn't happen en masse and often elk move under cover of darkness, it is witnessed only by locals. Roger Lang, who formerly owned the Sun Ranch and has donated property to help keep the migration intact, has stood on a hill and watched three different wapiti herds numbering 1,000 each converge into a river of elk. "If Greater Yellowstone as a whole represents a huge dispersed Serengeti, this is a mini one," he said.

"Path of the Pronghorn" in Wyoming involved mostly federal agencies acknowledging the pathway and then making a commitment to protect it. Government actions that extend beyond federal and state lands are viewed as an intrusion, even if ranchers enjoy having wildlife on their land. And the vast majority do.

"Currently, when a wildlife corridor is designated, it is often received initially as bad news by affected landowners because they fear restrictions, regulations, increased public scrutiny, and potentially litigation," Allison said. "Instead, we need to recognize the benefits of the working lands, treat landowners as valued partners, and find ways to support rather than penalize landowners for providing that habitat," she adds. "This can mean a whole suite of things, from simple recognition and appreciation to management flexibility, regulatory assurances, risk mitigation, economic benefits, and a greater voice in wildlife management decisions."

Those things are crucial according to Brian Yablonski, chief executive officer of the Property and Environmental Research Center in Bozeman, which is recognized nationally for its conservation work centered around property rights. Before taking the helm of PERC, Yablonski served as chairman of the Florida Fish and Wildlife Conservation Commission From rallying to win citizen support for protecting coral ecosystems off the Florida Keys, to mangrove along the coast, to attempting to reverse colossal negative impacts to the Everglades, one of the largest freshwater ecosystems on Earth, Yablonski has experience addressing landscape-level issues. He moved his family to Montana because he believes that protecting the migration corridors is one of the most important wildlife conservation issues in America. "Greater Yellowstone is roughly the size of Indiana and we are blessed with this huge fabric of interwoven public land; but if we don't get protection right on private land, we could lose many of these passages."

Private land covers just a small percentage of Greater Yellowstone but its importance cannot be overestimated. Not long ago, I spoke with Abby Nelson, a wildlife specialist with the Montana Fish Wildlife and Parks Department. She said that more than 80 percent of public wildlife coming off public lands when the snow flies spends all or part of the winter on private land.

Migrations provide a larger lens for pondering why private lands, and private property rights, matter, and why broader thinking about how con-servation can succeed is necessary. As the latter half of the 20th century demonstrated, the old way of simply drawing a line around public lands and believing they are enough to sustain wide-ranging wildlife isn't enough. In fact, it's something ranchers have known for generations because every winter they have hosted public wildlife on their lands. Today, operating with thin profit margins and younger generations not wanting to adopt ranching as a profession, thousands of acres of private land, crucial to the health of migrations, are at risk of being converted into scattershot sprawl.

Fortunately, seldom in the storied history of Greater Yellowstone has there been a more united effort involving stakeholders from across the spectrum of interest groups. PERC has emerged as a leader because its raison d'être as an organization is identifying ways that market-based solutions, including economic incentives, can be applied to advance better conservation outcomes.

When thousands of elk, for example, head to lower ground they both cross and seasonally inhabit private ranchlands where they can compete with livestock for forage, can knock down fences, and carry diseases. A major focus is developing a corridor conservation strategy that values local on-the-ground knowledge that rural landowners possess and understanding their concerns.

"Most of the property owners I've spoken with care about these extraordinary wildlife values but they also face the practical concerns of how to make a living and how to care for the lands inside their fenceline," Yablonski said. "I've always believed that carrots make a better inducement than sticks. I've seen the results where economic incentives are more effective in winning allies and creating win-win scenarios than regulatory structures alone that stymie creativity and flexibility. And, in America, defending and protecting property rights matters. I believe that if we can provide a variety of rewards that both honors private property rights and makes migratory wildlife an asset rather than a liability or impediment to owning land, then we can safeguard many of these corridors."

What continues to amaze Kauffman is the huge public interest in the phenomenon of migrations. While many wildlife issues are divisive, mutual curiosity is bringing people together around common concern. The Western Governors Association issued a statement expressing its support for studying migrations, joining industry groups, hunters and anglers, recreationists, conservationists, and even local chambers of commerce.

There's no better example of the public interest than the tale of the doe mule deer, "Jet," a Red Desert to Hoback migrant the research team has fitted with a satellite collar. Postings about her over a seven-week period became a sensation on Twitter, also attracting tens of thousands of views on Facebook every time a new map reading was given.

Drama built as fans anxiously awaited word as Jet started her spring migration jaunt later than expected. "People were really interested. They wanted to know when she started to move. They worried that maybe she had died. If you look at who was tracking her, it was all mostly just regular Joe and Jill Wyomingites, from oil field workers to ranchers, sportsmen and college kids," Kauffman said. "It really reinforces the notion that in Wyoming interest in big game herds is a social phenomenon the entire state is trying to wrap its head around."

Montana and Idaho aren't aggressively mapping many of their corridors yet but it's coming, Kauffman said, noting that he's been meeting with wildlife officials in those states, sharing with them how the Wyoming Migration Initiative works. They know migration is important, especially for the performance of the big game herds that are treasured.

As Bob Keiter noted in his in-depth analysis of issues in the Greater Yellowstone Ecosystem, amazing political support for safeguarding corridors has been building. In 2007, the Western Governors Association adopted a groundbreaking resolution to protect corridors. And, in 2017, the Trump Administration went on record endorsing that corridors be considered when then Interior Secretary Ryan Zinke directed federal land management agencies to collaborate with the states "to enhance and improve the quality of big-game winter range and migration corridor habitat on Federal lands." Keiter notes that the Zinke order complements rules applying to the U.S. Forest Service through the National Forest Management Act that instructs forest managers in Greater Yellowstone to address habitat connectivity in the forest planning process.

However, and this is essential to note, the same Trump Administration through the Bureau of Land Management where the Pinedale Anticline and Jonah gas fields are located, issued new leases to oil and gas companies within known corridors and critical habitat for Greater sage-grouse. The acreage slated for development dwarfs the amount that Zinke and his successor David Bernhardt proposed for protection.

Keiter notes that a bill, the Wildlife Corridors Conservation Act, was introduced to Congress in both 2016 and 2018 but it languished in part owed to opposition from the fossil fuel industry that does not want to be hamstrung by regulations telling it to heed or stay out of corridors where it believes commercially viable pockets of oil and gas might be found. "In sum, ungulate management in the Greater Yellowstone Ecosystem is as fragmented as the habitat," Keiter notes.

Steve Belinda quit his job as a scientist with the BLM because the agency refused to heed his warnings. Within a decade after Belinda and I strode across the Pinedale Anticline before it was covered with gas wellheads, pump stations and pipeline, the size of a local migratory mule deer herd had plummeted by 40 percent. "The BLM was never really sincere when it said it would ensure that balance would be achieved between protecting wildlife and accommodating industry," he said. "The proof is on the landscape. Wildlife tells you if balance works or it doesn't. If wildlife disappears or populations drop, then you know the promise wasn't kept."

The good news is that Grand Teton's charismatic pronghorn herd, which spends warm months in Jackson Hole, is still with us. At the southern end of the route, the town of Pinedale, Wyoming, which bet its fortunes on a gas drilling boom that has gone bust, now touts itself as a proud gateway of Path of the Pronghorn that will endure as long as there is habitat. Soon, there will be a map speaking to corridors present in every valley on public and private land, where they start and terminate. Migrations not only hold the spirit of Greater Yellowstone together; they're magnets that help tether the nature-loving identity of human denizens, too. Will we squander this opportunity to keep them alive?

To Kill A Grizzly

INTO THE BRAMBLES WE WENT, cans of bear spray on our hips, my scientific shepherd holding a device in his hand with GPS coordinates. We were on the trail of a grizzly who then had only a number attached to her and she was destined to become the most famous mother bear in the world.

My introduction to Grizzly 399 started without fanfare. I had been writing about grizzlies in the Greater Yellowstone for years. In fact, not long after I arrived in the ecosystem after being a violent crime reporter in Chicago, I was visiting my friend, Steven Fuller, the famed Yellowstone winterkeeper at Canyon Village (where I had worked as a cook during two summers of college), and not far from his rustic home, a fatal bear mauling happened.

A photographer, who had been trailing behind a female bear with cubs along Otter Creek, apparently got too close. The protective mother at some point attacked him, killed him and ate part of him. She demonstrated aggressive behavior when investigators arrived on the scene to look for the victim and she was shot.

The tragic incident largely conformed to a story line that had dominated human thinking about grizzlies going back to the days when white mountain men made their first incursion into native homelands in the West. Grizzlies were labeled dangerous, temperamental and animals to be feared for their ferociousness, which, of course, justified the fact that they were killed to make landscapes safe and in defense of livestock and people and later, when their numbers dwindled, to be sport hunted for fun, their hides, skulls and claws turned into trophies—expressions of manliness.

On this morning, in the company of Dr. Charles "Chuck" Schwartz, head of the Yellowstone Interagency Grizzly Bear Study Team, we had parked our car along Pacific Creek near a place near the shared boundary of Grand Teton National Park and the Bridger-Teton National Forest in Jackson Hole. Shannon Podruzny, a young researcher, had given Schwartz coordinates of the general proximity of where a bear, wearing a radio collar and identified as "399" had been days earlier.

The intent was not to try and find 399 but I had asked Schwartz for an interesting bear that might be of interest. At that point 399 was a nine-year-old who had already had a cub that perished, believed to have been killed by a male grizzly. Like lions in Africa, male suitors will kill cubs so that females go into estrous and breed.

We talked loudly, not quietly, as we headed away from any established trails into the forest, keenly aware as off in the distance we heard sounds of branches cracking that could be a moose, elk, cougar, deer or bear. Eventually we reached a place and, assessing the small knoll, Schwartz and I inspected bear scat and in a place of matted grass, he said "bear day bed. This is where she must have rested a few days ago."

At the time, the federal government had moved, with enthusiastic cooperation from the states of Wyoming, Montana and Idaho to remove the Greater Yellowstone population of grizzlies from protection as a "threatened" animal under the Endangered Species Act. Soon enough, the delisting would be overturned by a court, based on arguments from environmentalists that not sufficient enough analysis had gone into assessing how the loss of a key wild food—the seeds found in the cones of whitebark pine trees—might impact the population.

Bears gorge on the seeds which as a mixture of protein and fat help them put on weight. The more physically robust a bear is the better its chances of survival and persisting healthily through months of winter hibernation in the den. Great nutrition is especially important for female grizzlies that are pregnant or heading into the dens with cubs.

Physical fitness can be a determining factor in whether the pregnancy is successful, whether mother gives birth to a litter of twin, triplet or even quadruplet cubs and whether yearling cubs can suckle on a ready supply of milk. Reproductive health is related to fecundity, the ability of a species to successfully reproduce.

Grizzlies are among the slowest mammal species to reproduce and whether a population grows or declines depends on whether a mother is able to give birth to, and raise young, that live long enough to reproduce themselves and replace her when she and others die. For a long time, reproduction of new grizzlies in Greater Yellowstone was not keeping pace with the number of bears that, by an overwhelming majority, were not perishing owed to natural causes but to factors related to humans. Among the most serious was killing of bears by people with guns.

In the day bed of Grizzly 399, I laid on my back and tried to imagine her lounging, sleeping, dreaming and what she saw from this vantage. Schwartz indulged my curiosity. I ended up writing a story that mentioned 399 and there were, in fact, a lot of grizzlies with radio tracking collars, part of bear research in Greater Yellowstone that is among the longest and most prestigious ongoing wildlife study projects in the world.

I reflect today on how strange it is that stories of people and animals and even populations of animals can turn on decisions. As of autumn 2021, grizzly 399 was 25 years old and in the decades since I strolled down her trail, she had found a way to survive. Together with the renowned Jackson Hole nature photographer Thomas D. Mangelsen, we produced a book titled *Grizzlies of Pilgrim Creek: An Intimate Portrait of 399, the Most Famous Bear of Greater Yellowstone*.

The book, distinguished by its extraordinary photos by Mangelsen, wouldn't have been possible were it not for the fact that 399 survived. Descended from her in her bloodline, as of 2021, were more than 25 bears—cubs born to her and cubs born to her daughter cubs. (We don't know how many of her male cubs might have impregnated other females). What's the value of having/keeping a single female grizzly bear alive?

Up to the time that 399 became well known, it had been the cultural dogma of government wildlife managers to dismiss the importance of individual bears, saying that "we manage for populations and not for individuals." On the hand, it's true. They claim to be objective, dispassionate, "scientific" and, by that standard, keep themselves at an emotional arm's length distance so as to prevent any emotional attachment to their subjects.

But Tom and I have always wondered, if a researcher isn't attached to wildlife subjects, doesn't feel a connection to them, and asserts that the lives of individuals don't really matter compared to overall population trends, then how can one really sympathize and empathize with their plight, to essentially treat an individual animal as if it matters, the same way that individual people do. While some scientists dismiss that as shameless anthropomorphizing, Mangelsen and his dear friend Dr. Jane

Goodall argue it is used as an excuse to not treat animals the same way we treat our pets—as sentiment beings capable of thinking and having emotions and, in the case of a mother trying to protect an offspring that is suffering or had died, protectiveness beyond mere instinct and, if death happens, grief and mourning.

In the beginning, some biologists in Wyoming dismissively called 399 as a "celebrity" bear who was bad because her presence attracted a huge number of human followers. Over the years, 399 gave birth to three different broods of triplets, a couple of doubles and in 2020, amazingly, a quartet of cubs. She was known around the world because of who she was and where she lived: along the roadsides of Grand Teton Park and the Bridger-Teton National Forest where she was visually accessible.

She more than any other grizzly bear in history has, by her actions, unknowingly debunked the frontier myths advanced and reinforced around grizzlies as a reason for humans to kill them, that grizzlies were, by their nature, bloodthirsty monsters of the night that exist to terrorize people.

But to return to a point I mentioned earlier: the persistence of 399 has twisted and turned on many close calls, in which human bad behavior might have resulted in harm, but there is one in particular. Earlier in her life, 399 mauled a hiker who accidentally wandered near a place where 399 was feeding on a carcass with her first set of triplet cubs. She was only protecting her cubs and their food. He got injured but not fatally. He told authorities the bear wasn't at fault. The superintendent in Grand Teton Park, Mary Gibson Scott, made the crucial existential decision to let 399 live, saying that she was only responding naturally, and it made all the difference.

399 carried on, teaching her cubs how to navigate a very perilous human world full of fast moving cars and treacherous highways to cross, people with guns, people who throw food to bears, people who get too close. She has demonstrated wisdom in navigating through the human world as humans have pinched in on hers. She has taught us that if we treat bruins with respect, give them the space they need, and understand how bears see us (especially how protective mothers with offspring regard us), the Greater Yellowstone bear population has rebounded from an era when many thought the best way to deal with a bear was with a gun.

For more than two generations now, it's been illegal to hunt grizzly bears for sport in the Lower 48. The late Joe Gutkoski was 48 years old when the U.S. Fish and Wildlife Service seized control over grizzly management from Montana, Wyoming, and Idaho in 1975, invoking its authority under the Endangered Species Act. Nearly half his life earlier, he had gone stalking a Great Bear with his rifle in northern Montana. He was on the trail "of a big boar I had seen and I was cutting his tracks through downed timber and I was so close I could smell him." He proudly reflected later that he was glad he didn't kill a grizzly.

In 1975, the entire Greater Yellowstone grizzly population was estimated to number no more than 136 grizzlies, if not fewer. Bears were dying mostly from: lethal removals by wildlife managers; bruins were being shot by ranchers for being livestock killers; elk hunters who claimed self-defense in killing them; and poachers. Grizzlies were perishing far faster than bear reproduction could keep up.

Most of those them were clustered in Yellowstone National Park. Many biologists feared that without emergency measures implemented to prevent conflict and stop humans from felling them, without actions that implemented harsher penalties to stop elicit shootings, the bears would disappear from the region just as wolves had, or they would be rendered to merely a handful.

"I never thought we would have the numbers and distribution of bears we have today," Dr. Christopher Servheen, the Fish and Wildlife Service's former national recovery coordinator, told me. "I thought we would be lucky to have *any* grizzly bears in the Yellowstone ecosystem."

That's how bleak it was and many say the turnaround orchestrated by Servheen and others, including vigilant advocacy from conservation groups, ranks among the grandest achievement in wildlife history. Yet even now, maybe 2,000 grizzlies roam the entire Lower 48, down from 50,000 that used to inhabit the West historically. Sizable, viable numbers—enough to ensure grizzlies persist for the foreseeable future—exist in just two regions south of Canada: Greater Yellowstone and the Crown of the Continent/Northern Continental Divide Ecosystem that includes Glacier National Park and federal wilderness in northern Montana, not far from where Gutkoski went hunting as a young man.

"Our culture, ever since Lewis & Clark came through in the early 1800s, has had such a distorted view of grizzlies. We treated them as expendable, as things we needed to eradicate," Gutkoski, a nongenarian told me when we sat in his living room a couple of years before he died in 2021, "I think we're smarter in that we know more about grizzlies than ever before. We respect them more. We value them more because they are rare. We know they are not the bloodthirsty creatures they were portrayed to be by our ancestors. But I still wonder, are we wise enough to co-exist with them?"

In 2017, with bear numbers having rebounded in recent decades to somewhere around 700 (and maybe a few hundred more) in Greater Yellowstone, the Fish and Wildlife Service completed a full circle, moving for the second time in about a decade to relinquish its control and giving management back to the states of Wyoming, Montana, and Idaho. Servheen says the Endangered Species Act proved it works as a law that fulfilled its original mission of moving the grizzly bear population out of the biological emergency room and into recovery. Immediately, Wyoming officials, which had always resented grizzlies being federally listed in the first place, announced they would hold a trophy hunt for around 20 grizzlies. Government agencies that carried out delisting were again taken to court and lost. Grizzlies remain federally protected and sport hunting still outlawed.

There remains several significant questions clouding the outlook for grizzly survival, including the deepening impacts of climate change, bears dying in alleged incidents of human self-defense often involving big game hunters, and rising human population pressure affecting the spaces bears need to persist. But paramount, and indeed the major point of contention for 650,000 Americans who wrote comments in opposition to giving states management authority, relates to hunting.

Should the most iconic population of wild bears on earth again be targeted as animals killed for sport, trophies, and thrill alone? All three states have expressed their desire to begin selling bear tags in the coming months or years. "I find the prospect of sport-hunting grizzlies again to be appalling," Jane Goodall, the famed chimpanzee researcher, global conservationist and admirer of bears in Greater Yellowstone, told me.

Matt Hogan, who has served as the Fish and Wildlife Service's regional director in Denver who went on to become head of the Interagency Grizzly Bear Committee, told me it is not his agency's prerogative to instruct the states on what to do yet he is sympathetic to the profound sense of attachment Americans feel toward grizzlies. Hogan, who previously had served as government affairs manager for Safari Club International, one of the largest trophy hunting advocates in the world, believed grizzlies should be hunted. But he added that if the Greater Yellowstone grizzly population falls below minimal numbers that the states agree to, the bear can be relisted and control wrested away again from the states.

So here is a question posed to you, dear reader: why do we *recover* species? Why is the United States of America considered an exemplar of trying to rescue species, some of them, such as large animals, hard to live with? And if we succeed in reversing a downward spiral of an animal, is part of the motivation so that hunters can kill those animals again?

The U.S., which is to say the government supported by citizens and their tax dollars, brought back bald eagles but they aren't hunted for sport nor are they mounted on the wall. Nor are peregrine falcons, nor whooping cranes, nor California condors, nor black-footed ferrets.

Stephen Herrero, professor emeritus of environmental science and biology at the University of Calgary and author of *Bear Attacks: Their Causes and Avoidance*, expressed his concerns about grizzly hunting in 1985. He remembered how Wyoming, which holds the bulk of grizzly habitat in Greater Yellowstone, fiercely resisted closing down its killing of bears for sport in 1974. In the 1970s, Wyoming issued hundreds of tags and if all of them had been filled, combined with bears shot to protect cattle and sheep, every grizzly would have been killed save for those inside Yellowstone.

"Since we have had difficulty in regulating the kill of grizzly bears in strictly protected areas, it should not be surprising that sustained-yield hunting outside of parks and reserves has been an even more difficult objective to achieve," Herrero wrote in *Bear Attacks*. "The grizzly is a highly valued trophy animal, the hunting of which can generate expenditures of many thousands of dollars. Yet opportunities to hunt grizzlies are limited by the bear's inability to survive with more than modest levels of killing. Very few grizzly populations have ever been substantially hunted without population decline." Herrero added, "One of the greatest difficulties we face in attempting to maintain grizzly bear populations and monitor their mortality is our inability to estimate how many grizzly bears there are in a given area."

Grizzlies are second only to musk oxen in large mammals slowest to reproduce. Cubs suffer a high mortality rate of 50 percent and if they survive it can take six to 10 years before a female gives birth to cubs that survive long enough to replace her.

Gutkoski was a living legend to those who savor Montana's wild back-country. He was described as equal parts Theodore Roosevelt *the sportsman*, John Muir *the preservationist*, and Aldo Leopold *the ecologist*, though, truth be told, Gutkoski could probably have out-hiked those conservation giants even on their best days. Feisty at five-foot-four, he covered thousands of miles on foot.

A solitary wanderer, his hardiness has earned him comparisons to a wolverine. Today, after seven decades of exploration, his name appears in the summit registers of peaks scattered throughout the Greater Yellowstone Ecosystem and points well beyond.

Gutkoski was troubled that one political party—he didn't name it—claims to own the allegiance of hunters. He was an old union organizer and said all of his blue collar colleagues were hunters. He says the National Rifle Association, Safari Club International, and the Rocky Mountain Elk Foundation, all of which have come out in favor of hunting Greater Yellowstone grizzlies promoting it as a states' rights issue, give what is, according to him, a distorted view of where sportsmen's sentiments actually lie. Those organizations above have implied that anyone opposed to hunting grizzlies or differing with their view is un-American.

No one questions Gutkoski's patriotism or his love of hunting. During World War II, he served in the Navy on a Destroyer and was anchored in Tokyo Bay in the weeks after the detonation of two atom bombs forced Japanese surrender. Following schooling at Penn State, he was hired as the first landscape architect in the history of the U.S. Forest Service's flagship Northern Region in Missoula, Montana.

Later, in 1964, he transferred to Bozeman and completed his 32-year tenure of government employment with the Forest Service, sometimes fighting off misguided timber sales and attempts to cover mountainsides with mazes of logging roads, safeguarding wildlife habitat that has benefitted hunters. He's also been a river protector, a wilderness crusader, and a catalyst in pushing to re-establish free-ranging bison herds on the high plains.

But of all his passions, none comes close to matching his zealous enthusiasm for stalking big game animals in the fall, packing out the bounty on his back, and feasting upon it throughout the year. When he and I rendezvoused recently in his humble home in north Bozeman, he was feeling a bit stiff and tired, having just returned from three rigorous bow hunts in the Gallatin Range. Although those were unsuccessful, it's worth mentioning that in 2016, as an 89-year-old, Gutkoski shot a bull elk and carried hundreds of pounds of fresh wapiti meat out himself.

Since the late 1940s, Gutkoski tracked every major mammal in the northern Rockies, including cougars, wolves, imperiled Canada lynx, wolverine, bighorn sheep, and mountain goats. He's taken black bears with his rifle, cooking them as roasts for supper.

However, he had never eaten grizzly; the mere thought causes him to recoil. Indeed, for most hunters, grizzlies have never been thought of as an animal killed for sustenance; bringing down a Great Bear has always been treated instead as the ultimate wildlife trophy: an expression of manhood among the macho set.

Gutkoski was among the few living Montanans who, when they purchased elk tags as young men, were also told they could take a grizzly no questions asked. Reflecting on a couple of attempts to shoot that elusive massive boar in the South Fork of the Flathead River drainage, Gutkoski offers this solemn confession: "I'm glad I failed."

Had he succeeded, it would have been "driven by my personal ego in downing a grizzly for nothing more than the thrill of the chase." Gutkoski said he would have felt ashamed today. "It's not something that, looking back, I would be proud to admit or something I'd ever want to have my name associated with. Not going to judge another hunter; it's up to their own conscience."

Exhilaration. Pride. Joy. Hope. Sadness. Cynicism. Disappointment. Outrage. Bravado. Quiet humility and reverence. This are just a sampling of the charged human sentiments that accompany discussions of the plight of the American grizzly and the prospect that bears will be hunted regularly in Greater Yellowstone.

Few issues in modern wildlife conservation have stirred such raw emotion and vehement disagreement over what the ethical and legal objectives should be in rescuing a high-profile animal from the precipice of regional annihilation. Passions are even higher because today no species is more synonymous with the country's first national park, Yellowstone, and its sister preserve, Grand Teton, than *Ursus arctos horribillis*.

Among more than 266 different foods grizzlies eat, four have been identified as being especially important for bear nutrition, especially pregnant females prior to entering the den. One key food in Yellowstone, spawning cutthroat trout, have been nearly wiped out by the illegal introduction of lake trout in Yellowstone Lake (read the first chapter in this book). Another, mentioned earlier, the seeds present in the cones of whitebark pine are becoming scarcer as whitebark pine trees are dying off from diseases, insect attacks related to climate change, forest fires, and drought. A third food is Army cutworm moths that drink nectar from alpine wildflowers and gather in mountain scree slopes where grizzlies eat them in late summer; not only are the wildflowers threatened by climate change but also the moths, considered pests to agriculture, are vulnerable to pesticide spraying. The fourth important food, meat, comes from wild game that can put bears on a collision course with hunters and occasionally from the bears killing livestock. Male bears especially feast on meat and if females approach carcasses there is heightened danger that cubs could be killed by those male bruins.

Ponder again ripple effects. When grizzlies do not have access to favored nutritious foods they wander more widely. Many of their desired staples have existed in backcountry areas well away from populated human areas. Many of those high-value edibles are not easily replaced in a bear's diet. When bears have to wander more widely, they have a higher likelihood of running into people or places where people live. And that's not good.

Members of the Wyoming Wildlife Commission say there are plenty of bears—too many in some places—and their citizens are owed the privilege of hunting grizzlies because the state has spent $50 million on management since the 1970s. That sounds like a lot. However, non-lethal wildlife watching in Greater Yellowstone is one of the ecosystem's biggest tourist draws, appealing to people from around the world. Between Yellowstone and Grand Teton alone, more than $1.5 billion annually is generated through nature-tourism. Seeing a grizzly ranks even higher on visitor wish lists, according to one survey, than witnessing an eruption of Old Faithful Geyser. Second to seeing a bear is catching sight of a live wolf.

Down in Jackson Hole, the allure Grizzly 399 has probably resulted in more money spent by tourists that would cover Wyoming's expense in managing grizzlies many times over. Yes, the mystique of a single living bear, worth exponentially more alive than dead with a hunting tag attached to her hide that cost a few thousand dollars at most to secure.

Like the global outrage that erupted over the killing of Cecil the African lion in 2015, downed by an American bow hunter after the big cat was lured out of Zimbabwe's Hwange National Park and felled for sport, the possibility of something similar happening to beloved Yellowstone and Grand Teton grizzlies is, for many, unthinkable. Mangelsen and Jane Goodall have shared that worry with the U.S. Congress, along with the concern that Grizzly 399 might possibly be killed and turned into a rug for the wall or floor by a sport hunter.

The decision of whether grizzlies in Montana, Wyoming, and Idaho will be hunted comes down to wildlife commissions in each state, with final sign-off coming from governors. The bulk of Greater Yellowstone resides in Wyoming and that state has aggressively noted that it hopes to cash in by generating revenue from selling hunting tags.

Scott Weber, a self-admitted local provocateur, onetime public school board member in Cody, Wyoming and member of an organization called Wyoming Sportsmen For Fish and Wildlife, put up a billboard in his town at the height of summer tourist season showing a camo-clad hunter posed next to a dead grizzly. When Weber was interviewed by the *Cody Enterprise* newspaper, he said, "The greatest trophy in the Lower 48 is a male grizzly. Now you won't have to go to Alaska to get a grizzly."

Most advocates of killing grizzlies are far more coy, knowing that opinion polls show Americans being overwhelming opposed to trophy hunting. During an interview with Mike Koshmyrl of the *Jackson Hole News & Guide*, a Wyoming outfitter Paul Gilroy, a Safari Club member who lives near Wilson, Wyoming, said he sees a commercial opportunity for his business. "It would be a very popular hunt and easily advertised and easily booked. We have some very large bears here, which would make for commendable trophies," Gilroy told Koshmyrl. "It would be nice to be able to whack one that's causing problems. But to go through the effort to go out and stalk one, I'm getting too old. I don't hunt much anymore, I just point."

I reached out to several outfitters and guides in the tri-state region. Few wanted to have their name appear in print as being in favor of hunting, for fear of being harassed by animal rights activists, even though some told me they support it. Instead, I spoke with Gutkoski and two other widely-respected hunters who openly shared their feelings.

Randy Newberg of Bozeman is an international celebrity in hunting circles. He is host of the *Sportsman Channel's Fresh Tracks With Randy Newberg* and, in addition, oversees one of the most popular web podcasts devoted to public lands hunting in America. Cumulatively millions of people have followed his hunting adventures.

Years ago, Newberg killed a grizzly in Alaska, part of a dream hunt he took with his 82-year-old grandfather. "It was the thrill of a lifetime," he says. Having done it once, however, he has no compelling need to repeat it again. As for his stance on whether Greater Yellowstone grizzlies should be hunted for sport, Newberg is in a unique position.

Almost two decades ago, he served on a blue ribbon panel of citizens in Greater Yellowstone that examined whether the scientific goals used to gauge bear recovery had been met. He concluded they had. Newberg supported the move to remove grizzlies from federal protection in 2017 just as he had in 2007 when the Greater Yellowstone population was temporarily delisted from safeguarding under the Endangered Species Act. But lawsuits from environmental groups reversed the government decision.

"I've told people that I am in favor of hunting being made available to states as a management tool but I've also said the state wildlife agencies need to proceed with extreme caution," Newberg said. "There is a lot at stake for the credibility of the states in the public's eye, there is a lot at stake for the reputation of hunting, and most importantly, there is a lot at stake for the grizzly."

Newberg is torn when pondering where hunts should occur: on the far outlying edges of the ecosystem or closer to the national parks where there are higher concentrations of bears and people and thus likely more conflict. The states have said they first intend to target "problem bears": those, for example that get into conflict with livestock, chronically wander into communities, or get into trash.

Any hunts, if they target grizzlies that would otherwise be destroyed, relocated, or sent to zoos, need to be carefully orchestrated and involve only highly skilled and qualified hunters, guides, and close involvement with wardens and biologists on the ground, Newberg says. "I have suggested to all of the states that hunts should not be carried out within the PCA (primary conservation area) that includes the national parks (hunting is prohibited inside Yellowstone) and adjacent national forests because it puts beloved park bears at higher risk."

Newberg worries about hunts happening anywhere close to where hunts themselves could be captured on camera and used by animal rights groups, using social media, to create a firestorm. He witnessed the black eye that Montana incurred when Yellowstone bison were gunned down in the snow right along the park border after the state carried out a hunting season.

Should a popular bear like Grizzly 399 get accidentally killed, should a bruin get wounded and die with agony, should a female grizzly be slain because a hunter mistook her for a male, it would be a public relations nightmare that would have internationally negative consequences for the image of hunting. "As someone concerned about hunting and its positive role in society, I am deeply concerned that hunting of grizzlies in Greater Yellowstone could make the backlash caused by Cecil the lion look like a on the Richter scale," Newberg said. "The moment somebody shoots a bear like Grizzly 399, by accident, out of spite or stupidity, this will turn into a disaster for the hunting community of an order of magnitude like the San Francisco earthquake of 1906. If hunters want to make sure hunting is embraced for future generations and not have society turn against it, then they need to respect the millions of people who value grizzlies and not talk about the animals with an attitude of defiance or hostility like 'Let's just go shoot the bastards.'"

In late 2015, Bill Addeo, a hunter who spends part of his year in the Hoback Junction area south of Jackson, Wyoming, responded to a newspaper column I penned about conservation. He knew I had written a book about Grizzly 399 featuring Mangelsen's photographs. A few months earlier, he shot a wolf, strapped it to the top of his truck and circled the downtown square in Jackson to demonstrate his hostility toward environmentalists who support wolf conservation.

Addeo also apparently has little regard for those who treasure grizzlies. "I KILLED BEAR 399," he wrote as a social media comment at the newspaper site. "So, if Wilkinson is doing a book on bear 399, he needs to talk to me about the bear's last moments gasping for air as the cubs ran about. I was there taking pictures and have all the inside information."

Addeo later claimed he was merely joking—Grizzly 399 was obviously not killed—but law enforcement officials took it seriously. The underground outlaw code of "shoot, shovel, and shut up" when it comes to predators is no laughing matter. In Montana in 2021, the state legislature passed a bill, signed into law by its Governor Greg Gianforte that makes it illegal to relocate bears that get into conflict with people, a hallmark of bear recovery that has enabled more bears to stay alive, including reproducing females. The state also passed laws liberalizing the killing of wolves by hunters and ranchers who can use bullets an even snares which pose a risk of catching grizzlies as well as imperiled wolverines and Canada lynx. For decades, Dr. Chris Servheen during his time at the helm of grizzly recovery for the federal Fish and Wildlife Service, stood steadfast in defense of states who promised they would be good stewards if bear management was handed back to them. It should be noted that states resented having bears brought under federal control in 1975. Servheen took regular rhetorical pounding from wildlife conservationists who said he was selling out to states that had long held a grudge against having to recover grizzlies and they said the states couldn't be trusted.

After the action of the 2021 legislature and governor in Montana, essentially legalizing actions to thwart progress that has been made in enabling grizzlies to expand their range, Servheen, who is vice president of the Montana Wildlife Federation and co-chair of the IUCN's North American Bear Expert Team, wrote an op-ed that appeared in *Mountain Journal*.

"The bill in Montana related to grizzlies signed into law by Governor does not allow relocation of any bear in any type of conflict if outside the recovery zones. This is contrary to 40 years of Montana grizzly management policy and would dramatically increase the number of bears killed in Montana. Another Montana bill would allow anyone to kill any grizzly that they thought was 'threatening livestock,' which would essentially allow anyone to kill a grizzly bear just for being in the general vicinity of livestock," Servheen wrote in a piece circulated across the country. "I understand the need for management of grizzlies and wolves, and that includes ethical, fair-chase hunting using science to set mortality limits. But these extreme anti-predator laws in Montana and Idaho are a relapse back into the dark ages of wildlife and nature exploitation."

In a poignant comment, Servheen told me, "You know, all these years the environmental groups were saying the states can't be trusted to professionally manage bears. And I always believed there was no way we could go back, revert to the thinking that resulted in species having to be listed in the first place. But I was wrong and they were right."

Some claim that if grizzlies aren't allowed to be hunted there will be more poaching. Studies debunk this. A counter argument also is that poachers who break the law need to receive harsh sentences and there is fear among conservationists that the states will be lenient if more bears start dying due to claims of hunter self-defense. Every year in Greater Yellowstone a few people are injured by grizzlies, the vast majority not fatally.

The invention of bear spray has markedly helped reduce injuries to both bears and people. Still, pervasive fear exists. With a few hundred grizzlies living in and passing through Yellowstone and a few million humans visiting the park when bears are active, the number of physical encounters is actually low. Responding to questions about the frequency, Yellowstone offers statistics. The odds of a grizzly bear attack in Yellowstone which four million people visit and where a few hundred grizzlies move through the park landscape:

- If a human visitor remains in developed areas, roadsides, and boardwalks: 1 in 59.5 million visits
- If a person stays in roadside campgrounds: 1 in 26.6 million per overnight stays
- To camp in the backcountry: 1 in 1.7 million overnight stays
- To hike in the backcountry: 1 in 232,613 person travel days
- All park activities combined: 1 in 2.7 million visits

"Since Yellowstone was established in 1872, eight people have been killed by bears in the park. More people in the park have died from drowning (121 incidents), burns (after falling into hot springs, 21 incidents), and suicide (26 incidents) than have been killed by bears," park spokeswoman Morgan Warthin said. "To put it in perspective, the probability of being killed by a bear in the park (8 incidents) is only slightly higher than the probability of being killed by a falling tree (7 incidents), caught in an avalanche (6 incidents), or being struck and killed by lightning (5 incidents). Since 1979, Yellowstone has hosted over 118 million visits. During this time, 44 people were injured by grizzly bears in the park."

From his home in Kelly, Wyoming, Ted Kerasote has clear views looking west to the breathtaking Teton Range and behind him the

Bridger-Teton National Forest, an area where he has hunted for decades. Grizzlies and wolves have ambled through his back yard and he routinely finds fresh tracks. When he moved permanently to Jackson Hole in 1986, grizzlies were incredibly rare and wolves were absent from Greater Yellowstone.

Kerasote is, in his own way, also legendary. For many years, he wrote a couple of widely-read columns for *Sports Afield* magazine and he is author of the acclaimed book *Bloodties: Nature, Culture and the Hunt.* Like Gutkoski and Newberg, he is a passionate defender of hunting when it is done to put meat on the table.

"People try to tell me that if I'm not in favor of killing grizzlies, then I'm anti-hunting. I've been called that even though I've shot more elk than those people who are making the claim. There's an atmosphere of tremendous polarization in this country. It's based on the belief that unless you are wholeheartedly with us, you are against us. Those who say we need to kill grizzlies for fun are on the wrong side of history. And they're not doing the cause of hunting any favors."

The states can't argue that hunting is an essential management tool because it isn't, he says. Grizzlies have been stewarded successfully in Greater Yellowstone without hunting for four decades. Further, they can't claim that the revenues generated through the sale of bear licenses will fix funding woes negatively impacting their agencies. Wyoming is in a severe budget crisis because of falling revenues from declining markets for coal, oil, and gas.

"Wyoming or Montana or Idaho are not going to maneuver their way through larger fiscal crises on the backs of dead bears. You can't kill that many bears through hunting, on top of the number already dying through a variety of causes, and not have a negative impact on the bear population," he said.

The deaths of a relatively small number of breeding female grizzlies can, over time, mean the difference between a rising or falling population. States say they won't target female bears in sport hunts. Dozens of bears each year are already being killed or removed in management actions. In the case of Grizzly 399, there are 25 bears descended from her. Sobering is that half of those two dozen relatives have died in various kinds of run-ins with people. One of her cubs was destroyed for eating a cow, another was shot by a deer hunter, and a few have been hit by cars.

"I agree that we should be celebrating the fact that conservation works in bringing back grizzlies but I find it obscene that we raise a toast to their recovery in one moment and in the next scramble to kill one," Mangelsen, a close friend of Kerasote's said. "When a person sport hunts a grizzly, that one individual comes to own it in death but meanwhile that same bear alive could be inspiring thousands of people and generations to care more about Nature."

Kerasote has traveled around the world and he has heard the reports that by the middle of this century, many large carnivores, including tigers in India and lions in Africa, as well as many other iconic species, could be rendered extinct in the wild. Given the trendlines of the global human population rising from 7 billion to 10 billion, the prospects are not good for species that need big space and human tolerance. Grizzlies are America's version of the tiger and lion and by showing the rest of the world how species can be ushered forward through this century with compassion and stewardship gives hope that it can be done in other areas, Kerasote predicts.

"I honestly don't understand why Wyoming keeps insisting that grizzlies need to be hunted. In practical terms, there's just no good reason other than appeasing a few people who just want the thrill of saying they killed a Greater Yellowstone bear," he adds. "To pander to that kind of mentality just makes the state look puerile. Is that the image that Wyoming really wants to project to the rest of the world?"

Hunters, he points out, also can't claim they've suffered a hardship or that their sacred tradition of killing grizzlies is somehow being impinged upon. There is no hardship or tradition because hunting hasn't happened for nearly half a century, he notes.

The values of the West have shifted markedly since 1975 when grizzlies were given federal protection. "There are many people who moved here who think that having bears is pretty cool. There is a large wild bear constituency that did not exist generations ago," Kerasote said. "The thought of bears naturally wandering outside a national park and then unsuspectingly getting blown away by a member of Safari Club International or a redneck wanting a bear rug is reprehensible to most people."

Aldo Leopold, in his age-old classic, A Sand County Almanac, writes about how the spirit of wildness left a mountain called Escudilla in the American southwest after the last grizzly was slain by a trapper enlisted to protect livestock interests. In gazing at that place, pondering the mere existence value of grizzlies, he observed:

"There was, in fact, only one place from which you did not see Escudilla on the skyline: that was the top of Escudilla itself … no one ever saw the old bear, but in the muddy springs about the base of the cliffs you saw his incredible tracks. Seeing them made even the most hard-bitten cowboys aware of bear. Wherever they rode they saw the mountain, and when they saw the mountain they thought of bear. We spoke harshly of the Spaniards who, in their zeal for gold and converts, had needlessly extinguished the native Indians. It did not occur to us that we, too, were the captains of an invasion too sure of its own righteousness. Escudilla still hangs on the horizon, but when you see it you no longer think of bear. It's only a mountain now."

Joe Gutkoski says that Greater Yellowstone is like a modern manifestation of Escudilla. "You don't need to possess an individual grizzly in order to know and appreciate its power," he says. "You don't need to claim its life for your own one-time personal benefit. I've run into grizzlies on hunts in the Gallatins and I've had profound moments of satisfaction seeing them and knowing they are there and may be there next time. They make me feel more alert and when you are more alert you feel more alive."

To him, no creature distills the essence of wildness more than a griz. "In this day and age, we are trying to hold onto that raw edge of nature as it slips away from us. Why would you want to kill an animal that is the emblem of the very thing we are trying to save? Why would you spend so many years, so much money, manpower, and resources bringing something back only so you can kill it again?"

At the end of the day, near the end of his life, Gutkoski pondered a series of questions: in the 21st century, why do we *recover* a species? What is our motivation and what does it say about us? Is it so we can eat them, as with an elk? Is it so we can sport hunt certain animals, like a grizzly, that we will never eat but instead turn into a decorative rug or have its head mounted on a wall and use it as a tool for giving us bragging rights? Is it to generate income as in non-consumptive wildlife watching?

Gutkoski believed the relationship between people and apex predators has come around full circle and it's time to chart a different course going forward. Can the states be trusted to do the right thing for *all* citizens, not just hunters, who revere wildlife? Newberg, who has an audience of millions, doesn't disagree with Gutkoski's assessment. "The grizzly is unique. States should take a lot of pride in the fact they've played a role in recovery. But grizzlies need to be treated like the special species they are, whether we manage them for hunting or not hunting. If we mess this up, then shame on us. The public will never forgive us if we do."

The Plague Is Coming

D R. MICHAEL OSTERHOLM SAVORS the outdoors in Minnesota. He's spent a lot of time ruminating about the thin permeable line that exists between human civilization and rare undeveloped areas of the planet, between livestock and wildlife, bats that dwell in caves and flying mammals "harvested" and served up in soup, between chimps and other primates living in African rainforest near the same places where humans emerged as a species, and markets in equatorial regions where the close cousins of *Homo sapiens* are sold as bushmeat. Osterholm also has reflected on the unappetizing prospect of people eating beef that came from cows fed forage comprised of ground up sheep and bovines, essentially making the grass eaters a kind of meat-eating cannibals. Unfortunately, the sheep and bovines put in the cattle trough were infected as disease called Bovine Spongiform Encephalopathy (BSE) also called Mad Cow and cousin to another nasty brain disease called Mad Deer or Mad Elk.

Osterholm is best-known and respected today for his nearly spot-on, prescient forecasts of how the coronavirus known as Covid-19 would spread and mutate in variant strains, infecting millions upon millions, making many sick and killing fewer but still a substantial number of humans. It is one thing to implement the best preventative procedures possible by public health officials, and have them heeded by humans who deny science and are led astray by people with political agendas, it is quite another to control another kind of pandemic. This one goes by the name of "hysteria."

Before Dr. Osterholm became known as a blunt-talking, plainspoken sage with Covid, he was spending a lot of time thinking about another potential epizootic menace that even today few Americans have ever heard of. Epizootic refers to a disease event in a nonhuman animal population that can cause an epidemic of disease in humans; in other words, disease spillovers from animals to people and, in some cases, vice versa as when Covid-19 strains were shown to infect deer and posed a serious threat potential to wild gorillas and other primates.

A couple years before Covid-19 appeared, I had a telephone conversation with Dr. Osterholm to discuss that other potential zoonotic threat. He had reached out after reading my reporting at *Mountain Journal* on Chronic Wasting Disease (colloquially "Mad Deer" and "Mad Elk" diseases) and he said to keep it up, that we had devoted more virtual ink to this emerging disease than any other journalistic outlet in America. Our chat reached a sobering crescendo when he said, "All we need is one CWD case in which a human gets sick and dies to show the jig is up, to provide it can happen and then people will go off the deep end. There's no way you'll be able to control the hysteria."

Chronic Wasting Disease, or CWD, is a disease that devastates the central nervous system of its victims, it resides within the same family of maladies as Mad Cow Disease, and for those infected there is no cure. CWD as of right afflicts members of the cervid or deer family, which includes white-tailed and mule deer, elk, moose and caribou. So far there has not been a documented case of CWD infecting people after they have eaten game meat, but Dr. Osterholm told me that he believes such transmission is inevitable as right now hundreds of thousands of people have or are eating wild game animals that been infected or carry CWD, which is caused by misshapen proteins, known as prions, that are agents of encephalopathy that alter brain function.

In fact, Dr. Osterholm testified before the state legislature in Minnesota, where he is based, that it is only a matter of time before CWD kills a human and when that happens it is likely to set off a wave of uncontrolled panic not only about human health, particularly with millions of hunters who eat game meat and serve it to their families, but also livestock and CWD prions potentially contaminating food crops, soils, water and having implications for trade.

The reporting at *Mountain Journal* has been focused on CWD reaching the largest and most diverse concentration of large wild ungulates in the Lower 48, which happens to be located in the Greater Yellowstone Ecosystem. Wildlife and disease officials recognize that the implications of CWD potentially reaching widespread infection rates in the region's elk, deer and moose could have far-reaching consequences for hunters and the guiding industry, wild game processors, wildlife-watching as part of a multi-billion nature tourism industry and of course the predator-prey system that makes it globally iconic.

If someone like Dr. Osterholm, who has also tracked Ebola and Mad Cow (BSE) in the United Kingdom, is concerned about CWD, leading public health officials in America say we ought to be paying attention, too. Of his talks before legislators and agricultural officials, especially those dealing with wildlife such as deer and elk being raised on captive game farms, he told me: "They had to hear the truth and I didn't spare a world. At the time I said this has all the makings of BSE déjà vu (the Mad Cow outbreak in Britain linked to humans eating contaminated beef) all over again. Even if it's not going to happen, there is nothing to keep us from being expeditious and responsible in saying that 'Let's at the very least, just do whatever we can to prevent humans from coming in contact with or being exposed to contaminated venison.'"

Looking west toward the Greater Yellowstone, Osterholm said that the state of Wyoming had created giant petri dishes, in the form of elk feeding grounds, where if there were ever ripe conditions created for a disease like CWD to spread with virulence among cervids, it is there.

On any given morning in Yellowstone's Lamar Valley, wolf watchers show up in force. Prior to the winter of 1995 when long-extirpated lobos were restored to the park following 60 years of being gone due to deliberate human-caused extermination, the dell used to be quiet and devoid of many people. Now in this new millennium, citizen naturalists are ever so happy to assist visitors in peering through spotting scopes and observing wolves interacting with other pack members, confronting rival packs, and hunting, for the most part, elk.

Not so long ago, P.J. White, Yellowstone's wildlife management chief, and I were discussing what was then a hypothetical. What happens when a haggard-looking elk, left emaciated by the stress of a hard winter, ambles forth in front of human onlookers and drops dead? While under Yellowstone's natural regulation policy, in which nature is left to play out according to its own devices, ordinarily nothing would happen, circumstances today are different.

Ordinarily, a winter-killed wapiti would drop to the ground and immediately provide sustenance for a variety of wildlife scavengers, turning the carcass into a buffet for many different species.

But in these times CWD is a silent menace lurking. It has spread into populations of cervids in more than half of all U.S. states and provinces in Canada. It is classified as a new disease and one of top epinootic concern Although, again, there have been no confirmed cases of CWD being transmitted to people, yet, the ecological effects could also be dire. One study in Wyoming predicted that were CWD to become widespread in elk many herds could be in danger of dying out. How did CWD begin its march toward Greater Yellowstone?

On a map, "Deer Hunt Area 17" is unlikely to ring any bells of geographic recognition, even for residents in hunting-crazed Wyoming. Located northwest of Gillette in the Powder River Basin—a sweep of rolling, mostly treeless high plains embedded in the largest coal-producing region in America—Hunt Area 17 on Monday, December 19, 2016 became one of the latest in Wyoming to have a publicly-confirmed case of CWD.

"If you see a deer, elk, or moose that appears to be sick or not acting in a normal manner, please contact your local game warden, wildlife biologist, or Game and Fish office immediately," Scott Edberg, then deputy chief of the Wyoming Game and Fish Department's wildlife division, said in a press release.

Game and Fish added this to its statement, deferring to the assessment of medical professionals at two major public health entities: "The Centers for Disease Control and the World Health Organization recommend that people should not eat deer, elk, or moose that test positive for CWD."

That is one example. Many more confirmations of CWD in deer, elk, and moose have since swept across Wyoming. It's not often that citizens receive advisories from a government agency cautioning them the wild edibles they have traditionally harvested from nature for generations should first be tested to determine if they are safe to eat.

But that's exactly what Wyoming's wildlife agency did. Not long before, Game and Fish also posted an additional bulletin, alluding to the findings of a peer-reviewed Canadian study in which macaques (primates with a genetic makeup very similar to humans) were fed deer meat contaminated with CWD and fell fatally ill with disease.

CWD is on the minds of countless hunters in North America. Randy Newberg knows. "Am I worried about CWD?" he asked as another hunting season was getting underway. "Yes, I've been worried about it for years in terms of what it means for the health of wild deer, elk, and other animals." He acknowledges widespread confusion among hunters and that "public discussions about CWD are all over the map."

"There are deniers and there are overreacters," he said. "Where I am with CWD comes down to the expert opinions of scientists, many of whom believe we could be setting ourselves up for disaster."

Ever increasingly, in the rapidly-expanding reaches of the U.S. landscape becoming classified as CWD-endemic areas, huge numbers of outdoorspeople have trepidation about the wholesomeness of big game meat they bring home to the family dinner table. The laboratory study with macaques in Canada mentioned above, if the results are confirmed by second and third parties and replicated in months and years ahead, would represent a frightening watershed moment in thinking about CWD's ability to cross species barriers. It's a malady whose seriousness as a possible risk to humans has often eclipsed discussion of its already real impacts to nature.

Indeed, the potential consequences of CWD spreading throughout Greater Yellowstone's migratory wildlife has been downplayed and minimized for years in Wyoming. Numerous experts whom I interviewed said Wyoming's hands'-off approach to dealing with CWD is one of the most glaring examples in modern wildlife history where a preponderance of growing scientific evidence, supporting the need for aggressive intervention to slow a potential catastrophe, has been willfully dismissed to fit entrenched political agendas and commercial interests.

Like the expanding impacts of human population growth and climate change in the Greater Yellowstone Ecosystem, CWD represents a true test, they say, of whether public and private land managers, elected officials, and citizens in the region can really come together to address landscape-level challenges.

As of now, testing to determine if game meat is infected with CWD is made only *after* an animal is dead, yet living carriers of the contagion can appear normal and asymptomatic even when stricken with the disease that will kill them.

Endemic zone classifications for CWD applies to areas where the disease is now believed to be present in animals. But as with the testing mentioned above, lack of confirmation of a CWD-infected ungulate being present in a given area does not equate to absence of disease.

While Wyoming Deer Hunt Areas 17 was a few hours' drive from Greater Yellowstone in 2016, CWD endemic zones today are on the doorstep of Yellowstone and Grand Teton national parks, the adjacent National Elk Refuge in Jackson Hole, and inevitably will extend to all of ecosystem's national forests. The Powder River Basin, notably, also spills northward across Wyoming's border into Montana. Within months of CWD reaching Wyoming Deer Hunt Area 17, the disease would be confirmed for the first time ever in Montana, in a mule deer, and since then has turned up in dozens of deer, elk, and moose across the entire state, making it one of the swiftest progressions recorded yet for the disease.

Incurable, progressive, often slow to incubate, and except in the rarest of circumstances always-fatal, CWD has been described by epizoologists have confirmed Newberg's opinion of it being "a slow-motion wildlife disaster" in the making.

CWD causes individual victims to become emaciated with telltale symptoms: "vacant stares, drooping ears, stumbling movements, and drooling." Internal physiological effects can include transforming brains into the consistency of mushy Swiss cheese. Animals withering in the last phase of CWD behave and look remarkably similar to humans incapacitated in the final stages of severe dementia. Their haggard, bony appearance could also be mistaken for animals emaciated from hard winters.

Scientists say CWD can take years to assert full impact at a population level. It has been spreading steadily in individual animals westward across Wyoming after it was diagnosed in the southeastern corner of the state decades ago. CWD at present is in nearly 30 states in wild public herds and privately owned animals in game farms. There currently are neither vaccines available to stop it nor curative medicines that can be dispensed to hosts having it.

Whether a person hunts and consumes big game or is among the countless millions of Americans who simply enjoy having healthy wildlife on the landscape, CWD is creating impacts that scientists say they are just beginning to comprehend. The only hope for potentially dampening its impact in Greater Yellowstone, according to leading wildlife authorities, is taking actions that just happen to cut against the fundamental grain of how Wyoming has approached wildlife management for generations. In a nutshell it means halting century-old public feeding of wildlife and viewing predators, namely wolves, as allies in fighting diseases instead of as scourges that Wyoming would just as soon wipe off the landscape.

The origin of CWD is inexact. Some believe it is related to a scrapie outbreak which afflicted domestic sheep and then jumped species. In 1967, CWD was affirmed among captive deer kept at a research facility near Fort Collins, Colorado and then spread into wild deer and elk herds in that state.

Wildlife experts say the prevalence of CWD in some southeast Wyoming mule deer herds already ranges between 20 and 45 percent. Most victims die within two years of becoming infected but can live for half a decade. CWD is more common in bucks than does and prevalence oscillates differently in deer than elk, but some outbreaks of CWD in both captive deer and elk have been equally severe.

In the 1990s, the late Jim Posewitz, a revered sportsman in Montana and lifelong conservationist who worked for the Montana Department of Fish Wildlife and Parks, expressed concerns about CWD to me around the time that voters in his state went to the polls passing a ballot initiative to outlaw wildlife game farms.

Game farms are private facilities where wildlife is husbanded like livestock, sometimes to serve as trophies in canned hunting behind fences, sometimes to be used as breeding stock, or sold as meat to restaurants. Some horns from male deer and elk at game farms have been exported to Asian markets where they are marketed as traditional medicines and aphrodisiacs.

The campaign to ban game farms in Montana was prompted by rising concerns about epizootic diseases. One game farm deemed especially problematic was a fenced compound operated by Welch "Sonny" Brogan just outside of Gardiner, Montana near the northern border of Yellowstone and right in the middle of a wild elk and bison migration corridor. Bison, under laboratory conditions, have shown they can become infected with CWD but there have been no confirmed CWD cases in wild bison, yet. The late Mr. Brogan, who became known as "the granddaddy" of Montana game farms, was charged in 1989 with capturing wild elk and having poorly maintained fences that could result in captive elk escaping. Brogan fought the charges but his conviction was upheld by the Montana Supreme Court in 1993.

The reason the fencing issue was so important is that Brogan at one point was accused of selling some of his captive elk to a game farm in Canada—animals that later became sickened with bovine tuberculosis, a virulent disease that not only kills wildlife but is a hazard to humans. An investigation resulted in Brogan's facility being placed under quarantine and him ordered to pay $100,000 to the game farm with whom he did business.

Around the same time as Montana's ballot initiative, a Canadian biologist named Dr. Valerius Geist, who passed away in 2021 and was professor emeritus in Environmental Science at the University of Calgary, was on the stump warning about the consequences of epizootic diseases flaring among captive animals in game farms throughout the Canadian prairie provinces. He and I had many long conversations and he warned that CWD was more frightening than any other malady he was tracking. A major scare arrived in 1999 with the discovery of nine captive CWD-infected elk at an "alternative livestock" facility near Philipsburg, Montana. For a time, some wondered if any had escaped to the wild. Geist's jeremiads helped sway public opinion in Montana to realize the serious risk of disease. Echoing Geist, Posewitz said two decades ago that "once, and if, CWD ever arrives in our wild deer and elk herds in Montana, all bets are off. You won't be able to control it; it's going to forever change how we think about those animals."

Game meat is revered as a wholesome staple. He worried CWD would tarnish that image and could ultimately negatively impact the level of affection hunters and non-hunters alike have for those emblems of the wild Rockies.

Many believe the tipping point moment with CWD, predicted ominously by Posewitz and Geist, has already arrived. Because of the way elk are controversially managed in western Wyoming, it represents a case study, scientists say, for how **not** to steward public wildlife in the face of an advancing pandemic.

Dr. Thomas Roffe, a veterinarian and former National Chief of Wildlife Health for the U.S. Fish and Wildlife Service, told me this: if scientists were tasked with designing an experiment to create ideal conditions for a pandemic to take hold, involving a transmissible infectious disease in wildlife during winter when they are most stressed by the elements, one example would be having game farms. The other would be creating a complex of artificial feeding operations identical to those operating today in western Wyoming. Dr. Osterholm didn't disagree.

Indeed, CWD has never arrived in a healthy, still-functioning wild ecosystem with so much going on in terms of interactions between predators and prey, sheer numbers of potential victims, and complicated migrations happening over long distances on a high-profile public stage with a global profile. The stakes are high. Hundreds of thousands of wild elk, mule and white-tailed deer move in herds or small bands, circulating throughout Greater Yellowstone across jurisdictional boundaries of land management agencies, intermingling seasonally and dispersing again across huge, mind-boggling expanses of terrain. Those animals, in turn, come in contact with other herds up and down the northern Rockies.

Dr. Thomas Pringle, a molecular biogeneticist and respected authority on CWD and prion diseases, said mammal-to-bird transmission is highly improbable. He also said that birds such as raptors, corvids, and other avians are not carriers. The Wyoming feedgrounds, he and others say, represent a point of tightly-packed unnatural confluence for several herds in winter, meaning that if animals get sick there, they will carry diseases with them elsewhere. Similarly, if stricken animals arrive on the feedgrounds, there is a much stronger probability, given the notoriously high densities of animals, that they could be seeds to an outbreak. This is one of the golden rules of epidemiology involved people and it applies to animals.

Roffe has pondered the optics: what happens if, and when, elk, deer, and moose in Greater Yellowstone start dropping dead from CWD, whether in the valleys and geyser basins of Yellowstone Park in front of tourists, the middle of the Elk Refuge along busy U.S. Highway 191 in Jackson Hole, the flats of Grand Teton, or even within the city limits of Bozeman, Cody, Lander and Rexburg?

Will dead animals be quickly retrieved to prevent them from causing accumulating environmental contamination? Will the carcasses be dumped in landfills or incinerated? Does it mean that every live deer, elk, or moose that looks lean and weakened after surviving the winter will be treated as a possible CWD carrier?

How does having CWD-infected herds affect the public perception of wildlife? It's a grave prospect on the minds of Yellowstone Superintendent Cam Sholly and his staff. Sholly, however, admits there is no plan, no coordinated strategy existing between state and federal agencies for how to confront CWD. The very government entity that was created to formulate regional strategies, the Greater Yellowstone Coordinating Committee, does not have a unified plan.

For many years, Roffe worked as the equivalent of Dr. Anthony Fauci in his own field. Fauci is director of the National Institute of Allergy and Infectious Diseases and is currently advising The White House on how to deal with novel coronavirus. Roffe spent his career with the U.S. Fish and Wildlife Service, rising to the rank of chief veterinarian for animal health. His post was a prestigious and influential one, hard earned.

Apart from CWD's deadly consequences for members of the deer family, concerns abound about CWD's potential for crossing other species barriers. There is fear about it potentially infecting mammalian predators, ranging from grizzlies, wolves, coyotes, and foxes to other scavengers that feast upon dead animals. Yet the real wild card is what risk, if any, CWD and its possible mutations pose to human health? That risk appears to be remote, but it might or might not be.

Some scientists, like Dr. Don Davis, professor emeritus at Texas A & M University and a vocal defender of game farms in Texas where CWD is a growing issue, claim the risk is nominal, that raising the threat of CWD to human health is nothing more than media hyperbole. He wrote a couple of pointed push-backs after media reports about the Canadian macaque study.

In a recent op-ed, Davis highlighted the important fact that there hasn't been a single verified case of humans contracting CWD by eating an infected big game animal. "As a research scientist with 40 years of experience in the area of wildlife diseases, I have been regularly disappointed, disgusted, alarmed, and amazed at both the amount and frequency of alleged facts reported on CWD. These 'facts' are based entirely on totally unsubstantiated rumor or—even worse—on horribly misquoted science by misguided or misinformed individuals," Davis wrote recently in an editorial widely circulated to newspapers by an organization called The Exotic Wildlife Foundation.

Dr. Davis' assessment, however, is far from universally shared by peers working in wildlife medicine, including biogeneticist Pringle. In fact, people I spoke with say Davis' opinion would be in the minority. A far greater danger is minimizing the seriousness of the possible threat, suggests Dr. Michael W. Miller, formerly the senior chief wildlife veterinarian with the Colorado Division of Wildlife and a noted CWD authority. With prion diseases, increased likelihood of human infection is really a matter of a lot of people eating a lot of contaminated game meat.

"For a long time, some have been clinging to the naïve hope that if we just ignore chronic wasting disease and do nothing, it will go away," Dr. Miller told me. "The problem is that CWD has not gone away. It is not becoming rarer in the wild. In fact, it's become measurably worse over time. It is becoming more prevalent in wildlife, not less."

Miller, known for his cool-headed discussions about risk, acknowledges that he is concerned foremost about its impacts on wild ungulates and the domino effect of direct and indirect impacts it could set off for other species.

The more that new information has emerged in recent years, the level of concern has risen, not fallen. Some contagious diseases over the course of time run their course, leave behind survivors that carry immunity and then die down. Scrapie in domestic sheep is an example of that, Dr. Miller says. But CWD is accelerating in its geographic reach.

Wyoming for years predicted it might take a long while before CWD reached one of the most famous elk herds in the world. Like many of the state's prognostications, that one was wrong. Late in 2020, CWD was confirmed in a cow elk in Grand Teton National Park. Confirmation that the animal, killed by a big game hunter, had tested was announced Friday, Dec. 18 by the Wyoming Game and Fish Department's Wildlife Health Laboratory.

Scientists say that whether Jackson Hole CWD Elk Case No. 1 represents the start of a troubling new era. Although CWD's arrival in Jackson Hole elk has long been anticipated, it is important to mention that solid evidence comes with no small amount of bitter irony.

Early in the 20th century, Jackson Hole rose as a beacon in American wildlife conservation history when, in 1912, the National Elk Refuge was established as a rescue mission. Following winters when thousands of elk died from starvation owed to the fact they were unable to migrate out of Jackson Hole due to settlement blocking their traditional passageways, stranded wapiti on the flats stretching north of the town of Jackson were given supplemental rations of hay. As a result, it created an unnatural massing of elk in the high-elevation valley that previously did not exist prior to the arrival of white homesteaders.

Now, in more ecologically-enlightened times, this management practice is highly controversial. It is under withering scrutiny as disease experts say feeding, which puts elk at grave risk of catching CWD, could actually lead to the destruction of animals it was intended to save.

Western Wyoming is home to the largest unnatural wildlife feedground complex in the world. Along with the Elk Refuge, there are another 22 elk feedgrounds operated by the state of Wyoming. In total, more than 20,000 elk will congregate in close quarters at those locations until spring, whereby they are highly likely to come in close contact with other CWD-infected wapiti or deer, experts say.

Most worrisome to Roffe and others is that Grand Teton Park, where Jackson Hole CWD Elk Case No. 1 was confirmed, is located immediately *adjacent* to the Elk Refuge where thousands of wild wapiti are again present. As soon as the infected animal was confirmed, the Elk Refuge immediately started adhering to its "Disease Response Strategy" that is 19 pages long, Refuge Manager Frank Durbian told *Mountain Journal.* "I was not surprised [by confirmation of a CWD-positive elk]. I've studied the progression of CWD both within the state of Wyoming and across the country. It was not a matter of if CWD would get here but when. Unfortunately the when question just got answered." Neither the Elk Refuge nor Wyoming Game and Fish have any plans to curtail feeding this winter—positions that have drawn sharp rebukes.

The Elk Refuge, in response to court action brought by the environmental law firm EarthJustice, its senior attorney Tim Preso and conservation groups it represents, has been actively engaged in what it calls a "step-down" plan to wean elk off alfalfa pellets and hay over a course of years.

Roffe noted that the step-down plan grew out of the 2007 Elk Refuge's Bison and Elk Management Plan, which called for reducing elk numbers, to lower disease risk and prevent documented environmental harm to the refuge itself from elk overgrazing, has been a dismal failure. He said the "plan recognized that feeding wildlife (specifically elk) placed that resource at great risk of disease amplification and was antithesis to sound ecological management."

The agent that causes CWD is not a virus, bacteria, fungi, or parasite: not a typical living organism, but misshapen proteins called prions without DNA and RNA structure, which become harbored mostly in the brains and central nervous system of deer family victims.

As one researcher told me, "They [prions] are weird, they're not like normal proteins, and unlike viruses and bacteria they do not produce an immune response from the organisms they attack. We don't know what activates them and we don't know what the triggers are that could cause them to mutate, making them more conducive to move from one species to another." In this case, "mutation" means prions being altered in ways that increase the odds of transmission among wildlife, livestock, and people.

CWD is categorized among a general suite of neurological illnesses known as transmissible spongiform encephalopathies (TSEs). In cattle (and other hooved animals), the disease is grouped among a malady category called bovine spongiform encephalopathies or BSEs. CWD, also nicknamed "mad deer" and "mad elk" diseases, is a cousin of scrapie (which targets domestic sheep). To claim, as some do, that CWD won't proliferate within Greater Yellowstone deer and elk, and possibly represent a hazard to livestock or predators, which includes humans, is, in the opinion of experts I spoke with, to deny the reality of what has already been demonstrated elsewhere with prion diseases.

The best example of species barriers being breached with TSE prion diseases is found in Britain where around 200 humans who ate domestic cattle infected with Mad Cow died. The human version of Mad Cow Disease is a TSE called Creutzfeldt-Jacob Disease and another, variant-strain Creutzfeldt-Jakob-Jacob, both of which are very rare.

British cattle were believed infected after the remains of sheep suffering from scrapie were ground up and blended with feed poured into their troughs. The Mad Cow scare, which made headlines and caused panic around the world, resulted in the depopulation and incineration of millions of domestic cows that were potentially exposed to sickened animals. It also elevated concerns about lasting environmental contamination in the ground, a worry later validated by an experiment in Wyoming. Likely, millions of people in Britain and elsewhere came in contact with BSE-infected beef, hence the parallel to keep in mind with what Miller said about the likelihood of CWD transmission to people increasing with lots of hunters eating lots of contaminated game animals.

Were CWD to afflict humans, the most likely route of transmission would be from CWD-carrying wildlife infecting cattle or domestic sheep and then humans consuming those animals. There are no documented cases of prions that are shed by deer or elk then infecting cattle.

An advisory posted by the Centers for Disease Control in Atlanta, the nation's premiere authority on infectious pathogens, states: "Concerns have been raised about the possible transmission of the CWD agent to domestic animals, such as cattle and sheep, which may come in contact with infected deer and elk or CWD-contaminated environments. If such transmissions were to occur, they would potentially increase the extent and frequency of human exposure to the CWD agent. In addition, passage of the agent through a secondary host could alter its infectious properties, increasing its potential for becoming more pathogenic to humans."

Prions are notoriously hard biological particles to destroy. Cooking does not kill or immobilize them. They can remain actively infectious in the tissues and fluids of living and dead animals. "I'm very concerned about prion cross-contamination and it comes from some of my foodborne disease work, and has an overlay with prions," Dr. Osterholm says. "What the hell happens when you introduce CWD into meat processing environments? If somebody's deer or elk comes through and it's contaminated what does that mean for everything else behind it? I'll tell you: it's not good because it's not easy to sterilize and decontaminate places and surfaces that become tainted with BSE prions. I've been involved with several situations in hospitals where someone with Creutzfeldt-Jakob disease was accidentally operated on, had brain surgery, and they didn't understand what was going on. All of that medical equipment had to be land filled. There was no way we could adequately disinfect it. And now imagine the processing environment. I just finally said enough is enough here. We've got to speak out on this thing. I realize I have a voice in Minnesota and to some degree around the country; if I put my name to something, I typically think it's pretty important. I finally spoke out and said this is it."

Prions also leach into the environment through feces and urine and, as the carcass of a dead animal decays, contaminate soils and water for long, indefinite periods of time. Recent scientific studies in controlled settings also have shown that prions shed into the ground, especially in clay soils to which they bind, can even be taken up in living vegetation.

And many believe that CWD prions could be dispersed more widely across landscapes by being bound up in alfalfa that is shipped far and wide as hay bales and then fed to livestock.

So, is it possible for CWD prions to mutate and thereby become transmittable from members of the deer family to people, or other creatures eating contaminated meat, or by merely ingesting infected brain, spinal fluids, plants, and water? Dr. Osterholm believes there is a chance.

What about elk and deer that might appear healthy, but actually aren't and are then consumed by people, or asymptomatic infected animals that come into contact with other animals being packaged at local meat processors? What are the odds that domestic livestock grazing on contaminated grass growing from contaminated soil, be it on public or private lands, could become infected?

The answers are that no one knows yet, but some of the emerging indicators keep the level of concern heightened. Uncertainty is why the CDC and World Health Organization have for years offered their cautions against human consumption of cervids that test positive for CWD. Whether actual risk of prion transmission to humans is low, as Dr. Davis suggests, or higher, if mutations occur enabling CWD to jump species, it is a calculation that individuals must make in eating game meat.

Although it is admittedly a small sample size, a dozen different people (scientists, wildlife managers, and conservationists) well versed in the research of CWD and who also hunt elk and deer, told me they would not feed even healthy big game coming out of a CWD-endemic area to their families. That hasn't stopped deer hunters in Wisconsin.

Recent studies, like the research on macaques in Canada, suggest CWD jumping the species barrier to humans is possible. But Dr. Davis questions the techniques used in the studies and he points out that a similar earlier experiment demonstrated no linkage, a reference that will be explored in ensuing parts of this series. While the risk of CWD prions infecting people is low, threats to wildlife and landscape, however, are not. Some have alluded to CWD's arrival in Greater Yellowstone as a "ticking time bomb about to go off in the premiere wildland ecosystem in the Lower 48." Dr. Osterholm sees a similar pattern between denial about Mad Cow in the U.K. and CWD in the U.S.

BSE-related prions have demonstrated their ability to transcend boundaries between sheep and cattle, and across deer family members, and even from cattle to bison and, as demonstrated by Mad Cow, to people. Undeniable, experts say, are the threats posed to wild ungulates. Ironically, the future health of Greater Yellowstone's vaunted migratory ungulate herds is being jeopardized by the very government agencies whose duty it is to protect public wildlife from harm, warned Lloyd Dorsey, the longtime conservation director with the Wyoming state chapter of the Sierra Club who has since retired.

Even a federal appellate court has rebuked the U.S. Fish and Wildlife Service for engaging in management malpractice and violating federal laws. Ground zero for this prima facie argument is the Elk Refuge. At the Elk Refuge alone during recent winters, more than 8,800 elk converged around artificial food rations given to them. Combined with the state feedgrounds, upwards of 21,000 wild wapiti are congregated unnaturally together in western Wyoming, leaving them more vulnerable to catching not only CWD but bovine tuberculosis, septicemic pasteurellosis and hoof rot. High rates of brucellosis infection found among wild elk nourished at feedgrounds prove the point.

Wyoming for a long, long time has justified its refusal to close down feedgrounds by, more or less, portraying CWD as merely a hypothetical risk. In August 2004, the Wyoming Game and Fish Department released what it called a comprehensive white paper titled "Elk Feedgrounds in Wyoming." Its authors were: Ron Dean, Mark Gocke, Bernie Holz, Steve Kilpatrick, Dr. Terry Kreeger, Brandon Scurlock, Scott Smith, Dr. E. T. Thorne, and Scott Werbelow. "Many people are concerned that elk on feedgrounds may mimic the circumstances of elk in captivity and suggest that feedgrounds will result in high CWD prevalence resulting in drastic population declines as implicated by the disease models. Although this may happen, a perfectly acceptable alternative hypothesis is that CWD will have little or no impact on elk populations based on the known low prevalence rates for CWD in wild elk. Although there are many opinions, no one knows what will happen if elk on feedgrounds become infected with CWD."

In short order, Americans have become educated, in ways we never were before, about the thinking that goes into containment of zoonotic disease. Think now of the concepts firmly embedded in public consciousness with a purpose generally understood: *Social distancing. Sheltering in place.* Orders issued from on high directing humans not to gather in large groups.

Protocols, based on science, were devised by public health officials as a response to the deadly Covid-19 pandemic; the point is that in the face of a spreading communicable contagion the worst possible action is herding large numbers of humans together and concentrating us in single locations. At first, the appropriate limit set for massing was no more than 1,000 people, then dialed down to 500, then later reduced to 100, 50, and 10. Now the strategy, informed by epidemiology, is that we stay at home, or move about sparingly at no closer than six feet; if we grocery shop or order take out from a restaurant, it is smart to do so wearing a mask. The very same strategies for preventing disease transmission from human to human and animal to human apply for animal to animal, be it pets, livestock, or wildlife, experts have advised.

Jackson Hole valley folk, some of whom hail from the same families who in the 1930s and 1940s fought creation of Grand Teton Park, have also taken out full-page ads in the local newspaper condemning fellow citizens and public servants who speak a different reality that does not comport with their own world view and economic self-interest.

Bruce Smith, who spent decades at the National Elk Refuge rising to the rank of senior biologist and who wrote an acclaimed book, *Where Elk Roam: Conservation and Politics of Our National Elk Herd*, dared on several occasions to publicly declare the era of artificially feeding elk has to end.

That was met by calls for his firing as a civil servant and later as an alleged speaker of heresy in local newspaper ads.

If Wyoming believes it will be able to market its way out of a CWD crisis or deny culpability for a problem it has known is coming, Smith told me recently, then it is in for a rude awakening. This isn't just any region. It is the Greater Yellowstone Ecosystem, with Yellowstone National Park at its wild heart. It has a national constituency. The public will demand answers and accountability; citizens will want to know the names of who was in charge and did little to prevent disaster from happening.

To nature-adoring onlookers, the sea of elk gathered every winter on the National Elk Refuge in Jackson Hole, Wyoming appears to be an enchanting vision of wapiti nirvana.

Across generations, countless people have taken sleigh rides offered to tourists who visit the Elk Refuge. There, they can watch thousands wild elk being fed dry hay and alfalfa pellets. Elk are an iconic part of Jackson Hole's identify. Indeed, the town of Jackson, Wyoming's four rustic elk antler archways in its central public square are built from antlers shed by bull elk on the refuge.

Many readers here might reasonably wonder what could possibly be wrong with this tranquil picture? How could anyone question the magnanimous gestures of local folk and U.S. taxpayers offering these majestic creatures nutritional charity to get them through the snow season?

After all, many Americans, on the sly, put out corn and other grains for deer in winter, defying state laws against feeding yet believing they, too, are doing the animals a favor. In an age of CWD, looks can be perilously deceiving, scientists say.

As CWD rapidly expands its geographical reach in North America, those seemingly benign practices of feeding, experts warn, could be hastening disastrous consequences. Still, old-time residents of Jackson Hole get emotional, even misty-eyed, when discussing why the sight of so many elk is part of their culture and sense of place. They see the feeding of elk in heroic terms, the result of ancestors stepping forward and rescuing a national animal treasure, similar to what happened when Theodore Roosevelt, William Hornaday, and others emerged as saviors against the total annihilation of bison.

Artificial feeding at the Elk Refuge was initiated more than a century ago. Thousands of elk starved to death on the flats north of town, causing a public outcry that stretched all the way to Washington D.C. In response, a campaign to acquire land and create a national refuge in 1912 where elk could be fed was cemented.

There is even an apocryphal tale about the die-off years, that a human could have walked on the backs of dead elk in the snow for more than a dozen miles and never had one's feet touch the ground. The justification for feeding is based on the following rationale: because so much elk winter range in Jackson Hole has been covered by human development and because private ranches do not welcome elk, regarding them as unwanted competitors for grass consumed by cattle, the offering of alfalfa chow lines beyond what nature provides is essential.

Keeping wild elk reliant and semi-tamed on unnatural forage in fenceless feedlot conditions draws many—but not all of them—away from private property. Similar artificial nourishment of elk happens on 22 other state-run feedlots dotting the adjacent federal Bridger-Teton National Forest, on tracts administered by the Bureau of Land Management and state lands scattered across western Wyoming.

What the controversial feeding program stands in contradiction to, however, is the conclusion of virtually every major professional wildlife management organization which warns that bunching up animals fosters conditions that are ripe for deadly disease outbreaks. Wyoming's rationale for feeding stands in contrast to other valleys across the West, including Greater Yellowstone's Madison Valley in Montana, where wild elk persist in abundance and are not given boosts of alfalfa pellets to keep them alive.

Elk start arriving on the National Elk Refuge and the state's unfenced feedlots in droves in November, pushed out of the mountains by deepening snows. Remaining until April, they disperse again to distant summer calving and autumn breeding grounds in the high country following green up.

Dorsey looks upon the Elk Refuge regularly. In fact, when I spoke to him recently, he was on his way to hunt big game in the Gros Ventre Mountains, passing by both the Elk Refuge and a state-run feedground on the Bridger-Teton National Forest called Alkali Creek.

"One of the prevailing frontier-mentality options was killing off wildlife that was regarded as a competitor or threat to livestock; another was putting wildlife figuratively into boxes and, in this case, feeding elk like you would cattle in a pasture, semi-domesticating them. I get why it was done," Dorsey said. "Feeding elk in the early 20th century made sense because it mitigated conflicts and kept more elk alive to hunt, eat, and make money from."

But he and many others say it should have been a short-term solution, phased out when the science became clear decades ago. Recently, an official with the Wyoming Game and Fish Department admitted as much in a meeting with conservationists from Montana. Still, due to political resistance, feeding has continued. Some rural Wyomingites today insist their "way of life" and financial livelihoods depends on state and federal governments spending millions annually to feed elk.

"Intolerance toward free-ranging elk became official policy, and still is," Dorsey notes. He and others say there is still plenty of natural habitat on public land to sustain elk in western Wyoming without artificial feeding. Big game hunters, especially Wyoming outfitters and guides who profit by giving clients higher hunter success achieved through inflated numbers of animals to harvest, have vigorously defended feeding, at the same time denying that CWD is a serious issue.

Some vocal pro-feeding activists in Jackson Hole, like those arrayed around a group called Concerned Citizens for the Elk, have asserted, using Manichean logic, that it is better to keep feeding elk to prevent them from dying than stop feeding elk even though feeding leaves them highly vulnerable to catching a deadly non-eradicable disease. A local Jackson Hole veterinarian has even accused the Elk Refuge of deliberately starving elk whenever federal managers have made an attempt to reduce the amount of artificial feeding.

Harold Turner is the patriarch of a family that sells outfitting services and guided hunts on the Bridger-Teton National Forest. The Turner operation is based out of the Triangle X Guest Ranch in Grand Teton National Park, a tourist concession operation owned by the federal government. The Turner family sold the ranch to the federal government more than half a century ago, though it is a common misperception among Jackson Hole residents that the Turners still hold the deed.

Mr. Turner has long opposed cessation of feeding elk. "If the elk feeding grounds were shut down, we would not only lose our base, our economic base, but we will lose our heritage," he claimed on camera in filmmaker Danny Schmidt's acclaimed documentary *Feeding the Problem* that examines the feedground dilemma.

Wyoming's ongoing motivation for doing all it can to halt the proposed elimination of feedgrounds is no mystery. Elk and deer hunting generates tens of millions of dollars for the economy of gateway communities in Greater Yellowstone. By the numbers, the amount of money generated annually by selling guided elk hunts in Greater Yellowstone is a small fraction within the overall pie of income generated through non-consumptive nature tourism in northwest Wyoming. Meanwhile, the number of big game hunters continues to dramatically decline nationwide in America, exacerbating the sense of desperation among outfitters and guides that their tradition is fading away with changing times. And it does not bode well for the Wyoming Game and Fish Department that gets operating revenue from the sale of hunting licenses.

One hunting outfitter and guide in Jackson Hole, without offering any scientific data to substantiate his contention, claimed CWD is merely a "bogeyman" disease. That same individual has also claimed that wolves would devastate wildlife, an assertion proved by facts to be false. Concerned Citizens for the Elk has taken out full-page ads in the Jackson Hole News & Guide trying to call into question the science of infectious disease.

Turner suggested on film that the most prudent strategy for dealing with CWD is to wait until it arrives rather than taking preventative action such as closing down the feedgrounds. Fellow rancher and hunting outfitter/guide Glenn Taylor, also interviewed for Schmidt's documentary, chose to deny the science of wildlife epidemiology.

"I've been asked about Chronic Wasting Disease before and I don't think it's as serious as they try to make you think," Taylor told Schmidt. "Maybe today there's too much scientific demand [reliance on science]. Maybe we need to manage from the seat of our pants is a good term, I think. Let the animals kind of do their thing. We may be better off that way than trying to initiate or use too much science to manage maybe what science shouldn't be doing that."

Wyoming and the Elk Refuge stand accused by scientific experts as managing wildlife by the seat of its pants and critics assert that if wildlife were left to do its own thing, as Taylor suggests, feedgrounds would be shut down for the good of the public herds.

To willfully ignore 21st century, peer-reviewed research, conservationists like Dorsey note, is to embrace ignorance, the kind of thinking that prevailed during the era of bloodletting in the Dark Ages. CWD is not the only example of science—which does not comport with politics, culture and the agenda of special interests—being rejected in Wyoming. From members of Congress to state legislators and the governor on down to local school boards and chambers of commerce, many of Wyoming's elected officials also deny human-caused climate change is real and that carbon emissions being sent into the atmosphere by the burning of Wyoming coal is a problem.

They deny the clear body of evidence showing that domestic sheep spread deadly diseases to wild mountain sheep (bighorns); they deny data showing both the ecological and economic value of predators (wolves, grizzlies and other species, even bobcats) in the ecosystem; they deny data showing the severe impacts of energy industry disturbance on sage-grouse habitat; and they deny the profound role that conserving federal public lands, by keeping them in an undeveloped condition, plays as a positive sustainable engine of prosperity and enhanced quality of human life.

In his book, *Pushed Off The Mountain, Sold Down The River: Wyoming's Search For Its Soul*, writer Samuel Western takes note of a prevailing cultural belief among Wyoming citizens. They are convinced that Wyoming exists as an exception to laws of nature which apply to every other place in the world. That mentality is known as "the Wyoming way" and it holds the conviction that by denying truth, one can alter reality.

Except, as Dorsey notes, it doesn't. It certainly doesn't apply to Wyoming's defiance of prevailing scientific conclusions related to feedgrounds and CWD. Glenn Hockett, a lifelong sportsman and volunteer with the Gallatin Wildlife Association in southwest Montana, claims that Wyoming's incalcitrant stand toward feeding threatens not only the health of wild ungulates in Greater Yellowstone, but in all of the northern Rockies.

On a day in January, about a year before he was proved true, Eric Cole, a longtime Elk Refuge senior biologist, delivered a corroborating shot across the bow. Cole circulated information via email to wildlife colleagues and interested citizens that left many shocked. Cole's informal report stated that CWD "infection in the Jackson elk herd is inevitable and possible at any time."

Verbatim, his written assessment: "Population modeling predicts a wide range of CWD prevalence and effects on Jackson elk herd population growth rates in the short term (within five years) following introduction of the disease, but in the long term the effects of CWD on the health of the Jackson elk herd and recreational opportunities dependent on the Jackson elk herd will likely be significant and negative. For example, at any level of CWD prevalence, current levels of cow elk harvest could not be sustained. The current supplemental feeding regime will exacerbate the effects of CWD on the Jackson Elk Herd because elk density at NER far exceeds elk density reported at Rocky Mountain National Park, which was the source of the annual infection rate used in the model.

"Elk are fed on the same 5,000 acres of [the National Elk Refuge] each year, and given the persistence of CWD prions in the environment, these areas will likely become heavily contaminated with the CWD prion over time if status quo management continues. Sixty to eighty percent of the Jackson elk herd use NER feedgrounds each winter, which will regularly expose these elk to CWD prions at these sites. Various elk migration studies and research on another disease prevalent on [the National Elk

Refuge] (brucellosis), suggest that the current feeding regime and its associated high concentrations of elk could be a source of CWD infection for cervids throughout the Greater Yellowstone Ecosystem."

Cole's blunt acknowledgment, contradicting Wyoming's sanguine stance, repeated warnings made by a number of his predecessors who spent careers in Fish and Wildlife Service uniforms.

Former Elk Refuge chief managers Mike Hedrick and Barry Reiswig noted as far back as the 1990s that CWD's arrival in Greater Yellowstone was certain and that its spread would be exacerbated by the feeding of elk. Reiswig was roundly attacked by Wyoming outfitters, guides, and politicians as being an alarmist. His opinion, however, was backed up by Roffe who presided over wildlife health issues for every national wildlife refuge in the country. It was highlighted, too, in the acclaimed book by former senior Elk Refuge biologist Bruce Smith. "I know the national and regional offices of the Fish and Wildlife Service were well aware of the concerns because in the 1990s I helped Mike Hedrick draft a letter informing them," Smith told me.

A 30-year, top-level official with the Fish and Wildlife Service, now retired and who asked not to be identified, added this, "I recall briefings by Roffe when we met as Regional Refuge Chiefs. Also a meeting in Jackson Hole at the Elk Refuge where we heard about the feeding program. Seems like a bad idea that should have been stopped long ago. But, long-standing feeding programs like these can be incredibly difficult to dislodge," he said. "I've wondered about the impact on hunting in the region but the ecological impacts are even more concerning."

Smith said there is no federal law that orders the Fish and Wildlife Service to feed elk at the Elk Refuge.

Jamie Rappaport Clark, today president of the national conservation group Defenders of Wildlife, took a tour of the Elk Refuge when she was the Fish and Wildlife's national director in the 1990s. She understood the wildlife health issues in play. "She went back to Washington with a small elk antler that she found during her visit and I hoped it would be a reminder," Smith said.

Clark told me in an interview a few years later that she tried to bring reforms. The refrain has always been that as long as Wyoming is opposed, the ending of feeding will never happen. Even a stinging rebuke in court to the Fish and Wildlife Service, a lawsuit brought by Defenders and other conservation groups, and supported by Clark against her former federal employer, has not broken the inertia. In 2008, the environmental law firm EarthJustice and its lead attorney Tim Preso sued the Fish and Wildlife Service on behalf of Defenders, the Greater Yellowstone Coalition, Jackson Hole Conservation Alliance, Wyoming Outdoor Council, and the National Wildlife Refuge Association over management plans for elk and bison on the refuge.

The Fish and Wildlife Service, instead of heeding the expert opinions of its own senior staff, opted to essentially maintain the status quo. "In its final decision ... the Service reversed itself, elevating the political preferences of Wyoming over the biological needs of the Refuge and its wildlife populations. In so doing, the Service acted arbitrarily and unlawfully," EarthJustice wrote.

The DC Circuit Court delivered this stinging assessment of facts to Interior Secretary Ken Salazar in President Barack Obama's cabinet: "The whole point of a National Elk Refuge is to provide a sanctuary in which populations of healthy, reproducing elk can be sustained. The Refuge can hardly provide such a sanctuary if, every winter, elk and bison are drawn by the siren song of human-provided food to what becomes, through the act of gathering, a miasmic zone of life-threatening diseases."

During the late 1980s, Wyoming rancher Thomas Dorrance, best known for being an heir to the family that created Campbell's Soups, pressed to open a game ranch for exotic wildlife near Sundance, Wyoming. Dorrance wanted to create a Texas-style fenced-in compound on about 4200 acres inside his 17,000-acre ranch. Among the possible species were non-native Russian boar; red, roe, sika, axis and fallow deer; ibex, chamois, Barbary, mouflon, and Marco Polo sheep. Native animals such as elk, moose, pronghorn and bighorn sheep would also have been part of Dorrance's menagerie and featured in a drive-through wildlife park, harvested for meat production, traded and sold as breeding stock, and some made available to hunters.

As a young policy analyst in Canada, Darrel Rowledge came under the tutelage of Dr. Valerius Geist and others who initially welcomed game farming but quickly changed their views in the wake of several disease outbreaks including brucellosis, bovine tuberculosis, and in recent years CWD.

Rowledge, who became director of the Alliance for Public Wildlife in Calgary, is intimately familiar with the controversy that ensued over Dorrance's proposal. "When Dorrance submitted his application, Tom Thorne and Beth Williams responded by saying 'You're going to do what? Put wildlife in confinement, create a massive disease factory? Not in Wyoming, you're not.'"

How does Rowledge know this? He was invited down to Cheyenne from Canada to provide briefings to Wyoming wildlife officials and lawmakers on the dangers of game farms, based on his experiences with outbreaks of disease in Alberta and Saskatchewan.

For many years Dr. Thorne served as Wyoming's chief wildlife veterinarian and his wife, Dr. Beth Williams, was a widely respected CWD researcher who worked with Dr. Mike Miller, the nationally-renowned researcher in Colorado. Their concerns were shared by Robert Lanka of Wyoming Game and Fish who was lead author of a report about Dorrance's application.

Wyoming officials, their decision based largely on the findings of Lanka, Thorne, Williams and world-class consulting colleagues, turned down Dorrance's permit application. "We've got three or four options. We can accept it, we can take it into the court system, attack it legislatively to seek some changes in the Wyoming statutes or a combination of the last two," Dorrance, angered by the decision, told a reporter. "If we pursue it [a court challenge] and win we are still faced with the Wyoming Game and Fish Department. They might be very bitter and vindictive. They could make our life impossible."

Ultimately, Dorrance sued the state—and lost. "Wyoming's justification withstood every single challenge. It was the only government that ever did a comprehensive cost-benefit analysis on the dangers of game farming and congregating wildlife," Rowledge told me. "It was the overwhelming conclusion, based on the best of the best scientific minds, that it would be a disaster."

At the time, Wyoming Game and Fish Commission President Don Scott defended the state's position: "We have wild and free-ranging herds that are truly a national treasure and we just don't believe that that treasure should be placed in jeopardy, even a remote jeopardy. We don't want to turn Wyoming into Texas."

Horne and Williams, members of the Wildlife Disease Association, died tragically in a traffic accident in 2004. Rowledge argues that Wyoming over the past 25 years has lost its vigilance in aggressively trying to prevent sources of disease. "It's kind of crazy what the state position is today on keeping feedgrounds open. In terms of what they do, there's really no difference between them and game farms, except the feedgrounds involve larger numbers of animals and public wildlife that is free-ranging," he said.

Still, he remembers Drs. Thorne and Williams with fondness. "I have tremendous respect for them. They were willing to alter their perspective in accordance with new scientific discoveries," he said. "Had they lived, and were they to know what we do today about CWD, I have no doubt they would conclude that operating the feedgrounds is a terribly bad idea."

More than a quarter century ago, around the same time that the Dorrance case was playing out, another one hit the courts. This one involved a trial and the Parker Land & Cattle Company near Dubois. It had filed suit for damages after its domestic cows became infected with brucellosis and were ordered destroyed. The plaintiff's lawyer was former Wyoming Governor and Interior Secretary Stan Hathaway who foreshadowed the opinion of the D.C. Circuit Court two decades later. Hathaway referred to management practices at the Elk Refuge and, by association, the state feedgrounds as "a cesspool of disease."

Greater Yellowstone is supposed to be an American beacon for smart custodianship of America's public lands, and it's fair to say many Americans believe it to be true. But the feedground controversy has numerous negative ripple effects and is laden with epic levels of hypocrisy, Preso notes.

For example, the Elk Refuge continues to feed elk that during some winters are in numbers 50 percent over its own management objectives. Right next door across an artificial boundary in Grand Teton Park, park officials sanction a controversial elk hunt inside the national park boundaries (the only one of its kind in a U.S. national park) to reduce the number of elk.

That, in turn, causes dangerous encounters between hunters and grizzly bears. In fact, the Fish and Wildlife Service, which oversees management of the Elk Refuge and until recently was in charge of managing imperiled grizzly bears, said it fully expects that bears will die in run-ins with elk hunters inside Grand Teton.

Ironically, Wyoming Game and Fish assembled a CWD action plan and put it out for public review. The state offered only vague generalities for how it will respond when disease strikes the feedgrounds, yet the plan included these acknowledgments: "Disease transmission can be related to density of animals in a given area as well as the frequency of contact between animals. Artificially concentrating elk on feedgrounds may result in more rapid spread of CWD and contribute to increased persistence of prions in the soil and uptake by vegetation. Based on WGFD hunter-harvested CWD surveillance data, CWD prevalence levels in non-fed elk populations remain significantly lower than those of sympatric mule deer and white-tailed deer populations in the core endemic area of Wyoming."

The draft report added that "recent modeling based on a combination of captive and free-ranging elk data suggested that feedground elk may survive in the face of CWD at significantly reduced numbers through a combination of genetic selection and elimination of antlerless elk harvest."

Moreover, the department stated that "even though [CWD] eradication is not feasible at this time, the WGFD will consider management actions to slow the spread and/or reduce the prevalence of the disease statewide, especially west of the Continental Divide, based on accepted scientific information and wildlife management practices."

Like the Fish and Wildlife Service, Dorsey notes that Wyoming cites the science and then willfully disregards it. In 2019 when it released its action plan, the state refused to take action to phase out feeding. In a career of practicing environmental law, EarthJustice's Preso says that seldom has he encountered more egregious mismanagement from government land and wildlife agencies: state and federal working together. "I don't know that anything else exists with management policy in the Greater Yellowstone Ecosystem so blatantly contrary to the science, the law, and common sense and involves a state that is so resistant to change," he said.

What is the truth no one is willing to publicly admit? Politicians in Wyoming fear that if they support closing the feedgrounds, they won't get elected or re-elected. It's no different from being a politician in a coal-producing state and denying human-caused climate change or coming from a tobacco-growing state and refusing to publicly acknowledge that smoking cigarettes causes cancer.

But it's more than that: many don't want to say anything that challenges the beliefs of culture, whether based on fact or not. There is huge pressure in local communities to conform to the status quo or face shunning and being socially ostracized.

Eventually, Preso says, truth prevails and with CWD he fears it will only emerge from a preventable crisis. For now, he wants to know why federal civil servants working for the Fish and Wildlife Service and Forest Service would knowingly break the law. Further, why would Wyoming knowingly shirk science?

Another profound irony that will be explored later in this series is that Wyoming's state wildlife research facility at Sybille Canyon along the foot of the Laramie Mountains was renamed the Tom Thorne/Beth Williams Research Center. There, an experiment involving CWD and elk confirmed just how lethal the disease risk is, but a Wyoming veterinarian minimized its dire implications.

Brian Nesvik, new director of the Wyoming Game and Fish Department, continues to present the state position that the feedgrounds will continue to operate because there's no hard evidence that CWD will cause the problems some contend.

"We've had a lot of discussions about where that ought to go down the road, and for a long time the department's position on that has been that we should look for opportunities to reduce our reliance on supplemental feed where we can," Nesvik told reporter Mike Koshmrl with the *Jackson Hole News & Guide*. "But there are three things that have not changed. One is that without feedgrounds there's still potential to transmit disease to domestic cattle. Number two, without feedgrounds it's inevitable there'd be damage to private property and stored crops. And number three, there's a large constituency of folks that want to have hunting opportunity for elk, and eliminating feedgrounds would dramatically reduce that opportunity. Those things are not changing rapidly, and our priorities for why we feed haven't changed."

Critics say Wyoming's continuing denial of CWD's impact runs against the prevailing opinions of disease and professional wildlife management but that its credibility has already been called into question. Some believe that if CWD harms wildlife populations beloved to hunters, a basis for a lucrative wildlife watching and big game outfitting industry, and one day results in infections of livestock or worse, humans, there could be justification for decisionmakers being held subject to criminal liability.

Osterholm left some citizens who heard his testimony before the Minnesota state legislature shocked when he cited an estimate made by the Alliance for Public Wildlife that huge numbers of CWD-contaminated animals are likely consumed annually. Some believed that Mad Cow would never move beyond domestic cattle herds, Osterholm reminded us. It proved not to be true. In people, Creutzfeldt-Jakob disease is a human TSE that is extremely rare. The disease that crossed the species barrier from infected cattle [Mad Cow] to humans is Variant Creutzfeldt-Jakob or vCJD.

"Since 1995, when it was identified, 178 deaths have been attributed to vCJD. It's thought that one in 2,000 people in the UK is a carrier of the disease," BBC News reported in a story published in October 2018. "But it appears that relatively few who catch the infectious agent that causes the disease then go on to develop symptoms."

Some 4.4 million cattle, suspected of coming in contact with sick animals or facilities harboring them, were slaughtered. British ag producers for many years afterward suffered economic losses because other nations imposed a ban on British exports of cattle and beef.

In a study that appeared in Journal of Wildlife Diseases in 2018, evidence showed cattle resisted CWD in either of two challenge situations: 1) when exposed to the disease by oral inoculation, and 2) when cattle were placed in pens where CWD contamination was known to be present. Among the five authors cited were the late CWD scientist Elizabeth Williams and Terry J. Kreeger who had been a longtime veterinarian with the Wyoming Game and Fish Department.

While scientists noted that domestic cattle are susceptible to CWD-associated prions in an absolute theoretical sense, it was instructive that when domestic cows were exposed to enclosures where 89 infected mule deer and 83 infected elk had been kept over a ten-year period—all of which perished from CWD—no infections happened in cattle.

This is important because many experts believe cattle could function as intermediary vectors by which CWD could mutate into a strain more likely to be transmitted to humans. And it is that possibility that worries Osterholm and others because that's what happened with Mad Cow in the U.K.

Kreeger and others wrote in their journal article: "Of secondary concern, passage of the CWD agent through cattle or other livestock hosts could lead to transformation of cervid-adapted prions to a new prion strain with greater potential infectivity for humans." They noted that scrapie, a prion disease known to exist in domestic sheep for hundreds of years, had not been linked to human cases, though some suspect that scrapie transmission to cattle could have happened when beef and dairy cows were fed feed composed of ground up infected sheep.

"The possibility remains that a scrapie strain adapted to cattle after its inadvertent introduction became the BSE prion strain which—unlike the scrapie agent itself—eventually proved infectious to humans," the Journal of Wildlife Diseases article states. "Whether CWD infection of cattle would present a significant public health issue is unknown, but the potential risk would need to be evaluated. Considered in total, the improbability of cattle becoming naturally infected with CWD suggested by our and other studies should diminish concerns over these secondary transmission risks."

Osterholm, having been involved with investigation teams in the U.K, isn't so sanguine. In fact, people concerned about CWD reaching wildlife feedgrounds in Wyoming have criticized Kreeger for downplaying the risk of a catastrophic outbreak in elk. Over time, he and some of his research colleagues have acknowledged that CWD could result in the extinction of local mule deer herds carrying a specific genetic makeup and they've modeled the potential for that happening in elk.

Dr. Osterholm says the number of unknowns relating to the pathogenesis of CWD—the pathways it takes to infection—should not be a basis for relief but pondered for what coming revelations about the potential communicability of CWD could be. "Something that's been very concerning is the lack of national leadership, whether it be on the wildlife side or on the agricultural side. Clearly, I think we have some serious challenges here with what it means to the bovine world," Osterholm said. "Is there going to be potential cross exposure [to cattle] and would that happen? The ag people can't just back out of the conversation about it potentially reaching livestock and, of course, public health officials need to be paying attention to the human side. Right now there is no effective message coming forward from public health about the importance of this other than "just don't eat it."

The World Health Organization and CDC advisement to not eat suspected meat is limp compared to what we need. A lot of CWD-infected deer and elk may not look sick. I'm not telling anybody this [CWD] is going to be a BSE crisis but I am suggesting that it *could* be. Why do we want to experiment with ourselves to find out?"

Darrel Rowledge recalls having conversations with Thorne and Williams about the public trust doctrine and the precautionary principle, the latter being a governing tenet to err on the side of caution when dealing with consequences of possible actions that could prove catastrophic. Nameless, faceless bureaucrats don't make decisions, he says. Individual people do. Rowledge points to recent criminal charges involving public officials and an outbreak of Legionnaires' Disease, a bacterial disease, in and around Flint, Michigan. The assertion is that the disease outbreak can be traced to known problems with the city's water supply that those in charge of public health agencies ignored.

"Governments and individual people that dare to ignore the precautionary principle and public trust doctrine can face criminal charges," Rowledge said. "Could it happen with those who look after the welfare of public wildlife? Could it happen if one day people come down with a prion disease caused by eating a CWD-infected deer or elk? Who will be called to answer when injury comes to the public good and those in charge are shown to have either ignored the truth or looked the other way?"

At the Wyoming Game and Fish Department, officials have made it abundantly clear they frown upon "the celebritization" of wildlife. Over the years, field personnel have been dismissive whenever members of the general public have given individual animals nicknames, such as the case with famous grizzly bears in Jackson Hole.

Game and Fish managers insist that naming wildlife causes humans to anthropomorphize animals, and it puts too much emphasis on individuals when the department, they say, is devoted to stewarding species at the population level. Not long ago, Game and Fish researchers broke their own rule when they bestowed a moniker on a wild wapiti mother kept in captivity. She wore ear tag No. 12 and they dubbed her "Lucky." Lucky was born a wild cow elk who initially survived a close brush with doom. For those studying CWD, she represents either a cryptic symbol of hope for the persistence of elk in the Greater Yellowstone Ecosystem, or, in the eyes of scientists thinking about zoonotic diseases, a frightening potential harbinger.

In 2002, 39 healthy elk calves were captured at the National Elk Refuge in Jackson Hole, Wyoming and transported across the state to a research facility at Sybille Canyon near the town of Wheatland. There, the young ungulates were placed in pens. Over the course of a decade, every single one contracted CWD and perished—all except for Lucky.

The rate of CWD's lethality, involving wapiti guinea pigs like these, speaks to the disease's virulent progression, especially among deer family members grouped in tight quarters and exposed to disease. Similar outcomes have been mirrored in game farm settings involving captive privately-owned deer and elk.

Lucky the elk was two years old when Thorne and Williams died tragically in an auto wreck in 2004. Along with colleagues, Thorne and Williams were key proponents of the elk experiment at Sybille, intended to provide insights into how animals catch CWD, how it is spread and what prospects, if any, there might be for carriers surviving it.

So what is the most disturbing aspect of the Wyoming study involving Lucky the elk that CWD experts find so unsettling?

Lucky's wapiti cohort group contracted CWD naturally, simply by being placed in an environment where diseased animals previously had been. Researchers didn't have to do anything to overtly expose the elk to CWD through feed or injection; they merely kept them in pens where CWD had been present and yet its disease-causing prions persisted after sickened animals had been removed.

Prions had entered the soil at Sybille, shed through urine, feces, saliva, possibly in tissue decomposition of dead animals, and likely also became bound to surfaces in Sybille's captive settings. Even modest attempts at decontamination, paralleling what's happened at other sites in other states, did not kill them off. Prions are notoriously difficult to destroy.

Today, this is the question—the big one—looming over the heads of public land managers, wildlife officials, private landowners, public health officials, hunters and the general public dealing with the specter of CWD. It has implications for the northern Rockies and every other corner of North America where CWD has become endemic or will be.

If environmental contamination could happen at Sybille with such devastating results, what could CWD's arrival on the National Elk Refuge in Jackson Hole and Wyoming's 22 feedgrounds mean? At the feedgrounds, wapiti hordes come in close physical contact with each other; they urinate and defecate onto the artificial feed and available natural grass they are ingesting; in turn, their wastes seep into the soil. That is why disease experts became alarmed when the first elk was confirmed to have CWD on the edge of the Elk Refuge. How many more animals today are CWD-positive. It may take years to find out how deep the infection rate is. The first animals with prion infection are likely to be asymptomatic. The disease can have long incubation times lasting between months and years in a host. A doomed elk may appear healthy yet its wastes will get deposited into the ground and linger; for how long no one knows.

With more animals getting exposed and then sickened, prion contamination would, ostensibly, bio-accumulate, becoming established in the land, carried potentially in surface water and, as studies have also demonstrated, possibly be taken up in living rangeland plants. Laboratory research has shown that prions can exist in plants including tomatoes, alfalfa, and corn: one of the most universally-used grains in food production.

Think of this happening winter after winter, year after year: contamination at the Elk Refuge and feedgrounds would start modestly with one animal that creates a tiny toxic hot spot to which hundreds or thousands of other elk and deer would be possibly exposed over time, veterinarian Roffe says.

Infected CWD animals don't even need to come in direct contact with other elk, deer, or moose, because they can shed and leave behind infectious prions in the environment. Stricken ungulates only need to have been there. If infection sets in at the feedgrounds, CWD would also be transported through living animals to distant summer ranges across lines humans draw on maps, seeding prions shed via feces, urine, saliva, and death into other landscapes, creating new environmental zones of infection and exposure.

Dan Vermillion, former chairman of the Montana Fish, Wildlife and Parks Commission, said there is growing indignation toward Wyoming over its operation of feedgrounds. "We've been so focused in this state on brucellosis and trying to do spatial and temporal separation to keep elk and bison away from ag producers. CWD was kind of placed on the backburner of worries. Now we have cases and it's time to confront it head-on," he said.

Brucellosis, Vermillion noted, is not a population-limiting disease; CWD as it settles in can be devastating and the best strategy is to stop any activities that would make it worse. "To me, the arrival of CWD is terrifying and it's heartbreaking the more I learn about the science and the potential it has to harm our game herds which have contributed to the state's reputation for being the last, best place. Common sense, in the face of a disease event, points to getting rid of the feedgrounds. It's clear that they [feedgrounds] increase the probability of making CWD's impact a lot worse and affecting the progression of disease so that it moves into deer and elk a lot faster."

Vermillion compared CWD to a massive outbreak of exotic weeds originating on one landowner's property and bearing down on adjacent ranches, threatening to overtake their rangeland.

"We've been courteous to Wyoming and respectful of the argument that states don't interfere with the way other states do business, but when another state does things that affect the quality of life and resources that citizens in Montana value and hold dear, there comes a time when you run out of patience," he said.

Early in November 2017, a test confirmed Montana's first-ever case of CWD in a wild cervid. The diagnosis was based on tissue samples taken from a dead mule deer buck harvested near Bridger just north of the Montana-Wyoming state line. Confirmation came ironically on the same day the Montana Fish Wildlife and Parks Department began circulating a draft CWD action plan for public review.

Before we progress further, a journalist's acknowledgment is in order. One challenge in writing about CWD is balancing the significant fears being expressed by those involved with tracking the disease against those who claim that because CWD isn't an ecological or human health problem, and never will be.

The topic that wildlife managers are wary about discussing publicly is this: If hunters worry en masse about the potential risks of exposing themselves and their families to disease, they may stop hunting and buying licenses, the fees of which fund their agencies. They also note that hunters are a key tool—human harvest of animals—that adds an option that managers have for reducing ungulate herds.

Another area of controversy is the reluctance of state wildlife agencies to acknowledge the important role wildlife predators and scavengers—

wolves, grizzlies, cougars, and coyotes—play in slowing infectious disease progression by killing weak and sickened prey species.

Now with CWD in Montana, there is wide speculation about how the state will respond and the rate at which infections will deepen. If 38 elk out of 39 at Sybille became stricken and died, how might that rate of infection be extrapolated to wild settings? The elk calves removed from the Elk Refuge and raised at Sybille have a genetic make-up, an MM genotype, that is widespread and the most common in western Wyoming elk herds. Lucky had a different genotype, LL, that exists in two percent of a normal population. Some elk also carry a third genotype (ML) that, for some reason, has a resistance characteristic that delays infection but infection is still 100 percent lethal.

Montana has its own checkered past involving hypocrisy with the way it confronts wildlife diseases, says the Gallatin Wildlife Association's Glenn Hockett. Montana's strategy toward confronting another disease, brucellosis, was focused for decades almost exclusively on wandering Yellowstone bison known to be carriers of the *Brucella abortus* bacteria. However, a panel of scientific experts recently noted that the state has been focusing on the wrong animal. Elk represent the greatest possible threat for wildlife transmitting disease to cattle.

Some argue that CWD should not be discussed as a human health risk because there has never been a documented case of the disease sickening and killing a person. There also has never been a single documented case of a wild Yellowstone bison transmitting brucellosis to a domestic beef cow, yet more than 12,000 bison, members of the most iconic bison herd in the world, have been felled since 1985—and more will be this winter—based on the mere possibility that transmission *could* happen.

Tens of millions of public tax dollars have been spent targeting and slaughtering wandering park bison based on that premise, but it's a premise that has been scientifically disproven. Every case in which brucellosis has been transmitted from wildlife to cattle has involved elk, not bison. As the findings of a major fact-finding study, released in 2017 by the National Academies of Sciences revealed, the greatest threat of possible brucellosis transmission from wildlife to cattle comes from infected elk. The National Academy is the most respected scientific body in the world.

Within the ranks of professional wildlife managers, there's no disagreement that feedgrounds have made the amplification of brucellosis in wild elk herds worse. And there is little disagreement that CWD infection is likely to follow the same pattern. The coup de grace of Eric Cole's frank remarks was this, for it has direct implications for Montana and Idaho, whose elk herds mix with those emanating from Jackson Hole: "Various elk migration studies and research on another disease prevalent on the Elk Refuge—brucellosis—suggest that the current feeding regime and its associated high concentrations of elk could be a source of CWD infection for cervids through[out] the Greater Yellowstone Ecosystem."

Along with the National Academy, the most reputable professional wildlife management organizations in the U.S. say that supplemental feeding of wildlife goes against the best management practices of maintaining health in big game herds.

When the National Academy released its report on brucellosis, this was one of its highlighted findings: "Evidence suggests that incremental closure of feedgrounds could reduce the prevalence of the disease in the broader elk population and could benefit overall elk health in the long term. The committee recommended that state and federal land managers take a strategic, stepwise, science-based approach to analyzing and evaluating how the closure of feedgrounds would affect elk health, risk of transmission to cattle, and brucellosis prevalence."

A scientist on the National Academy review team said it also applies to CWD but there no regionwide plan for containment. Who is in charge of confronting CWD throughout the Greater Yellowstone region? Answer: no one is. Consider this: Yellowstone Park officials are gravely concerned about the consequences that CWD may have on wildlife in the most famous nature preserve in the world. However, the future of Yellowstone depends on the attitudes and actions taken by her neighbors.

Piecemeal approaches to managing big landscapes like Greater Yellowstone are costly, inefficient, and ineffective, especially with wildlife issues. The legacy of management approaches to logging, mining, and oil and gas development on national forests and BLM lands, and livestock grazing inside Grand Teton Park are evidence of that.

The impacts of CWD will reach into every corner of Greater Yellowstone, across state, county, and community lines, affecting quality of life for the region's 450,000 residents who share a common love for wildlife values. It will affect hunters and wildlife watchers, safari company operators, and the experience known to millions of visitors each year.

"With CWD upon us in Montana now, the number one goal should be to end the largest wildlife feeding program on the planet; it's a ticking time bomb and its destructive aspects are well known," said Nick Gevock, conservation director at the Montana Wildlife Federation and former environmental journalist.

Behind closed doors, local depopulation scenarios have been discussed as options not just to swiftly remove CWD-infected animals but to prevent perpetual CWD contamination zones from being created in the environment. During the 1990s, when Montana voters outlawed private game farms due to zoonotic disease concerns, Idaho too started to worry about CWD; in fact, one aspect of Idaho's CWD action plan lists aggressive deposition within a radius of where CWD turns up.

In an article written for The Wildlife Society, retired Elk Refuge biologist Bruce Smith noted that "Colorado tried to reduce CWD in wild mule deer through experimental herd reductions. Wisconsin went a step further: after finding CWD in deer in 2002, the state's Department of Natural Resources sought complete eradication by killing thousands of white-tailed deer with special hunts and culling programs designed to reduce deer densities. Unfortunately, those states' efforts have met with limited success."

In early 2017, Dr. Valerius Geist, David Clausen, former chair of the Wisconsin Natural Resources Board, Vince Crichton, former co-chair of Canada's National Wildlife Disease Strategy, and Darrel Rowledge, director of Alliance for Public Wildlife, published a white paper titled "The Challenge of CWD: Insidious and Dire."

"Left unchecked, the prospects for wildlife are bleak. CWD has clear population impacts; some models suggest extinction. Disproportionate impact on mature males carries implications for hunters and wildlife economies let alone populations. Still more bad news: efforts for vaccines have failed, and evolutionary or adaptive salvation is unlikely and would be too late in any case," they write. "CWD is now deemed to be the largest-ever mass of infectious prions in global history, and experts sum up the threat (to wildlife, agriculture, our economies, and potentially to human health) in two words: 'insidious and dire.'"

They estimate that hunting families in North America are presently consuming between 7,000 and 15,000 CWD-infected animals annually. The number is growing exponentially. Many are probably unaware their harvested animals are CWD carriers.

If readers aren't concerned about CWD yet, they will be after digesting what's in the report—a distillation of both comments from experts and articles published in the scientific literature. One cause for concern, off the radar screen of ranchers and even food consumers, is the ability of prions to bind with plants, such as alfalfa (hay). Therefore, it means not only could exposure increase via plant material being consumed by livestock (which people eat) but also products that show up in restaurants and the grocery store. And what about the widespread practice of moving hay around the landscape? Would hay produced in a CWD area need to be tested?

The report features excerpts from Dr. Christopher Johnson, a scientist with the US. Geological Survey: "Vegetation is ubiquitous in CWD-contaminated environments and plants are known to absorb a variety of substances from soil, ranging from nutrients to contaminants. The uptake of proteins from soil into plants has been documented for many years and we have been investigating the uptake of prions into plants in vitro. Using laser scanning confocal microscopy, we observed root uptake of fluorescently-tagged, abnormal prion protein in the model plant Arabidopsis thaliana, as well as the crop plants alfalfa (Medicago sativa), barley (Hordeum vulgare) and tomato (Solanum lycopersicum)."

Studies showed that prion uptake occurred in roots and was transferred to stems and leaves of those plants as well as corn. "Both stems and leaves of A. thaliana grown in culture media containing prions are infectious when injected into mice, and oral bioassays are underway for A. thaliana and other plants," Johnson wrote. "Our results suggest that prions are taken up by plants and that contaminated plants may represent a previously unrecognized risk of human, domestic species, and wildlife exposure to CWD and scrapie agents."

How will farmers and ranchers respond to elk and deer in their pastures if they suspect the wild animals could be infecting the soil where their livestock eats grass and alfalfa and other crops grow? What kind of a backlash could there be against public wildlife?

In states like Wisconsin, wildlife officials have, at times, resorted to depopulating local white-tail deer herds and incinerating the carcasses to kill prions but the geographic area where CWD is found in Wisconsin continues to expand. Why? Most experts say because of environmental contamination, exacerbated, too, by the fact that property owners feeding deer still happens prolifically in Wisconsin.

Smith added that "In Illinois, on the other hand, 10 years of government culling of white-tailed deer in areas of new CWD infections has limited disease prevalence to 1 percent. By comparison, prevalence climbed to 5 percent after localized culling in Wisconsin ceased in 2007. A prescription to similarly limit CWD infections of elk crowded on feedgrounds would compel the culling of very large numbers of animals."

In evidence submitted during a lawsuit brought by EarthJustice attorney Tim Preso against the Fish and Wildlife Service and National Elk Refuge, he introduced a document in which a regional refuge chief for the Fish and Wildlife Service admitted that even a reduced feeding operation would, with CWD present, threaten to "create a Super Fund Disease Toxic Site on the [National Elk] refuge that would remain contaminated for a very long time."

When former Elk Refuge Manager Barry Reiswig was asked by superiors in the Fish and Wildlife Service's regional office if he had a plan after the first CWD case was confirmed, he said, "One, dig a big hole with a bulldozer or obtain an incinerator. Two, you round up and shoot all suspect [diseased] animals. Three, you cover the hole with dirt or incinerate all killed animals."

Wyoming, in its recent CWD action plan, does not prioritize depopulation but what is its strategy for attempted containment? The state already is carrying out two things that are contrary to what most experts say is responsible wildlife management: it is running feedgrounds and shooting predators, namely wolves, allowing open season on lobos across 85 percent of the state, for any reason, at any time of day, by any means.

Wolves could help slow the spread of CWD because they take out sick animals. (So far, it appears wolves, like people, cannot get infected).

I reached out to another global disease expert, Dr. Andrew Dobson, who has done research both in Greater Yellowstone and the Serengeti. "CWD presents an expanding and increasingly worrying threat to elk, mule deer, *and cattle*. It's a consequence of loss of coyotes, wolves, and other predators from the West over the last fifty years, combined with early attempts to ranch stock on really poor soils where they are so nutritionally deprived that they gnaw on old carcasses and become infected with prions from animals that have died from CWD," he said. " I think the artificial feeding of wildlife in Wyoming is really dumb. It's much better to let natural regulation reduce elk populations down to levels naturally supported by the landscape. Aggregating elk on feedgrounds at the time of peak *Brucella* transmission and with CWD looming is arguably the stupidest form of animal management I can imagine."

I then asked him about the role of predators. "Wolves and coyotes are our strongest defense against CWD, particularly wolves; they are pursuit predators who always focus on the weakest animals in a group of potential prey. As CWD manifests itself by reducing locomotory ability, wolves will key in on this and selectively remove those individuals from the population. These animals are then not available to infect uninfected individuals in the herd, so there's a bonus knock-on effect of selective predation."

One thing is clear: Wyoming knows what is coming. A few years ago, Wyoming Game and Fish representatives reached out to managers of the Teton County trash transfer station in Jackson Hole, inquiring about the possibility of operating an incinerator there to process the carcasses of CWD-infected elk and deer. Incineration is the only sure way of destroying prions; however, what good is it to incinerate carcasses if those same animals, over the course of their abbreviated living lives, were shedding prions via urine, feces, and saliva across the landscape?

"From what I've heard about Chronic Wasting Disease, it's not a pretty thing to watch. And I have to believe that tourism would suffer, a lot, if people driving by on the highway past the Elk Refuge saw animals dying from Chronic Wasting Disease in the hundreds or the thousands," said Jackson Hole rancher Brad Mead in an interview he gave to Danny Schmidt for his documentary *Feeding the Problem*.

To prevent that scene from materializing, which would be a public relations disaster for a valley that promotes itself to the world as a mecca for wildlife watching, how will agencies respond?

During the past few years, some Wyoming Game and Fish officials expressed optimism that hope for dealing with CWD might reside not in shutting down the feedgrounds but in development of a vaccine. However, results of that effort were reported and they are bleak. Not only did the vaccine not prove to protect cervids from catching CWD but inoculations caused some cervids to actually get sick and die.

Which leads us back to Lucky. In that study involving her at Sybille, the wild elk calves taken from the Elk Refuge were shown to have three different genetic makeups. Most had MM genotypes and are representative of about 70 percent of wild wapiti in the Elk Refuge herd. All of those died relatively quickly from CWD when exposed to environmental contamination.

Then there were elk with ML genotypes, representing about 28 percent of the herd. They survived longer before getting infected and succumbing but they all died, too.

And then there was Lucky, a rarity with an LL genotype. Just two percent of elk have a genetic code like her. Kreeger tried to put a positive spin on the results when he still worked for the agency. His is a belief in "evolutionary adaptation"; i.e., the premise that CWD infected mothers will produce offspring before they die and CWD-resistant elk will be giving birth to seed-stock to rebuild populations if they crash.

Lucky and some of the other elk cows produced offspring and Kreeger speculated it was possible that reproduction could outpace death caused by CWD. However, the model showed that over a century, hunting would need to be curtailed if not eliminated and that elk with genomes MM and ML would likely vanish.

To put that in perspective, what if in a human community, 3800 out of 3900 people died due to a pandemic like the Black Plague and the restoration of civilization would rest on the surviving 100?

Would that be a cause for optimism or existential gravity? For Rowledge, it's the latter. As he and his fellow authors note, healthy wildlife populations are more resilient when they have more genetic diversity. CWD actually destroys and reduces diversity, leaving surviving gene pools potentially more vulnerable to *other* maladies and possibly less capable to deal with environmental factors. He says it's an incredibly risky proposition to bet on one genotype; moreover, it completely evades the reality that CWD would mean the loss of elk and deer abundance, as we know it today, by the end of this century.

In fact, some researchers in Wyoming have in recent years been mentioning the dreaded "e-word"—extinction—in recent discussions of what the future may hold for today's dominant elk herds in Greater Yellowstone.

Steve Kallin retired from his post in January 2017, though he validated an assessment from the Sierra Club's Dorsey in saying the consequences of CWD's arrival could be devastating. It isn't like there will be one epic dying event; herds will winnow over time and giving animals more feed will not mitigate the mortality; in fact, experts say it could intensify the impact of CWD's arrival.

"We have to remember this is an always fatal disease for cervids," Kallin told me. "It's slow moving but it's a serious disease. We have to look at it honestly and pragmatically and address it head on. This is not a manufactured scare tactic to promote a political agenda."

Wyoming wildlife filmmaker Shane Moore, whose Emmy-award-winning cinematic work is known around the world, and who has made tracking the science of CWD a personal passion, says the general public isn't aware of how "game-changing" CWD's arrival in Greater Yellowstone could be. The impacts will register in wildlife and for people, from tourists to hunters, who travel from far away to experience the ecosystem's charismatic deer family species and the things that eat them.

Moore and Dorsey have been outspoken in their reproach of the Wyoming Game and Fish Department. Their concerns are shared by Reiswig, Smith, and Roffe. In Yellowstone, managers have no plans for how they will deal with haggard-looking elk and mule deer in the spring that might be thin from enduring a winter in Yellowstone or potentially stricken with CWD.

Will they shoot the animal? Will they test all winter-killed animals? Will they remove carcasses on the ground that serve as valuable food sources for predators and scavengers? Will they start marking the place where CWD-positive elk have fallen and test the soil for prions?

If CWD strikes the Lamar Valley and the northern range, which has been compared to a mini-American version of the Serengeti, how will it disrupt the food chain? Park officials don't know what they'll do. Public health officials don't know how to respond if there's a spillover event either.

Osterholm told me that he's "a data-driven guy" but the more that gets revealed about CWD, it hasn't calmed his concerned but heightened it. I asked him directly about whether he thought bunching up large numbers of Greater Yellowstone elk together in the face of a potential CWD outbreak was irresponsible?

"Absolutely," he said. "It's setting the table for research into how a CWD pandemic could affect a regional population. We need to be looking at that. Some people say that if we don't feed them then they are going to die. Well, the people who say that to rationalize doing nothing must not know what it means to have CWD taking hold in their wildlife. This is where we have to start having dispassionate conversations and asking what are the factors and to what end. Part of the problem is discussions about CWD have been siloed, almost as an over-response to make sure there isn't alarm."

Noting that his predictions about the progression of Covid were deadly accurate, I asked what he thought the consequences might be of simply letting CWD run its course and continue wildlife management as usual? "I don't know. Soon we will, though," Osterholm said. "Feeding wildlife and bunching animals together concerns me greatly. That to me is as close as you're going to get in a cervid to migratory waterfowl and when disease affects migratory birds it gets moved around quickly. What happens in place A means nothing about what might happen in place B, C, D and E. You can't predict. But I will note that white-tailed deer don't move as much as mule deer and elk."

The potential ecological consequences of CWD on beloved wildlife populations should wake people up, Osterholm noted, and then added, "Regardless of whether CWD reaches humans, it's going to be a hell of a wildlife disease problem no matter what. But it could be a lot more than that. We could have a BSE nightmare, an American version of it, all over again. I think it would be a real challenge," he said. "The way the numbers are going up should be a concern. If we keep seeing the expansion of CWD in white-tailed deer, the numbers could be astronomical around the country. In North America in general and with elk on top of it. We have to pull ourselves out of the sand and understand there could be a real reckoning coming."

No Fairy Tale
(What Really Happened After the Pack Came Back)

O UTSIDE A RURAL FIREHOUSE in Alder, Montana, pick-up trucks filled the parking lot as a steady stream of modern ranchers and their range-rider cowboys packed the meeting hall to standing room only. Frustration was palpable in the air. An hour later, iPhone photos of dead calves and half-eaten heifers were projected onto the screen, which not long ago would have elicited gasps and fiery fighting words. Instead they were met by stone-cold silence in the room.

Gray wolves and grizzly bears were to blame for the depredations. But everyone conceded they are not going away. Cited time and again was a watchword that only a generation ago would have been culturally impossible to embrace in the Greater Yellowstone. The concept: co-existence between those who raise livestock and advocates for wildlife that have canid teeth and eat meat to survive.

Not long ago, the Greater Yellowstone region remembered a kind of big-bang catalyst that forced a cultural shift to happen: the 25th anniversary of wolf reintroduction to Yellowstone that happened in 1995. That year, some 60 years after they were exterminated by federal and state governments—wolves were brought back to Yellowstone and a separate central Idaho wilderness area in perhaps the most momentous restoration of an annihilated species in human history.

That it could have happened at all, many say, is a miracle. Even before the first lobo transplants from Canada arrived at holding pens in Yellowstone's Lamar Valley prior to release, boisterous predictions were made by ranchers and hunters that disaster would ensue—that wolves would lay bloody siege to cattle and sheep while also devastating big game herds and attacking people. And if that weren't enough, passionate advocates for *Canis lupus*, on the other side, claimed that wolves, as top predator and a missing link forcibly removed, would instantly reinvigorate a lost sense of ecological balance and yield the perfect assemblance of Eden.

After a series of unsuccessful legal maneuverings to block their reintroduction, a dozen wolves were brought to Yellowstone and by 1996 the two-year effort would reach 31 (separately 35 were released in Idaho). Today, their dispersed descendants can be found in five different states and the wolf population numbers upwards of 2,000.

Astonishing is how the convergence in Alder in November 2019 demonstrated how far the conversation about wolves has come, for inside the firehouse were descendants of cattle and sheep growers who believed in their day that completely purging wolves had been for the betterment of the West. On January 12, 1995, then U.S. Interior Secretary Bruce Babbitt, the late Mollie Beatty, head of the U.S. Fish and Wildlife Service, and Mike Finley, superintendent of Yellowstone, carried wolves into the park as a symbolic gesture showing humankind was righting an act of biocide.

Travel back to the early 1990s. While political winds had begun to shift, tempering the "wolves-will-never-ever-be-reintroduced-to-Yellowstone-in-my-lifetime" sentiments that prevailed in Wyoming, Montana, and Idaho, it still seemed that wolf reintroduction was, at best, a long shot.

In 1991, Yellowstone hosted a gathering of reintroduction advocates that I, as a young reporter, attended.

On a knoll rising above Tower Junction, L. David Mech, the world's foremost wolf researcher, joined Yellowstone interpretive ranger Norm Bishop who recounted events when the National Park Service was part of the wolf eradication campaign. Between 1904 and the late 1920s, 132 wolves (a number greater than the park population today) were destroyed. In 1926, trappers killed a pair of surviving wolf pups near a bison carcass at Soda Butte and it represented the last whimper for a species that had been there since the end of the Ice Age.

Bishop in the 1980s and 1990s gave more than 400 public talks, reaching tens of thousands of people and laying the groundwork for bringing the pack back. He met resistance from rural communities in the Northern Rockies, with some citizens vowing that any lobos would be greeted with "shoot, shovel, and shut-up."

Some politicians in the region wanted Bishop muzzled. "Nothing has been more satisfying to me than seeing the numerous ways that wolves have been demonstrated to affect the ecosystem and restore it to its normal working relationships, including the dynamics of predators and prey," Bishop said. "I thought it would be a rare person who would be able to see a wolf in Yellowstone but it's become an industry, a phenomenon. People come from around the world to see wolves in the Lamar Valley like they would go to the Serengeti to see African lions."

For his part, Mech says, "It's become the best lab for studying wolves in the world because you've had researchers and a huge involvement from a very engaged and enthusiastic public. Flowing out of it has been a bonanza of information."

Doug Smith is Yellowstone's senior wolf biologist and has been profiled on CBS's 60 Minutes. He is the lead author of Yellowstone Wolves: Science and Discovery in the World's First National Park, a tome featuring the perspective of 70 different ecology experts. It is unprecedented and offers the most intensive examination to date of the Greater Yellowstone wolf population. "It represents the state of the art and while it's a Yellowstone-centric book we took on all of the big themes for wolves and ecology," Smith said, noting that while a massive amount of information had to be cut to meet length limitations, it will be shared in the coming years.

Inside Yellowstone, Smith notes, 80 percent of wolf deaths are caused by other wolves and outside the park seven of every 10 wolves die from having contact with humans. Wolves endure because they have high reproduction capabilities, according to Smith, because female and male alpha wolves produce new pup litters every year.

During the last quarter century, no one has been a more intent witness than now-retired park naturalist Rick McIntyre. He spent, during one stretch, 6,175 consecutive days in the field and put more than 100,000 wolf sightings into 12,000 pages of meticulous journal notes. He is a lobo ambassador nonpareil and his first long-waited book, The Rise of Wolf 8: Witnessing The Triumph of Yellowstone's Underdog, has received critical acclaim, as have subsequent works.

McIntyre's book reads like a lobo version of War and Peace and he uses Wolf 8 as a lens. Over the span of two decades, McIntyre rarely missed a day of observing wolves in Yellowstone. Between the year 2000 and August 2015, he logged 6,175 consecutive days. He compiled a family lineage covering hundreds of different lobos in different packs and contributed over 100,000 descriptions accompanying differing wolf sightings. "The story told in this book is an epic one, filled with heroes and heroines who struggle to survive and defend their families. A story that includes all the elements of a great tale: warfare, betrayal, murder, bravery, compassion, empathy, loyalty—and an unexpected hero," McIntyre writes in his prologue. It is a story that deserves to be told by a literary genius such as Shakespeare, Homer, or Dickens. None of those writers was available. If Shakespeare had written a play about these characters and their lives, he might have invented a prologue set at a wolf den, deep within a forest.

Wolves have helped transform Yellowstone, but perhaps their biggest impact is transforming the attitudes of people, and it can be seen in the tens of thousands of park visitors raised on the tale of Little Red Riding Hood and the "big bad wolf" mythology. "It can be magical, when you allow [the reality of wolves] to come in," McIntyre told me during one of our many chats over the years. "I once heard someone say, 'It is hard to hate someone if you know their story.' If I can tell the story of wolves, I hope to help people see them like I do and therefore treat them with the respect they deserve."

Ed Bangs, the former wolf recovery coordinator for the U.S. Fish and Wildlife Service, said that "working with wolves guarantees that you'll be either famous or notorious." Smith has been on the receiving end of public vilification, which has flared less as years of accruing scientific data have replaced the hearsay and emotion that has flowed as polemics from both wolf advocates and despisers.

Writer Paul Schullery made this observation about how the arguments surrounding wolves have shifted. "Here, as always, we struggle with the same mythic temptations of narrative as did our predecessors," he wrote in a 2014 edition of *Yellowstone Science*. "Ecologist David Mech has recently articulated a concern many of us have felt, over what he has called the 'sanctification' of wolves. Few beliefs have seemed so urgently overwhelming to many of us in the modern Yellowstone community as the apparent conviction that wolves are furry little Anakin Skywalkers who will finally bring balance to the Force. From that point of view, all that's left is deciding who in Yellowstone's colorful cast of characters is Darth Vader, and who is Jabba the Hutt."

Indeed, Mech has told me that wolves don't deserve their dastardly reputation, "but neither do they float across the landscape on angel's wings."

Along the eastern slopes of both the Tobacco Root and Gravelly mountains in August, Bob Sitz who attended the meeting in Alder expressed frustration about predators. The Sitz Angus Ranch outside Harrison is nationally renowned for selling prize Angus bulls. Each summer, Sitz trails a few hundred cows into the Gravellies and in recent years he and other cattlemen have contended with predation by grizzlies and wolves in their cattle allotments on the Beaverhead-Deerlodge National Forest.

Wolves, which sometimes descend from the Tobacco Roots onto his property, are dispersers from the original transplants in Yellowstone. Since 1995, Sitz has lost 40 confirmed cattle kills to wolves though he estimates the toll could be double that. Like other ranchers, he says more generous compensation to cover livestock losses might achieve more tolerance for predators and that the wolf and grizzly presence stresses out livestock and creates other hassles.

"We can live with wolves—well we have to whether we like it or not, but with all predators we want flexibility to nip problems in the bud," Sitz said. His sprawling private ranch provides habitat for public wildlife and in order for the ranch to stay undeveloped he needs to stay economically viable.

"Wolves are neither 'good' nor 'bad,'" Doug Smith says. "They are key players in wild ecosystems that help regulate the populations of other wildlife they eat, and if the goal is having a full complement of original species as an expression of a complete ecosystem with its main wildlife parts, then we have success. And the public today, for the most part, gets that."

A few years ago, I went to Idaho as the state was undertaking aggressive action to lethally control lobos. "Wolves are under siege in Idaho but the reality hasn't really gotten the attention that it deserves from wildlife-loving Americans," says Suzanne Asha Stone with Defenders of Wildlife. Few conservationists have the perspective Stone does. She was there during the winters of 1995 and 1996 when wolves were reintroduced. "While public attention has been focused on Yellowstone wolves because they're literally visible to millions of people who come to watch them, here in Idaho the saga has been largely out of sight and mind to most people," she said.

Stone pointed to one group that played a pivotal role in giving wolves a second chance and has quietly been an unsung conservation hero: the Nez Perce Nation. She introduced me to Josiah Blackeagle Pinkham, the Nez Perce's cultural resources ethnographer.

"We have our own stories about wolves, coyotes, and other animals that speak to our attitudes of coexistence," he explains of the animals known to the Nez Perce as *Hími·n*. "They go back to a time long, long before Europeans ever realized this continent was a place on the map of the world."

After a pause, Pinkham noted that in the Nez Perce lexicon there is no natural word for "eradication," meaning the deliberate annihilation of a species as was carried out by European settlers against bison and wolves and other predators. "That concept is foreign to us," he said.

A college-educated father, son of an author who once served as tribal chairman, grandson of a noted shaman, and a hunter, fisherman, and naturalist, Pinkham is keenly aware of two divergent world views that surround him as he pointed toward a spot on the horizon where tribal members recently spotted wolves.

When former Interior Secretary Bruce Babbitt gave the green light for wolf reintroduction to proceed, Idaho refused to participate in an attempt to stymie wolf recovery. Much to the state's surprise, the Nez Perce stepped forward. The tribe has primary jurisdiction over 760,000 acres of reservation in Idaho and, due to treaty rights dating back to 1855, has guaranteed access to more than 17 million acres of original tribal homeland covering a variety of federal public lands in Idaho, Montana, Oregon, and Washington, including wilderness areas where the federal government intended to release wolves transplanted from Canada.

"I visited the tribal council when the wolf reintroduction proposal was moving toward reality and asked for their advice and support," Stone says. "When the state of Idaho refused to support the restoration efforts, wolves needed involvement from the Nez Perce to monitor their survival and their response was, 'Count us in.'"

"The Nez Perce committed as full participants in wolf reintroduction. The Nez Perce approach involves asking the question: 'How am I going to restore this greater whole so that it can function on its own without my intervention?'" Pinkham said. "As 'land managers,' we're one of the few entities trying to manage ourselves out of existence, not in terms of our presence but in terms of the need to constantly tinker."

Carter Niemeyer, a retired federal predator control expert who oversaw efforts to kill wolves that came into conflict with ranchers, investigated reports of depredation and concluded many livestock deaths were blamed on wolves without evidence. He says the Nez Perce's patient, calm, long-term perspective—one that rejects rash, knee-jerk decision-making—is exactly what's needed in the social and political discussions swirling around wolves. It's a perspective Josiah Blackeagle Pinkham and the Nez Perce embrace with open arms.

Renee Askins earned a place in the hearts of many as "the wolf lady" of Yellowstone's modern age. An ardent conservationist, she founded the Wolf Fund in 1986. Its singular ad hoc mission was bringing wolves back to Yellowstone. She promised the Wolf Fund would close the second wolves were re-established.

Recalling a long list of characters who played pivotal roles in making reintroduction happen, Askins says several park officials, including former superintendent Bob Barbee, science chief John Varley, and naturalist-interpreter Bishop, risked their jobs by continuing to advocate for wolves despite fierce political pressure brought against them and orders that they couldn't promote wolf reintroduction—orders they defied.

Following the writing of a lengthy environmental impact statement, hundreds of contentious public meetings, and collectively millions of public comments submitted—the vast majority supporting reintroduction—the final pieces of reintroduction involved finding wolves in British Columbia and then navigating a gauntlet of legal challenges.

Askins was there at Roosevelt Arch in 1995 to welcome wolves passing beneath the famous portal, the homecoming accompanied by an armed escort from law enforcement that had been warned about possible troublemakers. "My favorite moment was watching all the Gardiner schoolkids, festooned in vibrant-colored mittens, rainbow snow boots, their scarves fluttering like bright prayer flags, as they gathered along the roadside to wave wolves in," Askins recalls. "I was told there were some displeased teachers that had resisted, but the kids charged out to line the route, oblivious to any adult trepidation."

Like biologist Smith, she was afraid that a last-minute court ruling would delay reintroduction or halt it. Many worried that wolves, confined to small cages, might not endure the journey. "There were some exceptionally tense hours while the Farm Bureau sued for an injunction to prevent the wolves from being released from their portable kennels into the park holding pens," Askins recalls. "Secretary of Interior Bruce Babbitt, there for the celebration, instead found himself speculating to the press about whether Yellowstone's first wolves would arrive not in kennels but coffins."

That didn't happen. An Interior Department attorney's approval, upheld by a federal judge, cleared the way over yowls of protest and predictions the western way of life was about to collapse.

At first, wolves occupied and thrived in the park and then in remote corners of the region away from people. Mech knew the real test would come when wolves left the safe confines of Yellowstone. It didn't take long. The thirty-one lobos released in Yellowstone swelled to more than four times as many in the first few years. Within five years, wolves began inhabiting places where rural people and their livestock live.

In Yellowstone, "wolf watching" is an anchor in the park's popular nature-tourism economy that generates around 7,500 jobs and close to $700 million annually for the region. In neighboring Grand Teton, the numbers are 8,000 jobs and $800 million. Two of the main attractions are grizzly bears and wolves that can be viewed from the roadsides.

In Yellowstone, wolf watching alone is estimated to generate at least $35 million in annual spending based on people who say they are coming to the park primarily to see wolves and the amount of money they spend to make it happen That's according to a study by University of Montana economist John Duffield, who notes the trickle-down effect could actually be worth twice that.

As wolf watching became a sensation in Yellowstone amassing a rapidly growing army of adherents, some rushed to tout the alleged ecological benefits of wolves. On YouTube, a video titled "How Wolves Change Rivers" and homemade spinoffs have been watched more than 100 million times.

Scientists long surmised that by restoring wolves, as the vital missing link extinguished in a less-informed ecological era, balance and harmony to the food chain—the so-called "trophic cascade"—would be restored, too. The problem of "too many" elk populating Yellowstone's Northern

Range where heavy browsing severely impacted aspen trees and willow in the absence of wolves would be remedied setting off a positive chain reaction, according to the video.

Wolves have knocked down a coyote population blamed for intense predation on the park's small pronghorn herd. By reducing elk numbers, aspen trees have rejuvenated and willow abundance is returning, bolstering beaver (that eat its branches) and they would create jams and more wetland habitat.

Both Mech and Smith, the latter of whom assigned experts to intensely review the data, said not so fast; indeed wolves are causing ripple effects but not enough to justify the idyllic narrative in the YouTube video. To state it simply, nature is complicated.

This doesn't mean the insights now emerging aren't astounding and that the dividends aren't dramatic. The elk population has the richest carnivore community in North America and is holding its own, Smith says. After the elk population of the Northern Range fell from a high of around 19,000 elk to around 4,000 in recent years it has grown to around 7,000, according to surveys carried out by the state of Montana and Yellowstone personnel. Simultaneously, the original wolf population there, supported by prolific elk numbers and reaching 174, has dipped and resettled to around 100 in 10 packs, existing with a sort of dynamic equilibrium. A lively debate exists among scientists. "The evidence shows elk do change their behavior in the presence of wolves and it involves both congregating in larger group size and adopting different ways to avoid wolves," Smith said.

Others have argued that wolf presence has resulted in elk not using prime-favored foraging areas. Some claim the combination of having to be on the move and poorer access to nutritious edibles has negatively affected cow elk pregnancy rates. And yet, data shows a high pregnancy rate in cow elk. Ironically, some ranchers now complain that too many wapiti are wintering in their pastures.

Mike Phillips, the original lead wolf biologist in Yellowstone who went on to co-found the Turner Endangered Species Fund with media-mogul-turned-bison-rancher Ted Turner, was mentored by Mech in Minnesota. And he went on to become an outspoken voice in debunking mythology about wolves. Phillips' oration skills helped him become elected to multiple terms in both the Montana House and Senate. In recent years he has served as a scientific advisor for efforts to put the question of whether wolves should be restored to the state of Colorado on the ballot after a long stretch when agricultural interests in that state have prevented the U.S. Fish and Wildlife Service from repeating what it did in Yellowstone and central Idaho. I asked him what's been most significant as he looks back. "That's simple," Phillips said. "It's their ability to inspire changes in thinking. Wolves have always been about more than wolves and Yellowstone about more than the park itself."

Phillips helped spearhead an effort to restore wolves to Colorado by putting the issue on the ballot and he's using the lessons learned to debunk the same kind of resistance he encountered in Yellowstone. "The Yellowstone wolf story has a lot to teach people," he said. "So much of our poor treatment of the natural world has been caused by ignorance. But we can do better and this proves it."

I asked Phillips this question: "You're a scientist but, like journalists, you push back against distortion of biological facts and contentions that do not hold up to scrutiny. What's the most troubling pertaining to wolves?" He responded, "The most egregious claims about wolves are that they represent a threat to human safety, the livestock industry, and the recreational, big game killing industry. They do not. The best available science, the most reliable knowledge gained over the last 50 years, makes clear that coexisting with wolves is a straightforward affair that requires only a modicum of accommodation."

Abby Nelson, a wolf management specialist for Montana Fish, Wildlife and Parks, has seen it all and many view her as a rising star in field biology. "From my perspective, living with wolves is 90 percent people and engaging with them where they are at and understanding the con-straints facing those who deal with wildlife conflicts," Nelson says. All of it revolves around a bottom line that, especially for mom-and-pop ranchers, can be thin.

Many people, including wolf advocates, might not fully appreciate how beneficial it is to all to help keep rural ranchers and farmers on the land. Their properties provide free habitat for wildlife and open spaces that contribute to inspiring views for all around.

Nelson has found that many ranchers have tolerance for wolves in the northern valleys that spiral out of Yellowstone—the Paradise, Madison and Boulder—so long as wolf packs don't become cattle and sheep killers.

Some will even admit candidly they kind of enjoy seeing wolves around but if leaders of the pack start keying in on livestock instead of wildlife, then producers want swift remedies. And that's where she comes in.

If non-lethal deterrents such as stringing flag-like fladry and electric fencing around cows at calving time, or employing loud horns and flashing lights with motion detectors don't work, decisions have to be made. Either the state or agents affiliated with the federal agency Wildlife Services might be called in to kill wolves. "We need to respect and work with ranchers," Nelson said. "That's how you build tolerance." The estimated size of the wolf population in Montana is 800, she says, and the average number of wolves killed over the last six years annually is between 230 and 260.

How wildlife is managed in Yellowstone National Park, where hunting isn't allowed, there is no livestock, and preservation is the objective, is very different from the reality outside the park. "My colleagues with other agencies jokingly say that I work in a wildlife country club," Yellowstone's Smith believes today.

"I agree with Doug that there is tremendous value to having places like Yellowstone where wildlife doesn't have to be subjected to constant and, in some cases, heavy-handed human management," Mech explained. "But the fact is, the majority of terrain inhabited by wolves in the West is found outside national parks. There, wolves fall under some form of management. The question is, 'What kind?'"

Since wolves were removed from federal protection, the Fish and Wildlife Service no longer assembles a comprehensive report; but the last one prepared in 2014 by the person who succeeded Ed Bangs, Mike Jimenez, is instructive because the numbers haven't fluctuated much. He wrote that there were an estimated 1,800 wolves comprising roughly 313 packs right in the heart of Western cattle country.

Wolves account for about 1 percent of total livestock losses, according to federal ag statistics. Noteworthy is that only 62 of the 300-plus wolf packs were involved in livestock depredation and the majority of those cases involved only a handful of livestock depredations at most. "What it means is that four of every five packs are existing without incident," Jimenez noted, suggesting that in the realm of perception for some, the opposite is true.

Lethal control of wolves outside of Yellowstone and Grand Teton was always part of the deal in bringing them back, though it still doesn't sit well with some environmentalists. For as many wolves as there are today living in the West, at least that many have been killed, mostly in lethal removals but also by hunters and trappers. The number of dead wolves exceeds the number of cattle that have been taken and millions of dollars have been spent in control actions, federal and state officials told me.

Generating huge amounts of controversy, inflamed by social media, the deaths of park wolves with radio collars around their necks have been important parts of research in Yellowstone where they live most of their lives. When those animals have wandered across the park's invisible line some have been shot and what's especially galling for advocates is that those wolves, because they spent a lot of time inside the park within eyesight of people, did not associate danger with humans.

Ironically, wolves and other predators may have a role in helping big game populations fend off diseases such as Chronic Wasting Disease, the always-fatal brain disorder affecting members of the cervid (deer) family that includes elk, moose, mule and white-tailed deer. For over two decades, researchers have watched wildlife predators hunting for prey in Yellowstone. Smith says there is no mistaking the way that lobos identify and target elk. To the human eye, an individual wapiti might appear perfectly healthy yet there is something—almost *a sixth sense*—that catches the attention of discriminating pack members searching for their next meal.

It might be an elk with arthritis carrying a slight gimp in its gait, or maybe a hint of winter-worn fatigue, a slowness brought on by advancing old age or illness, or perhaps naïve behavior exhibited by the young. There is no doubt, based on the accrued record of wolf behavior documented in Yellowstone—and the significant body of scientific accounts logged across the continent—that under normal conditions, wolves key-in on prey that is meek, infirmed, or vulnerable.

"Wolves pick up on stuff we can't see. They are most efficient at exploiting weaknesses in prey because their survival depends on it," Smith told me. "They are predisposed, by instinct and learned behavior, to focus first on animals that are easier to kill rather than those living at the height of their physical strength."

Does having predators on the landscape—wolves, bears, mountain lions and coyotes—provide a protective gauntlet that can help slow the spread and prevalence of deadly diseases? In particular, with ultra-lethal Chronic Wasting Disease now invading the most wildlife-rich ecosystem in America's Lower 48 states and spreading coast to coast, are these often maligned meat-eaters, which are frequently dismissed as worthless vermin in western states, actually important natural allies in battling CWD?

While the data and the assessments of most scientists clearly suggests yes, there remains fierce resistance by some to acknowledge the beneficial roles predators play. At one meeting of the Montana Fish and Game Commission, anti-predator biases were on full display, especially toward wolves. They surfaced as the commission pondered its next move in confronting CWD which, in 2017, entered Montana via sick wild deer for the first time in state history.

Weeks earlier, Ken McDonald, wildlife bureau chief at the Montana Fish Wildlife and Parks Department, raised eyebrows when he claimed that the advantages predators bring in weeding out sick prey is merely theoretical and unproved. Dismissing the notion of wolves as effective disease-fighters, he asserted that in order for lobos to truly make a difference in slowing CWD's advance, they would need to exist in such high numbers that it would be socially unacceptable to humans, namely ranchers and hunters.

In terms of Montana's strategy for dealing with CWD, McDonald said the state's primary method of confronting disease will involve enlisting hunters to aggressively harvest animals in emerging CWD endemic zones. Many claim McDonald's characterization of wolves demonstrates not only a personal anti-wolf bias, which also permeates the thinking of the department, but it shows a lack of understanding and appreciation for the natural history of the species. In other words, it denies what the very essence of a wolf is.

"I was disappointed with Ken McDonald's nonsensical bureaucratic response," conservationist and professional biologist Dr. Gary J. Wolfe wrote recently in comments that were widely circulated. Wolfe is a former Montana Fish Wildlife and Parks Commissioner appointed by Governor Steve Bullock. Notably, he is also the former project leader of the CWD Alliance founded by a number of prominent sportsmen's groups and former national president and CEO of the Rocky Mountain Elk Foundation for 15 years. He is widely respected in hunting circles.

"While I don't think any of us large carnivore proponents are saying that wolf predation will prevent CWD, or totally eliminate it from infected herds, it is ecologically irresponsible to not consider the very real possibility that wolves can slow the spread of CWD and reduce its prevalence in infected herds," Wolfe says. "We should consider wolves to be 'CWD border guards,' adjust wolf hunting seasons accordingly, and let wolves do their job of helping to cull infirm animals from the herds."

Strong evidence seems to bear him out. Not only do predators stalking large game species target weak animals, they can mitigate the impact of disease outbreaks, experts say. Further, by removing sick prey species, predators could, over time, though this is unproved, make herds more resilient and stronger, less susceptible to disease. While some may doubt this premise, illustrated in literature below, no one has provided evidence suggesting that having robust and stable numbers of predators will not aid in confronting the most rapidly spreading and fearsome new disease in North America.

Lloyd Dorsey, former conservation director for the Sierra Club in Wyoming, is a hunter and crusader against Wyoming's operation of elk feedgrounds. We spoke about predators and CWD after he had just returned from hunting in the Gros Ventre mountains east of the National Elk Refuge. He told me of how on the morning that he glassed mule deer and bands of elk, he found grizzly tracks in the snow and heard wolves howling a quarter mile away.

Citing reams of scientific studies to back him up, Dorsey says predators play an import ecological role in keeping prey species in check and in serving as vanguards in removing sick animals. Greater Yellowstone's "predator guild" of wolves, grizzly and black bears, lions and coyotes, he notes, also makes it a draw for wildlife watchers from around the world.

A disease like CWD that stands to significantly harm the health of deer family members over time—deer, elk, and moose—also has potentially grave implications for species that eat and scavenge their remains. In many ways, the biological integrity of Greater Yellowstone's large mammal populations depends upon the health of its ungulate herds and the biomass they provide in sustaining other species large and small: those with fur and feathers down to the microbial level. Diseases that threaten to dramatically diminish Greater Yellowstone's ungulates could have negative, far-reaching consequences for people and the environment.

To date, there is no evidence that CWD can infect predators, humans, or livestock, though geneticists who have studied the molecular make-up of CWD prions (misshapen proteins) believe it could change.

With CWD, Wyoming is perilously burning the candle at both ends and it has implications for Montana and Idaho, Dorsey says. Wyoming and the U.S. Fish and Wildlife Service continue to knowingly operate feedgrounds which makes the state and federal government guilty of game management malpractice by setting up public wildlife for calamity, he believes.

At the same time, Wyoming persists in destroying a natural ally—wolves—based upon no solid reason other than traditional cultural animosity toward these archetypal animals that earlier generations of settlers took great delight in eradicating to make way for livestock. "Our understanding of wolves has broadened in an age of greater scientific and ecological awareness," Dorsey told me. "They are not the animals of menacing myth they were portrayed to be in fairy tales. We can, and should, co-exist with them for mutual benefit."

Nonetheless, Wyoming, along with Alaska, is known for having the most notoriously hostile attitude toward wolves in America. In over 85 percent of Wyoming, lobos, like coyotes, can be killed year-round for any reason, no questions asked. Only in the northwest corner of Wyoming within the vicinity of Yellowstone and Grand Teton national parks are wolves classified as a game animal and even there it is state policy to keep their numbers suppressed to please outfitters, guides, and ranchers.

Beyond that small zone, they are classified as "predators" and treated as vermin. They can be trapped, poisoned, shot at any and all hours of the day, and targeted by aerial gunners in aircraft. Even if they are not threatening livestock, it's open season on wolves. The profound irony is that just as Wyoming condones a campaign of re-eradication against wolves, CWD has been rapidly spreading westward, faster than anyone expected across the state via infected mule and white-tailed deer.

Perfect conditions to amplify a CWD pandemic, experts say, exist on the National Elk Refuge and 22 elk feedgrounds operated by the state of Wyoming, many of them on U.S. Forest Service land. CWD's arrival is considered imminent. When the disease lands in the Wyoming feedgrounds, where more than 20,000 elk are unnaturally concentrated during winters, CWD is expected to not only take hold but have its spread accelerated due to the widely condemned management practice of bunching up wapiti. The conditions there are similar to game farms where CWD infections have been devastating.

This point was made in a letter sent from the Montana state wildlife commission (read it at bottom of this story) to counterparts in Wyoming, asking the state to take steps to shut down feeding. "We respect the fact that how Wyoming manages its affairs is up to Wyoming. However, Montana's ability to combat CWD will depend upon decisions that Wyoming makes about its wildlife management. Over the long term, the feed grounds make your wildlife populations less healthy, less stable, and much more vulnerable to a catastrophic disease event," the Montana Fish and Wildlife Commission wrote. "We implore you to begin the process of looking at alternatives to the present management regime that unnaturally concentrates wildlife in feed grounds each winter and increases the pace at which CWD infects both states' wildlife populations."

The letter ends with this warning: "If we do not address CWD, we will all be *culpable* in leaving a greatly devalued landscape to future generations." Culpable is a word with many connotations.

While Montana has escaped the intense scrutiny and public rebuke aimed at Wyoming over its operation of feedgrounds and controversial management of wolves, Wolfe and others say Montana isn't much better with regard to predators. Still, CWD has spread in deer, elk, and moose across the state with amazing speed.

Allowing unlimited wolf harvest "is probably not the best ecological strategy for containing CWD," Wolfe noted. "As a wildlife biologist who spent several years working on the CWD issue, I believe wolf predation is an important tool that needs to be recognized and effectively utilized, along with other tools, as part of Montana's CWD management plan."

Wolves, Wolfe says, ought to have their numbers safeguarded in areas that represent the front line of disease. The state of Montana eventually listened and has reduced the number of wolves allowed to be killed outside of Yellowstone. When the argument has been presented to the Wyoming Game and Fish Department, it has been met with deaf ears, though Dr. Mary Wood, the former state wildlife veterinarian who now works for the state of Colorado, has stated that predators can play a beneficial role.

Humans can invent any fairy-tale reason they want to despise wolves and justify their elimination, but that doesn't change the fundamental time-tested nature of the species, says Kevin Van Tighem, a hunter and former superintendent of Banff National Park in Alberta's Canadian Rockies. "I don't know of a single credible biologist who would argue that wolves, along with other predators and scavengers, aren't important tools in devising sound strategies for dealing with CWD." Van Tighem asserted it can be rationally argued that wolves provide the best line of defense since they are confronting infected animals.

Van Tighem told me, just as a dozen other scientists and land managers who hunt have, that once CWD is confirmed in the places where they go afield, they will no longer eat game meat from that area and may stop hunting altogether.

Mech, the eminent American wolf biologist, has authored or contributed to hundreds of peer-reviewed scientific papers on wolves and prey. We've been talking about wolves since the late 1980s when he came to Yellowstone in the years before lobos were reintroduced. There's no tangible argument he's seen that suggests wolves wouldn't be useful in combatting CWD. "In the main, the preponderance of scientific evidence supports the view that wolves generally kill the old, the young, the sick, and the weak," Mech said. "There's so much documented field data behind it."

He then made a point that exposes the limitations of relying on human hunters and sharpshooters alone to remove suspected CWD carriers. Wolves appear to target sick animals that, to the human eye, exhibit no overt symptoms of disease.

"There's a lot more going on than we can detect," Mech said. "They are killing animals that most people would say, 'That animal looks pretty healthy to me,' but in fact it isn't." Mech stays out of the political fray, though he says the value of predators is clear. "Based upon everything I've seen over the course of my career, I generally stand behind the assertion that wolves make prey populations healthier," he said. "The evidence to support it is overwhelming."

In the book *Wolves on the Hunt: The Behavior of Wolves Hunting Wild Prey*, Mech, Doug Smith, and co-author/editor Daniel R. MacNulty, undertook an exhaustive, unprecedented review of scientific studies and observations related to wolf behavior. They cite example after example of how wolves choose prey. They use intricately-detailed observations based on the work of Rick McIntyre. They also point to hours upon hours of accumulated video footage amassed by award-winning wildlife cinematographer Robert Landis who has recorded numerous wolf predation incidents in Yellowstone.

"Suffice it to say here, in summer, that it is well documented … that wolves generally kill calves, fawns, and older members of prey populations along with individuals that are diseased, disabled, or in poor conditions, or that have various abnormalities," the authors noted. "These types of individuals are physically less able to withstand long and persistent attacks like more healthy animals can."

In 2003, then *Denver Post* reporter Theo Stein interviewed scientists about CWD spreading though deer and elk in Colorado. Dr. Valerius Geist, who briefly became a darling of anti-wolfers when he raised the issue of tapeworms, made this assertion about the significance of wolves in containing CWD spread via proteins called prions. "Wolves will certainly bring the disease to a halt," Geist said. "They will remove infected individuals and clean up carcasses that could transmit the disease."

The impacts of historic predator-killing campaigns have been documented. Stein reported that Geist and Princeton University biologist Andrew Dobson theorize that killing off the wolf allowed CWD to take hold in the first place. Further, the Chronic Wasting Disease Alliance observed, "The spread of chronic wasting disease toward Yellowstone's famed game herds alarms wildlife lovers, but two top researchers think biologists will discover a powerful ally in an old frontier villain. The wolf."

Be it wolf, mountain lion, bear, or coyote, each different predator species has different approaches to both taking prey and scavenging. Besides the significant body of evidence in the Mech, Smith, and MacNulty book, there is a lot of brainpower that has been applied to thinking how predators could help head off CWD.

Mountain lions are known for being ambush predators, lying in wait to target mule and white-tailed deer. Wolves and coyotes are "coursers" meaning they chase prey across open ground. Grizzlies and black bears take elk calves and deer fawns and, like the others, feast upon freshly killed carcasses, cleaning them down to the bone. Of note is that Mech and others have documented that wolves, for example, take down larger numbers of deer bucks, which, according to CWD researchers, also have a higher level of CWD prevalence in wild herds.

In a 2010 peer-reviewed journal article, "Mountain Lions prey selectively on prion-infected mule deer," lead author Caroline E. Krumm with the Colorado Division of Wildlife's scientific research center and four colleagues noted how cougars appeared to select for CWD-infected deer because they were easier to fell. Their research examined 108 kill sites where the big cats ambushed deer.

"From the observations gathered across several studies, we hypothesize that although much of the 'selection' we observed may be attributed to infected mule deer being less vigilant or fit and thus relatively vulnerable to 'attack' of one kind or another, mountain lions may also learn to recognize and more actively target diseased deer," they wrote.

Echoing Mech's observations, they pointed out, "Other studies indicate that coursing predators like wolves and coyotes select prey disproportionately if they appear impaired by malnutrition, age, or disease." Just as other scientists have warned that once CWD becomes firmly established in wildlife population and its effects over time can be dire, Krumm and co-authors suggested predators can help minimize prion contamination. "Although theory suggests that removing infected animals could 'sanitize' and slow the rate of prion transmission, prevalence can be remarkably high in mule deer populations preyed upon by mountain lions. Prion transmission among deer can occur via several mechanisms, including indirect transmission from exposure to prions in the environment," they stated. "We observed that mountain lions typically consumed greater than 85 percent of a deer carcass, often including brain tissue, and this may be beneficial in decreasing prion contamination at kill sites. However, the extent to which selective predation by mountain lions alters the dynamics of prion disease epidemics in natural mule deer populations remains unclear."

That's why it's important to have the full predator-guild present, perpetually seeking out sick animals in different ways, in different parts of the landscape. In 2006, researcher N. Thompson Hobbs wrote "A Model Analysis of Effects of Wolf Predation on the Prevalence of Chronic Wasting Disease in Elk Populations of Rocky Mountain National Park." He created a simulation based upon meat consumption necessary to sustain a group of wolves and factoring the likelihood they would first target sick animals. Just as experts who deal with epizootic diseases warn that the Wyoming feedgrounds represent the worst possible conditions for CWD to take hold, likely to unnaturally accelerate an outbreak, wildlife predators can serve as a powerful counterbalance.

Hobbs explained how it works. "Increased mortality rates [by predators] in diseased populations can retard disease transmission and reduce disease prevalence. Increasing mortality slows transmission via two mechanisms. First, it reduces the average lifetime of infected individuals. Reduced lifespan, in turn can compress the time interval when animals are infectious, thereby reducing the number of infections produced per infected individual," he wrote. "The effect of reduced intervals of infectivity is amplified by reductions in population density that occur as mortality increases, reductions that cause declines in the number of contacts between infected and susceptible individuals. Both of these mechanisms retard the transmission of disease. If these mechanisms cause the number of new infections produced per infected individual to fall below one, then the disease will be eradicated from the population."

Granted, his analysis focused on Rocky Mountain National Park and Colorado where there is today a population-level outbreak of CWD under way and where there are no wolves. Rocky Mountain has densities of wapiti approaching 115 elk per square kilometer. The unnatural densities of elk on the Elk Refuge and Wyoming feedgrounds, Dorsey notes, are orders of magnitude greater, literally thousands of elk per square kilometer. It means that should CWD take hold, predators would be even more important in aiding to stop a potentially virulent spread.

According to one study, CWD rates in Rocky Mountain were as low as one percent in the early 1990s. Since 2008, the proportion of female elk infected with CWD in the park has fluctuated between six and 13 percent. CWD is today the leading cause of death in adult female elk.

Despite claims that predators decimate big game herds, there is, in fact, little evidence to back up those assertions, broadly speaking. It's true that under certain circumstances the presence of predators can result in a significant population decline compared to numbers of ungulates present after species like wolves were eradicated. However, predator sinks are gross anomalies in the Rocky Mountain West; moreover, ecosystems are dynamic and populations of all species are always in some kind of flux.

Again, based upon surveys compiled by state wildlife agencies in Wyoming, Montana, and Idaho, most elk hunting units—with wolves inside them—are at, close to, or above desired population goals for wapiti.

Hunter success is high, especially for hunters willing to work at stalking their prey. Outfitters/guides throughout the tri-state region tout hunter success and boast of having happy customers.

What anti-predator voices never acknowledge is that the very prey species they covet—large, muscular bull elk and deer bucks—are products of thousands of years of evolution and pressure applied by predators, ecologists note. Pronghorn (antelope) on the prairies are fleet of foot because, as a result of survival of the fittest, they became biologically engineered to outrun North America's version of African cheetahs before those big cats became extinct.

McDonald of Montana Fish Wildlife and Parks has asserted that human hunters will be deployed to eliminate CWD. In Wisconsin, the state has spent millions of dollars depopulating areas of white-tail deer and enlisted hunters to remove animals in an effort to knock CWD back, all to no avail. CWD has spread from Wisconsin into both Minnesota and Michigan.

In 2011, Dr. Margaret Wild collaborated with Hobbs and two other authors on a paper, "The Role of Predation in Disease Control: A Comparison of Selective and Nonselective Removal on Prion Disease Dynamics in Deer." This study was based on a model that examined the likely effects of wolf predation on CWD-infected deer and holds possible implications for states in the Upper Midwest. The simulation noted that wolves could prevent CWD from emerging at the population level and proliferating. A crucial step is allowing predators to perform their role in the early stages of the disease's arrival.

"Thus far, control strategies relying on hunting or culling by humans to lower deer numbers and subsequently CWD prevalence have not yielded demonstrable effects," they wrote, explaining that human hunters only remove sick deer randomly while predators actively seek out the infirmed.

"Doubling the vulnerability of infected animals to selective predation accelerated the rate of decline in prevalence," they noted, even encouraging the consideration of making sure predator populations were healthy in the forward zones of disease progression. "We suggest that as CWD distribution and wolf range overlap in the future, wolf predation may suppress disease emergence or limit prevalence," they added.

The noted American-Canadian mammal biologist Dr. Paul Paquet has been monitoring the geographic expansion of CWD relative to the presence of long-established wolf populations since the disease was first confirmed in the wild, decades ago.

"To date and in general, CWD has not thrived where wolf populations are active, although the disease has appeared on the margins of these populations. A simple mapping of the distribution of wolves and CWD is very instructive," Paquet told *Mountain Journal*. "I have not mapped the distribution of *all* large predators and CWD, but that would be an instructive exercise. In particular, a comparison of diverse multi-prey and multi-predator systems like Yellowstone with simpler systems like the Great Lakes would of interest, as well as comparing the mix and densities of predators with establishment of CWD."

Why is confronting anti-wolf bias as important as the significant body of evidence pertaining to predators and CWD? Because the opinions that are informing policy don't align with reality.

Here, it is essential to provide some context of wolf presence in the West, a quarter century after *Canis lupus* was reintroduced to Yellowstone and the wilderness of central Idaho and have since fanned out across a much wider area, reaching Oregon and Washington and possibly opening discussions of their return to Colorado.

In 2016, a record 243 livestock animals—154 cattle, 88 sheep, and a horse—were killed by wolves in Wyoming, which a year earlier had an estimated minimum wolf population of 377. Montana's wolf count was close to 500 and Idaho had almost 800 in 2015, according to the U.S. Fish and Wildlife Service.

The Fish and Wildlife Service no longer compiles a regional report for the northern Rockies/Pacific Northwest since wolves were removed from federal protection and management handed over to the states. Wolves account for about 1 percent of total livestock losses. Noteworthy is that only 62 of the 300-plus wolf packs in the western U.S. were involved in livestock depredation and the majority of those cases involved only a handful of livestock depredations at most. "What it means is that four of every five packs are existing without incident," former federal wolf biologist Michael Jimenez said.

Before he retired as the Fish and Wildlife Service's wolf field director, Michael Jimenez and I spoke annually about wolf losses—real and imagined—and this gets at McDonald's point about social tolerance and its connection to political rhetoric.

In April 2015, 36 Republican members of the U.S. House of Representatives sent a letter to then Interior Secretary Sally Jewell and Fish
and Wildlife Service Director Dan Ashe, both political appointees of the
Obama Administration, demanding wolves be delisted across all of the
Lower 48. "Since wolves were first provided protections under the
Endangered Species Act, uncontrolled and unmanaged growth of wolf
populations has resulted in devastating impacts on hunting and ranching,
as well as tragic losses to historically strong and healthy livestock and
wildlife populations," those members of Congress wrote.

The phrase "devastating impacts on hunting and ranching, as well as
tragic loses to historically strong and healthy livestock and wildlife populations" is, on the face of it, a fabrication. How?

In one of the last reports Jimenez compiled, he noted that at the end
of 2014 there were an estimated 1,800 wolves comprising roughly 313
packs. Across Wyoming, Idaho, Montana, Oregon, and Washington, all
those wolves in that year were confirmed to have killed a total of 140
cattle, 172 sheep, four dogs, one horse, and one donkey. In a vast region
where there are millions of cattle, sheep, dogs, horses and donkeys, and
thousands of ranchers and farmers, is this what members of Congress
mean by "devastating" and "tragic"?

Across the West, thousands upon thousands of domestic cows and
sheep perish each year from disease, weather, accidents, eating poisonous
plants, lightning strikes, and predation of all kinds, including killing by
feral dogs. Wolves account for about 1 percent of total livestock losses.

Those who possess a disdain for wolves have, for years, thrown up a
series of theories, all either discredited or unsubstantiated. The first was
that wolves would decimate big game herds. Fact: it hasn't happened and
most big game populations in wolf country are at or above population
objectives. Another claim is the lobos reintroduced from Canada were
the "wrong subspecies" and substantially different from wolves that existed
in Greater Yellowstone and central Idaho prior to their extermination.
Fact: also not true.

More recently, as those notions have been dismissed as absurd, two
new contentions have been advanced. There's one claim that wolves represent an imminent danger to humans, pets, and wildlife health because
they carry *Echinococcus granulosus*, a tapeworm linked to hydatid disease.
Not only is this dismissed as untrue and fear-mongering, but the tapeworm

is found widely in elk, deer, and moose. Hunters are advised to take precautions such as wearing gloves in field dressing animals.

The latest unproved charge, raised again at the Montana wildlife commission meeting, is that wolves may themselves be vectors for spreading CWD because they eat disease-infected elk and deer and might therefore disperse prions via their scat. Opinion is divided on whether prions, being hardy agents, can survive passage through a wolf, or bear, coyote, or mountain lion's digestive track. It's possible.

Nonetheless, ecologists say that the role of predators in removing CWD-infected animals and "cleaning-up" carcasses by scavenging them would more than likely offset any negative potential they have for dispersing CWD more widely via scat. Migratory deer and elk are already moving hundreds of miles seasonally across and between vast expanses of land, shedding CWD prions into the environment along the way via urine, feces, saliva, and decomposing tissue when they die. "Canids are not susceptible to prions, many millions of years of evolution as scavengers have insured this. During the BSE [Mad Cow Disease] crisis in the UK, it was estimated that a large number of domestic dogs in the UK was exposed to the prions. Not a single dog was ever recorded as infected," Princeton research Dobson said. "So wolves and canids do not transmit the prions/CWD in their feces and urine. It is nonsense to suggest so. Carnivores are also much more territorial in the West and, except for individuals, they do not cover as much terrain of the combined movements elk, mule deer and white-tails."

Critics say the denial coming from western states about the beneficial role predators can play in slowing the advance of CWD is driven by a backward cultural mindset—reinforced by politicians who perpetuate it to get elected—that has little or no scientific basis. In the case of CWD, states that continue to adhere to anti-predator policies may, in fact, be making disease impacts worse. Lloyd Dorsey of the Sierra Club chimed in. "At this urgent moment, when everyone is scrambling to do what's sensible, now is not the time to be killing off the very biological tools we need."

CWD is now literally at the gate of Yellowstone and its arrival has park officials worried. A decade ago, P. J. White and Troy Davis provided an overview of CWD for an article that appeared in the journal *Yellowstone Science*. Referencing the study by Wild and Miller, and noting that wolves could have "potent effects" in tamping down CWD prevalence, they wrote, "Wolves [in Yellowstone] are highly selective for elk throughout the year and bears are highly selective of neonatal elk during summer. If predators can detect CWD-infected animals, then selective predation and quick removal of carcasses by scavengers could reduce CWD transmission rates and, in turn, the prevalence and spread of the disease. Wolves could also reduce the risk of transmission by dispersing deer and elk."

With predators on the landscape, again based on simulations run at Rocky Mountain National Park, "compensatory and density-related effects could result in less net mortality than rates of infection and death from CWD would suggest. Thus, the net effect of CWD on the abundance, reproduction, and survival of deer and elk could be less than predicted based on data collected in areas with few large predators."

In March 2016, Yellowstone assembled its first "Chronic Wasting Disease Surveillance Plan." Looming large in the document is this acknowledgment by the three authors, Chris Geremia, John Treanor, and P. J. White: "If epidemics lead to widespread population reductions in Yellowstone, CWD could indirectly alter the structure and function of this ecosystem during future decades; adversely affect species of predators and scavengers; and have serious economic effects on the recreation-based economies of the area."

The authors note that Yellowstone, by law, is mandated to confront diseases that threaten its mission to promote the persistence of native species, but CWD represents a conundrum. "A primary purpose of Yellowstone National Park is to preserve abundant and diverse wildlife in one of the largest remaining intact ecosystems on earth. Disease management actions such as depopulation or substantial population reductions by random culling may be inappropriate for the park because they would remove many more healthy animals than infected animals, substantially reduce the prey base for predators and scavengers, and result in fewer benefits (e.g., scientific knowledge) and reduced visitor enjoyment (e.g., recreational viewing)."

No strategy has been effective at eradicating CWD from areas where the disease is present. Disease management objectives will focus on early detection and monitoring," park officials say. Yellowstone in summer is a mixing bowl where as many as 20,000 deer and elk from multiple herds converge, including animals from the Jackson Elk Herd that winters on the National Elk Refuge and state feedgrounds. Those animals, in turn, mix with tens of thousands more.

Yellowstone, along with officials in Montana, Idaho, the National Elk Refuge, and Wyoming state feedgrounds are on the lookout for sick-looking animals, testing carcasses of dead animals, and even removing asymptomatic elk. Wolves, lions, and coyotes are always on the lookout, prowling.

Gary Wolfe is hardly the only one who questioned Ken McDonald's claims about wolves and predators not being impactful. I asked McDonald if he really believed what he said. "I don't think predators are going to hurt our efforts in addressing CWD but I don't think they are going to make a significant difference in stopping the spread of it. You'd have to have a pretty significant population of predators to have a significant reduction on populations of deer carrying CWD."

McDonald has said that hunters are a better tool for trying to control CWD but it's clear most hunters cannot discern an asymptomatic CWD-infected deer or elk from a healthy one. In 2002 and just months before he died tragically in an auto wreck, Tom Thorne, who had served as Wyoming chief wildlife veterinarian, acknowledged to Theo Stein of *The Denver Post* that cultural hatred of wolves trumped science. "Emotions against wolves are so strong that I'm not sure this potential benefit, which I agree might be there, would sway the opinions of many folks," he said. "I think it would be a long, long time before people are used to wolves enough to admit they might be doing a bit of good."

Is the civic dialogue and the public conversation about predators in Montana any more evolved? Bill Geer, president of the Montana Wildlife Federation, praised state wildlife managers for their bolstered surveillance and putting in motion an attempt to stop CWD before its foothold deepens. And he, too, encouraged McDonald and colleagues to reconsider their attitude toward predators.

"The outbreak [of CWD] … speaks to the benefit of having apex predators like wolves and mountain lions on the landscape. Wolves and mountain lions often preferentially kill compromised animals, and once a CWD-infected animal starts to show signs of the disease, it will be easier to kill for wolves," Geer wrote on November 28, 2017. "That's the way every effective predator hunts. That does not imply that CWD-infected animals are not shedding the prions that spread the disease before they start to show symptoms. It does mean that predators could be a factor to help remove infected animals from the population. It's important that these predators play their role in a functioning ecosystem."

Few former civil servants in the world are more conversant on the topic of rural hostility toward predators than Norman Bishop. He spent 36 years with the National Park Service and played a vital role in Yellowstone's drafting of an environmental impact statement on wolf reintroduction. The document drew upon the best available wolf science going back half a century, including studies of how the animals stalk prey. Prior to wolves being brought back to Yellowstone, and afterward, Bishop gave more than 200 public presentations on the ecological role. He received many different forms of personal threats from people who refused to hear what he had to say and politicians even sought to have him fired for calling them out when they claimed wolves represented a pervasive threat to human safety.

In Montana, Bishop, who today is retired, attended the public meeting on CWD where McDonald asserted there is no evidence substantiating the value of predators. He is incredulous that McDonald made the claim. "Wolves are out there sweeping the landscape 365 days a year, rooting out sick animals. Why would you want to remove the best weapons you have? It makes no sense," he told me. "What do the states have to lose by bringing predators into this fight which basically means just leaving them alone to do their jobs?"

One of the state officials who attended the recent Montana Fish and Wildlife Commission meeting told me, "Wolf advocates have been trying to get the commission to recognize the positive role of predators and make it an official part of the CWD strategy but there are folks pushing back who say they can't handle anything that even remotely casts wolves in a positive light. People are reluctant to do it because they believe there would be a political downside."

"A political downside even worse than having Montana's elk and mule herds decimated by CWD?" I asked. "What we are witnessing with wolves is a battle of modern scientific data against entrenched Old West dogma and we are in a time in which data doesn't appear to matter to those who cling to dogma," Bishop said. "It is disheartening to realize how the states have abandoned good sense."

In their tome, *Wolves on the Hunt*, Mech, Smith, and MacNulty note in field observation after field observation how difficult it is to be a predator like a wolf making a living with its mouth. The vast majority of predator attempts to take down large game animals are unsuccessful: by some estimates more than eight of every ten tries fail, and each one comes replete with the very real possibility that the wolf could get killed or maimed.

Survival of the fittest has a huge upside for those who care about elk and deer. "And so it goes, day after day, as wolves continue their rounds, ever searching for more vulnerable prey animals, chasing, missing, trying again and again, and eventually connecting," the authors wrote. "The net result of all this sifting and selecting of prey over eons is that the prey gradually get faster, smarter, and more alert."

Sadly, conservationists say, the U.S. Fish and Wildlife Service, the agency that is supposed to be a global leader in professional wildlife management, has been an accomplice in the CWD controversy. The agency continues to unnaturally feed thousands of wapiti at the National Elk Refuge under its command and yet the agency willfully is breaking its own mandates pertaining to wildlife health as noted by a panel of U.S. Circuit Court judges.

Second, Dorsey and Bishop note, it was the Fish and Wildlife Service which, in removing wolves from federal protection, handed over their management to Wyoming, knowing the very essence of recovering a species. Never before in the history of the Endangered Species Act was an animal brought back only to, under state management, be immediately subjected to antiquated policies of re-eradication. If there were compelling reasons for artificially feeding wildlife, which is making the herds of Greater Yellowstone sicker, and for the gratuitous killing of wolves, some of it might make sense. But none of it does, they note.

Today, akin to many fronts of U.S. environmental policy, discussions about the ecological niche of predators appears to be yet another example in which science and natural history are warped or ignored in favor of carrying out political agendas. In the case of wolves, are politicians refusing to accept reality because it cuts against the grain of myths they have helped to perpetuate and because they are concerned they might lose votes from ecologically unenlightened constituents? If yes, what kind of wildlife management is it producing?

Hostilities toward wolves still flare. Regarding impacts of wolves on big game, a reference point can be found at Isle Royale National Park in the Upper Midwest where research has been ongoing for more than half a century, ever since a few lobos crossed the frozen ice of Lake Superior from the mainland and remained on the isle, which had significant numbers of moose.

Over decades, wolf numbers rose and fell, correlating to the size of the moose population. Based on the old premise that wolves will prey upon wildlife populations until they are destroyed, one would think the wolves on Isle Royale would have wiped out moose. But it didn't happen that way; in fact, wolf numbers tumbled on Isle Royale necessitating a wolf reintroduction in recent years.

In Yellowstone, emerging research does not implicate wolves as being the most formidable predators of elk. Field data shows that cougars, as ambush predators, are far more dangerous. During spring, meanwhile, grizzly bears take more elk calves. "When wolf reintroduction began, there were assumptions that major predation would be a wolf-driven dynamic, but it's not," Smith observed.

Tellingly, in the northern Rockies, the vast majority of elk hunting units with wolf presence are at or above population objectives, state wildlife officials say. There are more elk in the West today than in at least 140 years. Norm Bishop, after an examination of statistics, offers perspective.

In 1995 the elk population in Wyoming was estimated at 103,448 and the elk harvest that year was 17,695. In 2017, the elk population was estimated at 104, 800 (31 percent over objectives set by state game managers) and the elk harvest was 24,535. Notably the average hunter success rate was 35 percent.

In Montana the 1995 elk population was 109,500 and I could not find the harvest data for 1995. In 2018, Montana's elk population was estimated at 138,470 (27 percent over upper objective) and the 2017 elk harvest was 30,348, some 6,000 more than in Wyoming.

In Idaho, the 1995 elk population was estimated to be 112,333 and the harvest that year was 22,400. In 2017, the Idaho elk population stood at 116,800 (4,000 more than when wolves arrived). Notably, 18 elk units were assessed to be at or above population objectives set by the state, 10 units were deemed below objective for a variety of reasons that certainly included predation but also human harvest, agriculture, habitat degradation, and droughts. In 2017 elk harvest in Idaho was 22,751, which is 300 more animals that in 1995.

"Just as there are unsubstantiated claims that wolves have devastated big game herds in the northern Rockies, there are parallel false assertions that wolves threaten people and the livestock industry," he said. "Tens of thousands of visitors come in the shoulder seasons to watch wolves. From 1995 to 2018, Yellowstone hosted 101,070,722 visitors, none of whom was injured by a wolf. Among 2.7 million tent campers in Yellowstone from 1995 to 2018, no camper was injured by a wolf."

Regarding predation on livestock, Bishop cited federal ag statistics that showed there were about six million cattle in the Northern Rocky Mountains in 2014. The 140 cattle taken by wolves made up 1 in 43,000, or 0.000023 percent of cattle in the states. There were about 825,000 sheep in the Northern Rockies in 2014. The 172 sheep taken by wolves made up 1 in 4,800, or 0.000208 percent of sheep in the states. Several conservation organizations are providing effective proactive, non-lethal means of limiting livestock losses to wolves.

Although some ranchers, mostly sheep producers, have at times sustained losses of dozens of animals in a short time, such occurrences are in fact rare, doubly so given that wolf control measures have been swift. At the meeting in Alder, Montana last fall, Wyoming rancher Albert Sommers appeared as a special guest. Sommers, also a state legislator from Pinedale and a member of the Upper Green River Valley livestock grazing association, offered a confession. "I thought that wolves showing up would be a major nightmare but it really hasn't been. We can live with them. A bigger issue is grizzlies," he said. Other Montana ranchers echoed the sentiment.

Over the years I've had discussions with many different ranchers in the tri-state area and two of the most thoughtful were Wyoming cattlemen Bob Lucas and John Robinette, both of whom run cows on ranches in the vicinity of Togwotee Pass near Dubois.

Wolves haven't been as bad as they're portrayed to be nor are they as benign as wolf-adoring environmentalists contend, Lucas says. Most mom-and-pop ranchers operate on narrow bottom lines, and anything that eats into their profit margins is a concern. Robinette and his wife, Deb, have had wolves and grizzlies literally at the back door of their home in the

Dunoir River Valley. They've lost beloved pets to both predators, and they've had concerns about their grandchildren's safety. But they're not fearmongers. When they hear claims that schoolchildren waiting for buses in rural areas need to have protective shelters available to shield them from possible bear and wolf attacks, they roll their eyes.

Both being cowboy-boot-and jean-wearing wildlife photographers, the couple's preference has been to find ways to deter lobos and bears from getting into their cattle without using bullets. They've spent many long nights vigilantly looking after calves in the pasture, employing electric fences and flags, and flashing siren lights. In one incident, government agents came in and lethally removed wolves, against the wishes of the Robinettes; yet it was the Robinettes who received a nasty telephone call and death threat from a person who was upset that wolves had been killed.

Before Jimenez was tapped to oversee wolf management for the federal government in Wyoming, Montana, and Idaho a few years ago, he was based in Jackson Hole. His job was to resolve wolf conflicts in Wyoming, which were mostly with ranchers. As part of his duties, Jimenez killed hundreds of wolves that had killed livestock and pets. Environmentalists accused him of destroying too many wolves, and ranchers condemned him for not felling enough. "I've kind of gotten used to it," he says. "Being pilloried by both sides goes with the terrain."

"Part of this is an urban/rural divide issue in which people on ranches and farms don't feel like their concerns are being heard or acknowledged by pro-wolf people from cities who don't have to live with the animals. They're concerned about their own survival," Jimenez says. "It just seems like some of the hardcore conservationists are waiting for hardcore anti-wolf people to come around to their positions. They say, 'If only ranchers learned to like wolves.' But I can tell you that it ain't ever gonna happen—certainly not until rural people feel respected. People need to talk to each other more."

Askins says that distressing to her is how slow culture can be to change and how society arcs on an endless swinging pendulum struggling to find equilibrium. "What bothers me? The radio collars still being put on wolves to track them for research purposes, the traps, the ignorance, the hyperbole, the rhetoric, and the vitriol that is the product and terrain of bureaucrats, pandering politicians, and, too often in the West, wannabe cowboys. Against that type of foolishness, even the gods fight in vain."

The conflict revolving around wolves has never been between man and wolf, Askins said; it has always been, and will continue to be, a war between the parts of the human psyche that struggle to recognize and embrace who and what we are as humans. "The wolf, going back as far as the origins of language, has been the creature upon which we project the evil, the darkness, and the wild nature, which we are unable, or unwilling, to accept as our own," she says. "The story of wolf reintroduction in Greater Yellowstone is an archetypal tale, enacted on the unparalleled, pristine stage of our oldest national park and its surrounding public lands." Making good on her promise that the Wolf Fund would end when wolves hit the ground, Askins closed its doors on that day in January twenty years ago and then retreated from public view. She and her husband, the legendary folk singer Tom Rush, had a daughter, and they raised her in New England. But Askins recalls a sabbatical they took back in the West during the winter of 2007-08. They stayed at a home near the southern border of Grand Teton National Park.

An injured bull elk, left haggard by the elements, lumbered into the yard and died. Eagles, ravens, foxes, and coyotes helped themselves to the carcass. And then, as Askins recalls, savoring the thought, came an unexpected gift.

"A wolf showed up at about 2:00 one morning," she says. "A second about four days later. Nature took its course, and soon there was the genesis of a breeding pair, frolicking, feeding, and chasing ravens and coyotes not fifty feet from the house. A third wolf joined the pair, and my daughter got her first extended course in wolf ethology, watching three uncollared wolves play, mate, chase, and sleep in her front yard, not even needing binoculars or a scope. They came and went for several months, without incident or another human soul noticing."

No one knows for sure what brought down the 1,800-pound bison bull. The strapping behemoth was dead, its mortal end likely hastened by canid fangs applied to jugular vein. When Doug Smith arrived on the scene last August in Yellowstone's Lamar Valley, a battle was already ensuing between two of the national park's most formidable and charismatic predators, hungry for a meal.

As Smith describes it, a sow grizzly bear and triplet cubs had moved in first on the fresh carcass. Rising on her haunches, whiffing the air, the mother bruin took note of a six-hundred-pound male griz rapidly closing in across the sagebrush. Circling, too, were gray wolves, members of the Junction Butte pack, howling as they dodged the bears, and sending ravens and a pair of bald eagles scattering.

The commotion attracted a large crowd of human onlookers along the road one hundred yards distant. Even Smith, Yellowstone's senior wolf biologist, couldn't help but marvel at the scene. "This," he thought to himself, "is the picture of wildness that America's first national park is supposed to be in the twenty-first century."

Looking back, David Mech contends that reintroducing wolves to Yellowstone was the right thing to do. "Society should have brought wolves back and this should apply to more than charismatic megafauna, such as wolves, but anything we've extirpated where places exist that you can do it, we ought to," he said. "It doesn't mean it will be popular but the important thing is having a dialogue, using facts where you can, listening to peoples' concerns and addressing them."

As for his protégée Doug Smith, he's had an epiphany. "I've flipped my thinking on why all of this matters. I said 25 years ago that the reason to restore wolves was purely ecological. This was something done for nature, but in fact it has been a gift to our species, demonstrating what we are capable of when naysayers claimed it couldn't be done," he said. "We—humans—have been the biggest beneficiary. I think it's a sign of hope. If we can do it with wolves, we can do it with a lot of issues that divide us."

Being Loved to Death:
An Unnatural Disaster

I N THE STILLNESS OF A SUMMER MORNING, haze from wildfire smoke thickening the air, Randy Carpenter arrived for a hike up Sypes Canyon in the pastoral northern outskirts of Bozeman, Montana. Ascending into the Bridger Mountain foothills, we talked about how "crazy" it feels these days down there "in town"—America's fastest growing "micropolitan city" which rolls out across the land below; how quickly new subdivisions are springing up in fields that just a year ago were covered with planted wheat.

Carpenter then started in, reciting some jaw-dropping statistics that seemed abstract until we reached an overlook and gazed clear-eyed into an uncertain future. Before us, and stretching for nearly 40 miles to the next muted horizon is the booming Gallatin Valley. Apart from the main mass of urban-suburban-exurbia, scattershot enclaves of new real estate plays reign. Carpenter, known for his work as a career land use planner, says it won't be long, given current trend lines, before the vast chasm of space fills in with more development.

This was a dell that until the 19th century was revered as "the valley of the flowers" and a bison hunting ground for several different indigenous tribes. In a single human generation, the flanks of the Gallatin Range south of us held several thousand wintering elk, now mostly gone, and a robust mule deer herd winnowing along both sides of the Bridgers.

Yes, it's a fact in the Anthropocene: places grow and inevitably change. I've been fortunate to view some of the more spectacular undiscovered ones firsthand in my reporting around the world, but what Carpenter said has radically altered the way I think about the place I call home, the place that I assumed given the huge base of public lands would always be protected. It's made me realize no other models from elsewhere can be imported to resolve what's currently happening rapidly in Greater Yellowstone, the wildest corner of the Lower 48 states. Rather, the paradoxical challenge is that Greater Yellowstone's own salvation depends upon it becoming *the* example other regions with wildlands in their backyards emulate, Carpenter believes. But it means achieving something that's seldom been accomplished in the modern world: defying our human nature's urge to colonize, monetize, and tame as much of terra firma as possible.

Bozeman has been attracting modern "lifestyle refugees" from the coasts and distant urban areas because it has been special. Enrollment at the land grant Montana State University has grown 70 percent since the start of the new millennium. People are drawn to the "sense of place" and they want to possess it. Together with overarching Gallatin County, for which Bozeman is the county seat, there is a swelling number of human denizens in this dale about 90 miles north of Yellowstone Park's main entrance. One of every ten Montanans dwells here where it used to be one of every 30 in 1980. And it's growing like an Old West mining town; the key commodity isn't Oro y Plata—gold and silver, the slogan on the state flag—but land.

Whenever I'm doing interviews with the boosters of commerce, with elected officials who blindly push it, with public land managers, with professional conservationists pushing a surge in outdoor recreation that is rapidly crowding some trails, I ask them this question because it gives me a sense of where their thinking is, their ability to see the trajectory that I know from writing about how other places have been lost to credo that all growth is good. I ask them to soak in the trendlines and the datapoints and answer: "Where do you see Bozeman, the other wide open rural valleys currently uncluttered with sprawl being in 2050? What will the prospects for wildlife be?"

If it appears that they are capable of being prescient, I then ask, "So what can communities do to prevent that fate from happening?"

Bozeman is viewed as the capital city of Greater Yellowstone located in the northern third of the ecosystem. Where we are headed doesn't require radical speculation. We just need to do the math, use the statistics that are right there in front of us. Before you read the next line, know that it was written *before* the Covid-19 pandemic encircled the globe and it validated what Carpenter had earlier conjectured with an alarming exclamation point behind it.

Within 24 years, Carpenter told me initially, at a *three percent* growth rate, the number of 110,000 people in the Bozeman/Gallatin County will double. It means that by the 2040s, the city/county will equal the size of Salt Lake City proper (minus its suburbs, not the entire metro). Still, it means breathtaking change for a destination that was long considered an out of the way town in the middle of the American flyover. Salt Lake City, it must be noted, has the fraction of the wildlife values Bozeman presently does. Even more sobering, in less than half a century, meaning sometime during the 2060s and based on the same three percent rate of annual population growth, there will be a population of 450,000 (equal to all the residents of the entire Greater Yellowstone today) present in Bozeman/Gallatin.

On top of it, in just the next 18 years if not sooner, looking at the entire region, another 100,000 homes, along with their infrastructure accoutrements will be added to the landscape of the ecosystem, many of them pressed up against the very edge of public lands where wildlife roams.

That 450,000 that may inhabit Bozeman/Gallatin County/Big Sky is a concentration of people that is, to put it into perspective, *Minneapolis-sized* (again, the actual city, not including St. Paul and the suburbs), consuming much of the open space between the Bridgers where Carpenter and I stood and the distant ranch/farmlands around Three Forks, the town so named because it's where the Gallatin, Madison, and Jefferson rivers converge to form the birthplace of the Missouri River.

Many Bozemanians, Carpenter admitted, probably found the prospect of us becoming Salt Lake and then Minneapolis inconceivable or maybe, oddly, desirable, especially those boosters of growth who have steadfastly fought progressive planning and zoning, impact fees, placing conservation initiatives on the ballot for voters to decide, and anything else they find to be restrictive of individual liberty.

Point of fact, and this is the shocking part, Gallatin County is actually growing at better than a four percent rate—*not* three. Before the Covid-19 pandemic, I spoke with a local public health official who serves on a committee addressing the shortage of doctors in southwest Montana and the demographic data they are using suggests the growth rate for Bozeman/Gallatin is actually *eight* percent, meaning the scenario of sub-urbanization cited above could happen twice as fast.

Still, Carpenter used three percent to be conservative in his extrapolation, which is indisputable and very conservative, it turned out, given other wildcard factors, such as Covid-19 causing newcomers to scurry to the region and people fleeing climate-challenged places, that make the potential of Carpenter's original growth projections seem quaint. He makes his calculation using the "rule of 72" in which the constant growth rate is divided into 72 and it provides the number of years it takes a locale to double in population. Ironically, the same formula can be used for calculated return on investment.

A three percent annual growth rate means Bozeman/Gallatin will double in 24 years. Yet at a four-percent rate, it means it would take only 18 years to reach Salt Lake City and 36 years to match the population of present-day Minneapolis proper.

So, here is the breathtaking part. The 2021 U.S. Census Bureau stats showed that Bozeman/Gallatin actually have 120,000 residents and Carpenter projects that, conservatively, another 40,000 people will be added in a decade and 90,000 to Bozeman/Gallatin County in 20 or one human generation. That's equal to a population of Billings-Montana's largest city—being added to a mass of humans already transforming the landscape.

Growth, some opine, is always good, in that it's better to be booming in the West instead of busting. Old booms involved development of finite natural resources such as minerals and old-growth forests. This boom is different and from its landscape-level impacts, it is permanent and it's happening across landscapes that hold the last greatest wildlife migrations in the continental U.S and unmatched diversity of large species. The questions regarding blind promotion of growth are: good for whom, good *for what*, and how are growth's real impacts and hidden costs that really being manifested? Most importantly, *who* is paying for them?

Is more of everything better? Ask an angler who wade fishes or floats one of the globally-famous "blue-ribbon" trout streams if having twice as many people casting lines in the water is better. Ask drivers in cars if it's a good thing to have the drive time between Bozeman and Big Sky or Teton Valley, Idaho and Jackson Hole taking two or three times as long.

Ask trail users if it's better when quiet strolls in the forest suffer from their own forms of gridlock and a trip through Yellowstone yields tension-filled traffic jams like the ones they have in cities back home? Ask longtime residents of Livingston and Paradise Valley what it means to be invaded by refugees from Bozeman which is dealing with refugees from Jackson Hole?

I asked a friend, an ardent mountain biker, this question: what if Bozeman ends up with the best trail system for hiking, bicycling and riding e-bikes in the world, and the best pastry and coffee shops awaiting people after their outing, and affordable housing and great paying jobs for all people is achieved (though the record of history shows that is highly unlikely), yet wildlife vanishes as the bulge of development and number of recreation users grows? Would that be considered a success in preserving the essence of Bozeman that currently sets it apart? And after he replied that for some, wildlife considerations don't matter, I humbly suggested that if maintaining healthy wildlife populations doesn't factor in the character of Bozeman (or many other towns in Greater Yellowstone) then it would seem not to matter if Bozeman were located here or instead in California, Colorado or Utah.

Down in Jackson Hole, a place I used to live and work as a reporter before coming to Bozeman, there's a visionary thinker who was once a college professor and a longtime vaunted mountaineer and climbing guide. John "Jack" Turner wrote a book, *The Abstract Wild*, that is considered a classic and a mandatory read for those young people majoring in environmental studies. But it's another volume of Turner's, *Travels in the Greater Yellowstone*, that exposed his ability to be keenly prescient when advocating that leaders in Greater Yellowstone, including those at the helm of some non-profit environmental groups, whom Turner believes suffers from activist narcolepsy, need to wake up. He thinks of what has happened since the year 2000 and how Greater Yellowstone is regarded as a safer haven, not only for a new lifestyle diaspora involving well-heeled climate refugees, but for those wanting isolation from more crowded urban environs holding a populace more susceptible to Covid-19 and what other viruses may come. His biggest lament is that newcomers haven't a clue of the uniqueness of the region and that not even fun hog recreationists, among whom Turner himself was once revered as a demi-God, see it as a primo playground; they have no understanding of how or why it warrants the title "American Serengeti."

"Tragically or ironically, depending on your philosophical druthers, as our understanding of the importance of Greater Yellowstone grew, forces *inimical* to its integrity grew, too. Greater Yellowstone has become a battleground that in the years to come will make the conflict over drilling in the Arctic National Wildlife Refuge seem like child's play," Turner wrote. "It is the one great chance for us to preserve a large, relatively intact ecosystem that is embedded in our history and our hearts. But Greater Yellowstone faces problems; some might call them challenges, but I think they are problems. First and foremost is the American public's *ignorance of ecology*. Evolution is the foundation of biology, biology the foundation of ecology, and ecology the basis of informed conservation. How can we expect public support for sound conservation policy against a backdrop of such ignorance?"

All of us are here because we love to be outside doing various kinds of recreational activities. To scrutinize the impacts is not to be anti-recreation or being anti-physically fit or being anti-fun; it is no more anti than enjoying clean water and taking precautions to ensure it stays that way. Another way of thinking about it is not through the lens of being anti, but *pro-wildlife*.

I first came to Greater Yellowstone during two summers of college to work in Yellowstone Park as a cook for a concessionaire at Canyon Village. I am an outdoor recreationist—I identify as one—but my desires are secondary to the needs of wildlife. I accept that now more today than when I was young. And I understand the zeal that a young person, especially, has for blowing off steam, feeling free, pushing the limits of one's physical abilities, being a member of an outdoor tribe where one's standing is venerated based on the number of hair-raising or rugged quests you've accomplished or attempted.

Nobody likes to be told what they can't do; I get that, but I will assert that not accepting limits is juvenile. Every day we accept limits in order to achieve a better good or to preserve the essence of an experience. Such as: it isn't acceptable to roller blade through the National Gallery of Art though the smooth floors provide excellent terrain. I accept that I might be limited where I can hike, float, run, raft, hunt, fish, bike, ski, or build a home. If you told me there are places where I can never venture again, in order to give a little more space to a grizzly bear or elk and bison mothers with calves, or for struggling moose or bighorn sheep, I would gladly abide. I have innumerably more options to indulge my desire to be in the outdoors than a wild animal does which exists in a given homeland.

In 1982 when I worked in Yellowstone, some 2.3 million visitors passed through the park and in summer time the roads on many days seemed crowded. In 2021, Yellowstone notched over 1.08-million visitors in the month of July alone and more than 300,000 above the entire 1982 level with five months left in the year. Grand Teton Park to the south also notched a double-digit percentage increase. As Cam Sholly, the Yellowstone superintendent said, it's not a problem that his staff can build or engineer it's way out of. "Limits," the taboo word, are inevitable, the same as embracing "planning and zoning," the term treated as anathema by conservative county commissioners, must become an essential part of the good governance lexicon if communities dealing with a tsunami of growth are sincere about wanting to maintain their community character. Hundreds of paid conservationists dwell in Bozeman and Jackson Hole, the fun hog meccas of Greater Yellowstone, but there are few groups that have taken a big-picture approach that thinks across the region with a plan in mind and is not engaged instead in piecemeal approaches which simply are not keeping up with the pace of change occurring, especially on private land.

Though the ecosystem is world-renowned and chambers of commerces and state tourism agencies promote wildlife watching as an attraction to woo transplant businesses and tourists, there is not a single permanent ecologist on staff of the 20 counties composing Greater Yellowstone, or in the civil service ranks of the largest communities that is advising elected leaders on the consequences of growth impacts wildlife. There is not a single national park superintendent from Yellowstone or Grand Teton, a single national forest supervisor, a single top manager at Greater Yellowstone's national wildlife refuges, or a single state employee within the three state wildlife departments operating in our region, who have publicly stepped forward and noted how development trends on private lands located next to the public lands they administer are impairing the ecological function of the lands they are bound to administer on behalf of the public interest in perpetuity.

The latter will claim it's not their business, and privately they'll admit that doing so might harm their career politically, even though every public land official, if you ask them, will claim to be devoted to thinking beyond borders to advance the concept of ecosystem protection.

If the voice of ecology isn't taken seriously in planning decisions, if it isn't given a seat at the table of decision making and being fully heard, then the people in charge of shepherding us forward to a future, where our sense of this wild place has a chance of surviving, then we are operating blind. And, as Jack Turner says, ignorance, whether willful or innate, is not bliss.

This is why *Mountain Journal* was founded—to make palpable what the threats to Greater Yellowstone are before they reach an irreversible crisis stage, to remind people how the patterns of development have played out elsewhere and why wildlife-rich landscapes have been erased, and to spur those in a position to lead, to do so. If conservation groups are not applying pressure to public officials at the federal, state and local level—and to demand planning and zoning recognizes the failures of the free market to adequately protect nature—then who will do it? And if conservation organizations aren't boisterously demanding that agencies think and act more boldly to protect the only bioregion like this left in the Lower 48, then who will?

Plenty of scrutiny over the years has justifiably been directed at the timber, mining, energy and livestock grazing sectors on public lands by conservationists and journalistic entities, but not so much at private land sprawl or outdoor recreation (that is treated as conservationists' own sacred cow). My frustration was borne, as a writer who has worked for *National Geographic* and *The Guardian*, to found a journal that devoted constant, truthful in-depth focus on issues of Greater Yellowstone which wasn't happening with either the national or local media; moreover, it has been the intent to encourage conservation organizations to step up their game—to advocate for actions as inspiring as the daringness that resulted in Yellowstone Park being created over local opposition, including the local newspaper in Bozeman and members of Montana's Territorial Legislature who claimed preservation would devastate progress. A parallel argument was made in Jackson Hole with heroic efforts undertaken by John D. Rockefeller and others in expanding the boundaries of Grand Teton National Park.

Often, using other reference points are instructive. Imagine how the Serengeti Plain might look if the city of Nairobi existed astride of it or if a major interstate were blazed through the center of it. Imagine if Anchorage, Alaska were saddled into the Arctic National Wildlife Refuge, or Minneapolis/St. Paul were on the edge of the Boundary Waters Canoe Wilderness Area. Those wonders of Nature would not exist.

Bozeman, as the largest community does not exist in isolation; its trends have huge implications for nearby places in every direction and most importantly spillover effects of growth affecting rural valleys where wildlife still moves across and views are unblemished.

Again, Carpenter's growth estimates mentioned above of three percent equating to X population proved in the wake of Covid-19 to be conservative. While the effects of climate change and pandemics are considered so amorphous, that, for now, they're difficult to wrap one's mind around, projections for growth, based on extrapolations of hard existing data, are impossible to dismiss.

There is today a palpable sense of social unrest and angst welling up in Bozeman and Jackson Hole and Livingston and Red Lodge and Teton Valley, Idaho and even among ecologically-aware people in Big Sky related to the multiplying impacts of growth. It is accompanied by a widespread perception that developers, especially speculators who made fortunes in real estate development in states like California, Utah, Colorado, Oregon, and Washington State, have moved in for the kill, taking advantage of naive, provincial-minded planning staffs that are increasingly overwhelmed and codes that are lax compared to where the developers came from. But many of the developers are local and when I've had an opportunity to converse with them about the wildlife marvels of Greater Yellowstone, many are not literate in explaining what wildlife needs to persist. According to one estimate, nearly $2 billion worth of real estate changed hands around Bozeman, Big Sky, and Livingston, Montana in just 18 months of the Covid-19 lockdown.

Some more stats to chew on relating to how growth in Bozeman/ Gallatin may be impacting neighboring valleys. Livingston has grown in population from about 11,000 in 1970 to 16,000 in 2015. The increase, however, is deceiving. From 1970 to 2010, the amount of seasonal housing skyrocketed by 855 percent, Carpenter says, from 137 in 1970 to ten times that, 1308, in 2010. And that was a full decade before Covid-19 arrived. There are more houses being built than rising numbers of year-round residents and in Park County there are somewhere around 5,000 lots that have been subdivided but yet to be developed. Across Bozeman Pass in the Gallatin Valley, Carpenter suspects that the percentage of seasonal dwellings is higher than in Park County.

In Gallatin County, if there's good news to be had it's that two-thirds of the growth has occurred in within the general envelope of the city of Bozeman or towns whereas it was 42 percent 40 years ago. However, and yes, everything comes with an asterisk, the volume of growth still translates to a lot more people showing up at hiking trailheads and floating rivers and causing traffic. On many days, the traffic loads between Bozeman and Big Sky or Teton Valley and Jackson are bumper to bumper.

"What does an extra 90,000 people mean to water use needs and open space and wildlife habitat and air and water quality and traffic and property taxes?" Carpenter asks. While Montana legislators will not allow local cities like Bozeman to put a local sales tax up for a citizen vote in order to pay for rising costs of roads and other services, one thing cannot be denied. Millions of visitors put a serious strain on infrastructure and most other places in American would be trying to tax visitors to help pay for maintenance costs or reduce local property taxes. Having an adequate supply of money would be game-changing in addressing the impacts of sprawl if large landowners were incentivized to protect their holds for wildlife and scenic open space. Imagine if a real-estate transfer tax, which is really a consumption tax on growth, had existed and a portion of the $2 billion had been made available to secure conservation easements from willing sellers, or purchase outright key pieces of habitat or even to fund ecologist positions to advice elected officials and the planning offices on the impacts of development.

There's no denying the physical manifestations transforming a landscape like the Gallatin Valley that, since in the 1860s, has held some of the richest farmland in the state while providing key wildlife habitat for species synonymous with the ecosystem. "The impacts of growth are not only accelerating. The effects are *compounding*," Carpenter said. "This isn't just another boom that will eventually be mitigated by another bust."

Indicators about the impacts of population growth are everywhere and the one institution trying to make sense of them is academia. Montana State University, which is branding itself to be "the University of the Yellowstone," has a number of ecologists crunching data. The first com-

prehensive examination of growth impacts of Greater Yellowstone's ecological vital signs was published in 2018 in the scientific journal EcoSphere,
assessing snowpack, water flows in rivers, fire, wildlife, native species,
and invasives.

Like a patient that feels fine and looks fine, especially to the untrained
eye, Yellowstone National Park and its neighbors appear vigorous and
immortal yet the region is coming under the influence of serious stressors,
Dr. Andrew Hansen, a professor of ecology told me. Together with his
assistant and co-author Linda Phillips, he wrote: "Greater Yellowstone's
ecological health is challenged by growing use by people and changing climate. The human population has doubled, and housing density has tripled
in Greater Yellowstone since 1970 and both are projected to double again
by 2050. Human development now covers 31 percent of the ecosystem.
Temperature has warmed 1.5 degrees Fahrenheit since 1950 and is projected
to increase 4.5 to 9.4 degrees Fahrenheit by 2100." By the middle of this
century there will be more than half a million homes in Greater Yellowstone
and he believes that is probably an underestimation and does include
people living in multiple-person dwellings. While there are no precise
statistics Hansen over the years has studied various calculations of "human
footprint" and it is jaw-dropping, he says, the amount of land mass and
resources that it takes to sustain the consumptive habits of a single human
being. People complain about how much water, grass, and space is required
to raise a beef cow but a human engulfs far more space.

Hansen and Phillips pointed to a paradox involving simultaneous
forces that, if left unaddressed, will result in one dramatically negatively
affecting the prognosis of the other. While large mammal population of
migratory ungulates (such as elk, deer, pronghorn, moose, and bison) and
grizzly bears and wolves have increased in number and are expanding
their range from their historic human-caused lows, it is set against a backdrop of gigantic trends occurring on the landscape level.

"…changes in land use and climate have reduced snowpack and
stream flows, increased stream temperatures, favored pest outbreaks and
forest die-off, fragmented habitat types, expanded invasive species, and
reduced native fish populations," Hansen and Phillips noted.

A study in Canada that examines the impact of roads on grizzlies
alludes to human footprint which is a serious issue for all species and one
often on the mind of Hansen and others in Greater Yellowstone. "Natural

systems and wildlife have faced unprecedented challenges in recent decades resulting in accelerated loss of biodiversity and ecosystem function across the globe resulting in extinction rates approximately 100 times natural rates," six authors, including Dr. Mark Boyce who has done analyses on grizzly conservation in Greater Yellowstone, wrote in the journal *Ursus* in 2020. "These trends are occurring while a decades-long environmental effort sweeps the globe. This conundrum clearly suggests that protected areas are not mitigating the ever-expanding and intensifying human foot-print. The corollary is that if we want to maintain biodiversity and sustainable supportive ecosystems, we either need to increase and diversity the protected area system, ensure the varied types of protected areas are linked by functional connectivity networks, managing the intervening matrix of multiple-use lands to a higher standard, or some combination of the above. One sphere within the increasing human footprint is the ubiquitous presence of roads, which can have unintended negative effects on natural systems and wildlife populations." Another area of growing interest are recreation trails constructed to accommodate larger volumes of people. What's good for grizzlies, which are a barometer, is good for hundreds of other species sharing the terrain.

While Greater Yellowstone's categories of public lands with the highest level of protection—Yellowstone and Grand Teton national parks and surrounding federal wilderness areas—continue to function as important refugia for wildlife, especially during seasons of green-up, that is not the case in low elevation valleys providing critical winter habitat. Most of the lower elevation valleys, which connect public lands in the mountains and flank rivers, are privately owned and many, like the expanses of Gallatin, Paradise, Teton, and Madison valleys are already subdivided into small parcels, covered with lots lines visible at the court house but not to passersby who think they are protected. "Once you have a road and a power line it lays the groundwork for a subdivision and after that infill can happen fast," Carpenter says. "The person who moves to Greater Yellowstone and smugly says to themselves, 'I'm building my dream home in the middle of nowhere and how wonderful it is to see elk or moose doesn't realize that they have started an inevitable and irreversible pro-gression that will result in the landscape filling up, the same way that a mountain biker who naively thinks that making a new user-created trail on a wildlife game trail is benign and won't hurt anything. It's not the first person in who is the problem, it's the opening they've created that everyone else follows."

The eruption of development is unprecedented, permanent, and the impacts irreversible, Carpenter noted. Unless leaders in the region, from public land managers to city and county elected officials, become consciously aware of what's happening and try to get ahead of it, the consequences will be severe, ecologically and economically, he noted.

Carpenter, who works for the non-profit think-tank FutureWest which advises rural communities on how to remain vibrant while preserving their character and sense of place, is not known for speaking in platitudes. If and when the anticipated future lying before us arrives, scientists and planners like Carpenter, who have witnessed the results of runaway growth elsewhere in populous states, say a vital part of Greater Yellowstone, the most heralded complex of still-wild terrain in the West, will be lost.

"In the middle of a boom, we rarely hear about downsides," Carpenter, a native of Iowa, said. "The boosters don't want to hear it—the downsides. They choose to live in denial and their attitude works as long as it's not challenged. I've seen a lot of farms and wildlife habitat disappear but I've never seen a subdivision vanish. Concrete, asphalt, roads, traffic, noise pollution: they are *forever*. What we forget is that the Greater Yellowstone Ecosystem isn't just uncommon. It is an American treasure and the only one of its kind in the world."

Whether one is Republican or Democrat, a political conservative or liberal, Carpenter reckons that few enjoy paying higher taxes. One prominent expert on land use planning has described growth essentially as a Ponzi by which the economic costs associated with frenzied growth in the present are paid for by receipts generated from growth in the future.

Elected officials need to keep permitting new development to cover the costs of older growth that wasn't required to pay its way. The implication is that citizens unknowingly subsidize the very kind of costly growth and profits for special interests they don't want to pay for.

What's imperiled? In a word, *wildness*; more specifically, a rare quality of wildness capable of sustaining the survival of an unsurpassed biodiversity. A huge percentage of the wildlife species persisting in Greater Yellowstone rely upon undeveloped private lands for their survival. In their vital assessment, Hansen and Phillips wrote: "On private lands, in contrast, vital signs relating to snow, stream flow and temperature, river condition, native fish, and wildlife habitat were rated as deteriorating."

The paper's abstract states, "The Earth's remaining tracts of wildlands are being altered by increased human pressure and climate change. Yet, there is no systematic approach for quantifying change in the ecological condition of wildland ecosystems." Between 1993 and 2009, the footprint of humanity, which already had resulted in wild places being relegated to merely a fraction of the land mass that started the 20th century, expanded by 9 percent globally. "Even within designated protected areas, wildlands are being reduced due to downgrading, downsizing, and degazettement. Currently, 33 percent of the global protected area coverage is under intense human pressure," the EcoSphere article notes.

In 45 years the number of homes in Greater Yellowstone has tripled from 79,000 to 228,000. By 2050, that number will surpass half a million homes and corresponding footprints. Across Greater Yellowstone, Carpenter says there could be double the number of permanent residents—approaching one million—in 20 years. What that means is that Greater Yellowstone is becoming Colorado. Such footprints are more impactful ecologically (and more costly for the public to service economically) the farther outside of urban boundaries they occur. In 30 years, at current trends (which many demographers say are conservative) Greater Yellowstone will have suburban like feet several times greater than today.

On top of the above, the paper highlighted the rapidly rising number of outdoor recreationists inundating public lands, and through advances in machine technology (ranging from motorized to mountain biking), being able to reach areas once beyond reach and to traverse them faster. River traffic, too, has swelled. From 1984 to 2016, angler days on the upper Madison River rose from 51,000 to 178,000, prompting the Montana Department of Fish Wildlife and Parks to consider implementing restrictions. This number does not include rapidly expanding numbers of non-fishing recreationists ranging from boaters to packrafters and stand-up paddle boards.

At what point does the phenomenon of humans loving Greater Yellowstone to death and trying to capitalize on its amenity values impair the very foundation of the nature-based economy, including its wealth of fragile, intangible wonders and sense of place that does not exist anywhere else? Meanwhile, even as ski areas have pushed expansion, many of them on public lands, to support their profitability and using it to bolster the value of their real estate plays at the base of mountains, climate trends are for markedly shorter seasons. And summers are going to be hotter, meaning more fires and impacts on wildlife. Large ungulates can be negatively affected by impacts to what they eat and where the food is found. "More meaningful to plants and wildlife than annual average climate condition are thresholds based on daily climate Comparing climate metrics from the 1950s with those projected for 2100, the number of hot days (above 90-degrees F) is projected to increase dramatically, particularly at lower elevations where the projected increase is more than 4 weeks by 2100," the paper notes. "Annual growing degree days more than double in all vegetation communities. The number of days below freezing is projected to decline by 32 percent by 2100."

With regard to snow: "Projections for the coming century suggest more precipitation as rain rather than snow, which will have substantial impacts to snowpack across the GYE. The net balance of the projected increases in temperature and precipitation results in a 36 percent reduction of the average total annual snowpack during 2070–2099 relative to 1970–1999."

And with water, which also hold impacts for ranchers, farmers, and municipalities: "River flows have declined in the Greater Yellowstone Ecosystem, at accelerating rates since 1970. Despite high interannual variation, strong statistically significant trends in stream flow were found across Greater Yellowstone during 1970–2015. Peak discharge shifted 7.5 days earlier, summer minimum flows declined by 27.5 percent and total annual volume declined by 15.6 percent."

As for water temperature, vital to the multi-million-dollar, cold-water recreation fishing economy: stream temperatures have warmed across the region by almost two degrees over the past century. Stream warming during 2000–2009 exceeded that of the Great Dustbowl of the 1930s and represented the greatest rate of change over the past century. Stream temperatures are projected to increase another two to six degrees by 2069.

Water corridors, ecologists say, are the richest and most important for wildlife in Greater Yellowstone. What has spared Greater Yellowstone to date is its relative geographic isolation, the fact that it does not have a major urban area like Salt Lake City, Denver, or Boise parked on its doorstep. Indeed, the Front Range of the Colorado Rockies and the Wasatch Front are perhaps the poster children of how true wildness in the West has eroded and suffers in the age of the Anthropocene. Between them, Bozeman and Jackson Hole have the busiest airports in Montana and Wyoming and have been breaking records. Yellowstone and Grand Teton national parks have had a long streak of visitation rising year over year and the parks are busier longer than just the three-month summer season crunch.

Bozeman is positioned on the Greater Yellowstone Ecosystem's northern flank, but by dint of setting it is also a wildlife crossroads between wildlands to the south and north, east and west. The 20 contiguous counties composing Greater Yellowstone are, put together, the fastest growing rural region in the country. It's vital to note the caveat that not all of Greater Yellowstone's counties have significantly growing populations, but the ones that do have created a spillover effect that impacts their slower-growing brethren.

The growth in Bozeman/Gallatin is actually a harbinger, experts like Hansen, have noted. Parallel growth scenarios are playing out around the region: astride the Tetons in adjoining Teton County, Wyoming and Teton County, Idaho; the booming state highway 20 corridor between Idaho Falls, Rexburg, and Island Park, Idaho; the southern tier of Jackson Hole stretching toward Hoback Junction and Star Valley; a triangle of topography formed by Cody, Wyoming, Red Lodge, Montana and Billings, Montana. More people also are pouring into Paradise Valley between Livingston along the Yellowstone River and Gardiner, that is itself the northern gateway to Yellowstone National Park.

The average number of people per dwelling in Greater Yellowstone homes is about 2.3, half the number of two generations ago. Yet even with fewer inhabitants, homes are being built with more square footage; many are going up in the forested wildland-urban interface where they are more likely to burn in a wildfire and residents expect to receive expensive taxpayer-subsidized firefighting services. More than half of the U.S Forest Service's operating budget is consumed by firefighting costs, mainly to protect private homes built in fire-prone areas (akin to putting up a home in a flood plain) and that means less funds available for ecologists and rangers in the field doing research, preventing resource damage, keeping trails and campgrounds open, and trying to halt a growing problem of illegal trail building and trespass by recreationists who don't like to follow rules.

Some newcomers, craving views, will unknowingly and with no context provided by realtors, site their dream dwellings in important wildlife winter range or near riparian areas (river corridors) considered biodiversity hotspots. The space claimed by those homes in exurbia is not merely the envelope of the structure itself but it includes access roads and driveways, outbuildings, gardens and lawns fenced to keep wildlife out, barking dogs and pet canines chasing wildlife, housecats preying on songbirds, mini horse pastures, lawn watering, invasive weeds and herbicides applied to keep them at bay, and ground disturbance to accommodate essential services such as electricity, plumbing, and septic. Every human structure emanates its own bubble of influence that displaces wildlife. A grizzly bear expert told me that the presence of a single home can cause a grizzly to alter its behavior within a space equal to half a section of land.

Once infrastructure is bulldozed in for one subdivision, it fuels more adjacent access roads, and thus more infrastructure, accelerating the pace of exurban development and results in rising costs for counties, e.g., taxpayers, to provide public services. "Bozeman/Gallatin isn't considered a metro area yet but by the middle of the next decade it will be, and if we know anything about development trends nationwide, areas located at the edge of metro areas are growing fastest," Carpenter said. "Before a baby born this year graduates from the new high school in Bozeman, she will watch the valley where she's growing up add the equivalent of a Boulder, Colorado to the landscape."

Notably, the current 450,000 population figure for Greater Yellowstone's current population does not include the 160,000 people currently living in nearby Billings/Yellowstone County located just 20 miles beyond the official northeast edge of the ecosystem. This is important because with Gallatin and Yellowstone counties bookending 140 miles of U.S. Interstate 90 between them, in-fill of development on the landscape is expected to be rapid and some have speculated that by the middle of this century there could be between 800,000 and 1 million people living between Three Forks and Billings within two human generations.

Beyond Bozeman's coming sprawl, there is another stunning reality. Within a decade or two, the permanent/itinerant population in the resort community of Big Sky could be approaching the size of Jackson Hole's and will result in a complete biological east-west decapitation of the north-south running Madison Mountain Range. The Madisons have been an important passageway for wildlife. Big Sky, already bursting at the seams along the Gallatin River will be spilling westward out across the forested mountains into the Madison Valley. The enclave of Ennis will at least double. All of these figures do not include the large and increasing number of second-home owners who do not claim Greater Yellowstone as their primary residence with the U.S. Census Bureau.

During the 1990s, while working as a staffer for the Greater Yellowstone Coalition, Dennis Glick, who founded FutureWest where Carpenter works, was drafting the first comprehensive overview of the Greater Yellowstone Ecosystem. The 222-page document, *Sustaining Greater Yellowstone: A Blueprint for the Future* was published in 1994 and identified things worth celebrating, progress, and problems in advancing ecological health in the region.

In recent years, according to analysts, Big Sky's population has increased three times faster than Aspen, Colorado and Sun Valley, Idaho. Other mountain towns dealing with growth have already identified negative impacts on wildlife. In Colorado, at Vail, which Big Sky often draws comparisons to, the town of Vail and an entity called The Vail Symposium hosted a forum on wildlife issues. Numbers of elk, deer and bighorn sheep are falling. "The decline we're seeing in the elk herd goes from Vail Pass to Aspen," Bill Andree, a wildlife officer for Colorado Parks and Wildlife said. "It's not too tough to figure out why when you're looking at the levels of development, recreation, and roads."

That's the direction the Bozeman to Big Sky corridor is headed, Glick says, sharing the anecdote that many people have relocated to Montana from Colorado ski resort towns because their once intimate connection to nature has vanished from the bustle. He laments that over the years, with the exception of scrutinizing sewage spills in Big Sky and the possible release of treated effluent into the Gallatin River, none of the conservation groups in Bozeman (a burg that has one of the highest concentrations of paid conservationists per capita in America) has bird-dogged development in Big Sky and gauged its impact on wildlife, water and air quality, wildfire, and what eventual build-out will look like.

Metropolitan Salt Lake City, located only a few hours' drive from the southern reaches of Greater Yellowstone, is exuding a presence, both with people leaving the city and resettling in the ecosystem and vacationing there. Within a few decades, the connect-the-dots corridor of Idaho

Falls/Bonneville County, Idaho (currently 110K people)-Rexburg/Madison County, Idaho (40K)-Driggs/Victor/Teton County, Idaho (10K)-Jackson Hole/Teton County, Wyoming (24K)-Afton/Star Valley/Lincoln County, Wyoming (20K)-Pinedale/Sublette County, Wyoming (10K) will hold its own greater Salt Lake City equivalent of sprawl.

Cody/Park County/Powell/Bighorn Basin on the east side of Yellowstone, could be Bozeman-sized. The Upper Yellowstone River Valley, between Gardiner and Livingston, will also be approaching the Bozeman size of today. Further, Billings/Laurel will be spilling into Red Lodge along the flanks of the Absaroka-Beartooth mountains. Development is steadily pinching in at the same time ecological processes keeping the interior of Greater Yellowstone healthy need room to breathe. What is happening in Gallatin County, as just one example, does indeed have huge spill-over implications for the Madison and Paradise valleys, and the open space defining Bridger Canyon and even the Shields Valley along the western face of the Crazy Mountains. Several ecologists told me that even if public land remains unchanged and not significantly impaired—an impossibility with climate change and energy development—the effects of private land development will doom the major wildlife migration corridors.

While Greater Yellowstone is still ecologically intact, the way humans relate to it is multi-dimensionally fragmented. Again, among wildlife professionals there is widespread agreement that unless leaders (including public land managers, county commissioners, state legislators, and mayors) think big and cohesively, making conscious effort to avert destructive patterns of sprawl that have degraded natural environments elsewhere, Greater Yellowstone is destined to follow the same fate.

On top of the inward population migration of permanent and parttime residents, the front-country areas of Yellowstone and Grand Teton national parks, already choked with summer traffic, have broken visitation records almost every year for the last decade. Escalating recreation pressure is happening, too. Mountain biking and ATV users on national forests and BLM lands account for some of the largest growth in backcountry users and they are reaching remote places considered important and safe refugia for wildlife.

Another major problem is that local and regional media has largely been missing in action in writing about growth. To date, there has not been a single journalist or publication devoted to covering the big-picture issues of the entire Greater Yellowstone Ecosystem full time. Truth be told, the stories that have been written about growth in the region have been lacking in depth and analysis. How can the public engage in informed discussion about what's at stake if the media, which reaches the greatest number of people, examines growth myopically? In cases where the media has covered stories, the reporting has been misleading or notable for the questions that aren't being asked.

Here's an example: On March 30, 2017, the *Bozeman Daily Chronicle*, the largest newspaper of record in Greater Yellowstone, published the findings of a report assembled by a Bozeman-based economic development organization called the Prospera Business Network. Growth stats in the Prospera report were based on projections from the state of Montana, which, in turn, came from numbers provided by a national consulting firm. *Chronicle* journalist Lewis Kendall referenced Prospera's own description of its research as being "a comprehensive description of the regional economy."

Gallatin County, Kendall wrote, is expected to hit *145,000* residents by *2060*. But Prospera's projections and Kendall's reporting, were off. Way way off, in fact, by several times what the actual growth rate is. The data used by Prospera and the state were based on calculated growth rates in Gallatin Valley of 0.8 percent when, again, it is closer to 4 percent in Bozeman/Gallatin.

"I found their publishing of this data to be bizarre," Carpenter said.

The problem with the Prospera report, besides the faulty algorithms used to calculate the growth rate, is that elected officials have pointed to it in their assertions that growth isn't an issue. In fact, some vocal individuals claim that protecting public lands, and utilizing planning and zoning methods on private land that safeguard open space and the environment are impediments to job creation.

Together, the two national parks at the heart of Greater Yellowstone—Yellowstone and Grand Teton—infuse $1.5 billion in annual commerce driven by nature tourism to the region, with the marquee attractions being grizzlies, wolves, and big game animals. The prospect of seeing wildlife attracts people from around the world.

Nature tourism has yielded sustainable commerce more reliable than the proceeds in recent years generated by the other pillars: agriculture, logging, hard-rock mining, and coal (subject variously to the whims of weather and markets). The magnetic appeal of wildness in Greater Yellowstone's 22.5 million acres of land, an area equal to the size of South Carolina, and the preponderance of it taking the form of federal public lands, has a net annual economic value of more than $4 billion, suggests Headwaters Economics founder Ray Rasker.

Even Governor Greg Gianforte, a Bozeman resident and former Congressman, believes all growth is good. In an interview I did with Gianforte for the *Christian Science Monitor* when he headed a tech company, RightNow Technology (since acquired by Oracle), he claimed that Bozeman/Gallatin's clean and healthy environment was a major enticement for luring top-flight computer programmers to work for his firm here. Despite the growth-related challenges already here, there are some who would like to lure a major tech company to set up satellite manufacturing or tech services in Bozeman, bringing thousands of additional high-paying jobs which would only, from a landscape perspective, result in the same kind of sprawl around Boise, Salt Lake City, Reno, and the Front Range of Colorado.

No one, of course, is suggesting that good-paying jobs aren't good, but most of those jobs would likely go to outsiders and families relocating here, further taxing schools, roads, eating up more land. Were the prospect presented, would it be wise for city/county/state leaders to encourage it to happen, essentially pressing the accelerator on a speed of growth that is already explosive but being met with no coherent plan to deal with it?

Andrew Hansen told me for a story I wrote for *National Geographic* that within two decades an additional 5 to 40 percent of the ecosystem's most biologically rich habitats will undergo conversion from ranch and farmland to exurban development. As I mentioned at the start of this book, wild places are defined by the caliber of wild creatures that can persist there. Are black or grizzly bears that amble into town and eat fallen apples, only to then be removed or euthanized, really what we want when we visualize co-existence with wildlife? Should golf course fairways be counted as suitable elk winter range? Is having the occasional moose or mountain lion wandering down a stream corridor out of public lands into development an idyll of wildness?

Biologist Brent Brock, who operates a consulting business, HoloScene Wildlife Services, in Bozeman, thinks about the implications of human population pressure already being exerted on wildlife that inhabits both the front and backcountry. "The big issue is just the level of disturbance being caused by constant, rising levels of human activity and it gets complicated for wildlife pretty fast. By the time you recognize a problem, it can be too late," Brock said. "For the longtime survival of species at a population level, such as wolverines and grizzlies, maintaining connectivity between wild lands inside Greater Yellowstone and beyond is essential and it necessarily includes wildlife being able to get safely through gauntlets of development in river valleys and across highways."

The renowned guru of conservation biology, Reed Noss, has said nothing impacts the fabric of wildness more than roads or even recreation trails made bigger to carry heavy volumes of people. Based on his own research, Brock concurs. "The effects are insidious because impacts might seem minor in the beginning but they can escalate," he said. "Traffic volumes can cause animals to avoid moving through areas and they increase the probability of conflict. With development occurring in wildlife habitat or recreationists flooding into an area it's the same thing. Either you are taking habitat directly away from wildlife or indirectly because the infrastructure brings in more people and it diminishes the carrying capacity and creates population sinks. People might see wildlife around for a while but offspring aren't surviving so eventually the animals just disappear. The wildlife that do adapt become 'mid-wild' or habituated or it might mean, given the level of disturbance, that elk don't migrate anymore."

For those Greater Yellowstone residents who are indifferent to such impacts, unbridled growth has consequences for the very quality of life people are fleeing other areas to find here. As Carpenter and I stood on the flanks of Sypes Canyon peering into the wood smoke from forest fires, he mentioned that as Bozeman/Gallatin fledge into a full-fledged metro area, the beloved views of the Bridgers could, within a decade or two, become shrouded by smog that rivals Salt Lake City, seriously impairing air quality (and not including bad air made worse by forest fires).

That's not good news for asthmatics but the most precious natural resource in Greater Yellowstone is, of course, water. A few years ago, a working group examined water use in Bozeman and arrived at this conclusion: Soon, Bozeman will outstrip the capacity of its existing water supply that takes the form of three reservoirs.

"The water needs of the next fifty thousand people cannot be accommodated with the practices that supplied the first forty-five thousand," said former Bozeman city employee Lain Leoniak in a piece she wrote for the city's website; she is now working in the attorney general's office of Colorado, studying water issues.

Carpenter says water could become a limiting factor that cools Bozeman/Gallatin's growth. For those who say the answer is simply to build more reservoir capacity by damming more mountain streams, climatologists note that the outlook for climate change effects are for hotter and drier summers and earlier or less winter snowpack, meaning those reservoirs will be more challenged to fill.

But this, too, raises another tantalizing question: If Bozeman, which sits near the headwaters of a major river system, is looking at water challenges, what is going to happen in major urban areas like Phoenix, Las Vegas, Salt Lake City, Denver, and Tucson? Leoniak told me at a conference in Bozeman sponsored by FutureWest that those cities are located in desert states that are part of the Colorado River Compact and even now, prior to the biggest impacts of climate change setting in, water in the Colorado system is over-appropriated, bring major clashes between urban and ag users.

Will water shortages and nearly untenable hot temperatures there result in an exodus of people who head to Greater Yellowstone? Former Bozeman Mayor Chris Mehl worked as an analyst at Headwaters Economics and previously served as a Congressional aide. He is frustrated by the knee-jerk anti-government sentiment that proliferates in the rural West that is based on the trope that "big government" is trying to rob individuals of their freedoms. But should the costs of an individual's right to do business on private land be passed along to taxpayers and do individuals who are transforming landscapes have any responsibility to help protect assets valuable to the common good, such as wildlife? It is clear that the free market and laissez-fair capitalism have never resulted in a wild ecosystem like Greater Yellowstone staying protected.

In fact, there's a compelling fiscally-conservative argument that can be made for planning and zoning because it highlights predictable impacts and allows for crises to better be averted, like those that arise when towns run out of water, or a subdivision in the county discovers that its individual wells are contaminated by someone's raw sewage due to septic systems put in on the sly and the cheap. A group in Bozeman called PERC (the

Property and Environment Policy Center) is trying to devise ways to economically incentivize large private landowners to keep their land open for the sake of wildlife.

Mehl believed the only way that wildlife issues will resonate is if the threats are made tangible, not only in the eyes of citizens but the decision makers they elect. The media plays a crucial role. Paradoxically, at a moment in time when Greater Yellowstone most needs her residents to rally around a common vision, ideological divisions are at their deepest. "To think more broadly and longer term cuts against the grain of human nature in some people," Mehl said. "Frankly, I'm seeing a decline in the willingness of people to think long term. It's hard to get them out of their narrow mindset when they are scrambling to pay the bills."

If Bozeman/Gallatin/Big Sky are one of the main pistons in Greater Yellowstone, then Jackson Hole/Teton County, Wyoming is the other. Teton County is, per capita, one of the wealthiest counties in the U.S. because of the high concentration of uber-wealthy individuals who live there permanently and seasonally. For years, severe housing shortages have resulted in high home prices and rents so expensive that school teachers and firefighters can't afford to live there.

Part of the blame is because 97 percent of Teton County is federal or state land and just three percent is privately owned. Growth proponents have suggested that public land be divested to accommodate more development. But the truth is that the highway system in Teton County is already racked by urban-like congestion.

Today, more hotel rooms in Jackson Hole are being added to bring in more visitors who are shelling out hundreds of dollars a night while the service workers making the visitors' beds have to make long commutes in and out of the valley. At the same time, multi-million-dollar, 10,000-square-foot homes are being built not only in Jackson Hole, but also, up north in Big Sky, Montana, exacting huge footprints, and many are only inhabited for the equivalent of a few months out of every year. Meantime, development continues to fracture what remains of wildlife habitat with one indicator of the effects being a significant number of road-killed animals along the highways.

Packing more people into Teton County, critics of growth say, is not going to resolve any problems related to the impacts of sprawl and will only exacerbate the domino effects radiating in all directions.

"For better or for worse, Jackson Hole is the economic engine for Teton Valley, Idaho," says Shawn Hill, former executive director of Driggs, Idaho-based Valley Advocates for Responsible Development. His valley is located westward just over Teton Pass from Jackson Hole. "When Jackson overheats, we're the release valve, especially when it comes to housing. However, over half of the housing units in Teton Valley now sell to second homeowners or investors, which soaks up much of the already limited housing inventory here."

FutureWest, Teton Valley Advocates for Responsible Development and the Jackson Hole Conservation Alliance are three of the very few conservation organizations in Greater Yellowstone aggressively working on private land growth issues. A number of excellent land trusts are protecting land by brokering conservation easements in Greater Yellowstone, and an effort called the High Divide Collaborative is collaborating with ranchers and farmers to protect agrarian land, but none really engages in the contentious trenches of shaping public policy. Moreover, the pace of development is far outstripping the scope of protection being achieved by land trusts alone.

The High Divide, so named because it applies geographically to the path of the Continental Divide as it runs from Wyoming into Idaho and Montana, represents the western flank of Greater Yellowstone. It's a microcosm of the big picture. In the past 50 years, according to Headwaters Economics, 51 percent of new homes were built outside of town centers in unincorporated portions of High Divide counties. Since 2010, this trend has increased and 63 percent of new homes were built outside of towns.

"This trend of an increasing amount of development occurring outside of town centers will impact and compromise the future of important working lands, scenery, and wildlife habitat for many of the iconic wildlife species associated with the High Divide, including elk, pronghorn antelope, grizzly bears, and wolverine," Headwaters stated in a report.

Dispersed homes also restrict hunting opportunities, limit scenic vistas and open spaces, and increase potential conflicts with agricultural land owners. Among High Divide counties, a high degree of variability exists in the amount of out-of-town growth. For example, in Jefferson and Madison Counties in Idaho, 19 percent of homes built since 2000 were built outside city limits. By contrast, in Madison County, Montana, one of the agrarian jewels of Greater Yellowstone, 91 percent of new homes put up since 2000 were built outside city limits.

In the past 50 years, the number of new homes in the High Divide built in the Wildland-Urban Interface, prone to burning by wildfires, has increased by more than 300 percent, from 2,187 homes in 1963 to 8,915 in 2013. Who is paying for the costs of defending structures built in vulnerable places? The public. Sprawl is wreaking havoc on the budgets of some counties struggling to pay for law enforcement, fire protection, emergency services, roads and their maintenance, planning staff, and transportation for such things as school buses.

In the next 10 years, nearly 150 square miles of currently undeveloped private land on the west side of Greater Yellowstone is forecasted to experience low-density creeping "exurban" development. "Teton Valley, Idaho will not only be challenged by growth pressure, but also by correcting the mistakes of the past," Hill said. "When it comes to managing growth, the Teton Valley community is often characterized by its divisions, but the vast majority of its residents want to protect its quiet, rural atmosphere. My biggest fear is that we'll make the same mistakes again because we've lost sight of why we all choose to live here."

Mark Newcomb is a geologist, a rock climber, and an elected commissioner in Teton County, Wyoming. How can the Gordian knot of preserve what's necessary on private land versus develop it create more wealth be rectified? "Should we, can we, put a dollar value on the area's ecosystem, the area's ecological amenities, the area's open space, its wildlife, its life, its wildness?" he asked. "To highlight this struggle, let me ask you this. Defining 'the area' as Teton County, Wyoming, what is the dollar value for an intact, healthy, resilient ecosystem? If you're like me, you don't even know where to start."

According to Newcomb, Teton County has a bit over 4,000 square miles, or 2.7 million acres within its borders. Of that, roughly 76,000 acres are privately owned. Of that, roughly 21,000 acres are under some sort of conservation easement to protect some combination of scenic, agricultural, or wildlife values. The remaining 2 million or so acres—97 percent—are public lands, much of which are to be conserved mostly unimpaired for future generations. About 45 percent of the county lies within Grand Teton and Yellowstone national parks; some 51 percent lies within the Bridger-Teton and Caribou-Targhee national forests, including significant tracts of "Big W" wilderness in the Teton, Jedediah Smith and Gros Ventre wilderness areas. And about 1 percent lies within the National Elk Refuge.

"All that public land harbors substantial wildlife populations," he said, citing 15,000 elk in the area, hundreds of bison, grizzly bears, wolves, moose, bighorn sheep, and other creatures that in turn attract tourists from around the world. Public lands are crucial to their survival and so are private lands. Healthy public lands and the ecosystem services they provide also positively influence human health.

"While open space on private land, due to its valley-bottom location, tends to punch above its weight in per acre importance in supporting certain species, it's the undeveloped public lands that by and large deliver the bulk of the ecosystem services we value," Newcomb added. "Undeveloped public land keeps our air clean—imagine if all of the county were private, how much air pollution would be trapped in our valley during winter inversions. Undeveloped public land by and large keeps our water clean: runoff from mountains on public land creates an underground river to constantly flush our groundwater ensuring its purity. Undeveloped public land by and large harbors the wildlife in populations our private land couldn't otherwise sustain. And undeveloped public land by and large provides the bulk of our opportunities for recreation in all its modern forms."

So, taken as a whole, he asks, what is this area's ecosystem and the ecosystem services it provides worth to citizens? "Contrast that estimate, if you even tried, with the value of private property and associated private property rights held on the remaining 3 percent of private lands that compose Teton County. As of July 10, 2017, the State Assessor certified that the remaining private land in Teton County, Wyoming is valued at $15,222,990,853. Yes, that is 15 billion with a B. That's pretty precise."

He continued, "Our inability to value ecosystem services, let alone place a value on our ecosystem as a whole, is clashing over and over again with a system of private property rights rooted in principles of individual and economic freedom tracing back to the Magna Carta. Actually, I throw that out just to sound erudite. I gather politicians cite the Magna Carta when trying to look informed about such things as personal freedoms."

Again, the Teton County, Wyoming Comprehensive Plan is one of the most foresighted in the American West and yet ideological conflicts between personal rights and the larger public interest show that unless attitudes change, unless quality of life is measured differently than in maximizing profit, power, and personal freedom, a global treasure like Greater Yellowstone will not be saved.

"There are 75 or 80 pages of land development regulations that attempt to strike a balance between the exercise of property rights and the resulting impacts to the community. They lie in Article 5, titled Physical Development Standards Applicable in All Zones of our Comprehensive Plan. They are onerous. The late Justice Scalia once wrote regarding the reduction, in Supreme Court jurisprudence, of the protections afforded to property rights, that "economic (my emphasis) rights are liberties: entitlements of individuals against the majority. When they are eliminated, no matter how desirable that elimination may be, liberty has been reduced."

Newcomb, however, points out that Jackson Hole as a beautiful place and one of America's premier places for watching wildlife would not exist if Justice Scalia's interpretation allowing free-wheeling developers to exercise their self-interest to play out. "I guarantee that these 80 pages of regs in the Teton County Comprehensive Plan governing what you can and can't do with your property were not requested by the property owners trying to exercise their property rights," he says. "They were requested by neighbors, neighbors expressing a diminishment of their rights to natural amenities such as viable and healthy wildlife populations, natural soundscapes, and scenic vistas. But rarely is there a dollar value attached to said diminishment of ecosystem services, to that one-more-cut in the death-by-a-thousand-cuts of our ecosystem."

Newcomb's colleague on the Teton County Commission is Luther Propst, who founded a land-use planning organization called the Sonoran Institute devoted to helping communities maintain their character in the face of breathtaking development pressure. For a time, Dennis Glick worked alongside Propst. Propst says it's been a bumpy transition from the frontier-era, Manifest Destiny, natural resource extraction economy led by the robber baron "Lords of Yesteryear" to the era of the New West. In some ways, the New West is no less consumptive because development is yesterday's hardrock mine that polluted streams.

"The problem is that the Lords of Yesteryear never disappeared as we were promised and the challenges of the New West are far worse than we were promised. I don't want a West of man-camps and gas field booms, nor a West of precious tourist towns that exist to feed a global cowboy/ mountain man/Disney/ski resort/New Age fantasy, surrounded by busted towns that are ghettos for workers," he said.

Carpenter believes that Greater Yellowstone and the West need a hundred other Mark Newcombs and Luther Propsts. If county commissioners in the 20 counties of this region aren't together in addressing the costs and impacts of growth extending beyond their jurisdictional boundaries, and federal and state agencies aren't unified in addressing impacts on and beyond their public land boundaries, what are the options?

"There is a prevailing mentality that we as a region can deal with challenges the same way we handled them 20 to 30 years ago, and it's incredibly shortsighted," Carpenter said. "There is nothing preventing us from being smarter. It's really a test of whether our leaders have the will and the courage to show they are capable of consciously avoiding the destructive patterns that have wrecked other places. Of course, it really comes down to the quality of the people who citizens elect."

As Bozeman/Gallatin races toward becoming Minneapolis proper sized and the valleys straddling the Tetons turn first into Bozeman and then Salt Lake City, Carpenter acknowledges that it is recent events elsewhere that keep him up at night. Greater Yellowstone does not exist in isolation from what's happening in the rest of the world, and that is the frightening wildcard. "This is what's been haunting me," Carpenter said. "I worry about the deepening impacts of climate change not just in our region with water and wildfires, but how events from afar impact us. Will hardship elsewhere drive significant numbers of people here?"

Scientists have been discussing the consequences of an ice shelf the size of Delaware breaking off Antarctica, melting and raising sea levels a foot along coastal areas where half of the population in the U.S. presently lives, he said. "And then you look at Houston and Hurricane Harvey and Florida and Hurricane Irma, and Phoenix broiling in 120-degree heat, the water shortages coming to cities in the desert Southwest, and the fires in southern California," Carpenter explained from the slope of the Bridgers. "The current explosive growth in Greater Yellowstone is happening because the region is attracting a lot of people coming here with a lot of money wanting to live lives that are quitter and closer to nature. They are the first big wave."

That alone, he says, is creating a nightmare of cascading growth-related issues, to which leadership in the Greater Yellowstone Ecosystem is either unable, unwilling, or ill-equipped to confront. "But how are the counties and towns going to handle a flood of climate and Covid-19 refugees topping the current inundation?" Carpenter asked. He doesn't even need to speak the answer. As I began to close my notepad, he adds, "It is never too late. I want to keep telling myself that, though in a region like this we're really talking the best of the last, so what we must recognize is there's always something to save until there's not anything great left to save."

Giving Up Wildness for
the Fun of It?

(The Fate of the Gallatins are a *Yellowstonesque* Test for Our Time)

WHEN BART KOEHLER PULLED off U.S. Highway 191 and turned east toward the trailhead, he wasn't toting a guitar. He sported a King Ropes trucker hat and whistled the melody of a new tune. The modern ballad he'd been composing in his head would soon be debuted by his Country Western/folk band "Coyote Angels."

Koehler shared the lyrics and chorus as he gazed toward green ridges and the curving pathway of a creek that fell from snow-covered mountains:

Ridin' my old Appaloosa
There's one thing I know for darn sure
When it comes to the change of the seasons
Elk Valley will always endure
And I sing for the Wild Heart; The Wild Heart;
I sing for the wild heart of the range

Rest assured, the lyrics weren't delivered like a line in a Shakespeare sonnet. But they conveyed the unpretentious tenor of our meeting. "Elk Valley," he said, was his personal nickname for what lay before him—the twisting expanse of the Porcupine Creek drainage. Historically, after wapiti had been nearly wiped out by market hunters in the West, this terrain served as a sanctuary of sorts for the Gallatin Elk Herd that was known and beloved even by Theodore Roosevelt.

Playing gigs as a crooner was rare weekend entertainment for Koehler. By his 60-hour work weeks, though, he was a professional conservationist who could at once be charmingly persuasive and unwaveringly devoted to cutting the best deal for wildlife, like union attorney negotiating a collective bargaining agreement. Koehler's area of expertise had, even by then, earned him a national reputation as a firebrand. He had helped spearhead several successful campaigns to get American federal public lands elevated to full protection as "wilderness." Up in Alaska, he also had toiled to prevent biologically-rich old-growth trees on the Tongass National Forest from being toppled by timber and paper companies, an action subsidized at taxpayer expense; the trees were then sold at discounted prices.

Only a few months earlier, he had arrived in Bozeman, recruited as part of a special assignment for the Greater Yellowstone Coalition and its allies. His task: building public and Congressional support for a series of complicated land trades in the Gallatin Mountains: a range jutting through two states, Wyoming and Montana, that begins in Yellowstone National Park and extends 75 miles to the edge of the Gallatin Valley encircling Bozeman.

As Koehler's song alluded, he thought of the Porcupine as the Gallatins' "wild heart." Back then, in 1993, when Koehler stepped out of his pick-up, the circumstances were urgent and potentially dire. A once-in-a-lifetime opportunity was at hand to prevent the Gallatins from becoming heavily logged and peppered with residential development built for wealthy homeowners as was then happening directly across Highway 191 in Big Sky, the unincorporated town founded as a ski resort destinating, set beneath the loom of Lone Mountain.

There is no ski resort south of Canada that inhabits a neighborhood like this, certainly none whose viewshed looks across a busy two-lane federal thoroughfare, across a storied river and into a mountain range that is the antithesis of Big Sky. The irony: likely few inhabitants of Big Sky and the jet setters who arrive there to recreate, nor even residents of Bozeman an hour north, are probably aware of how special they are.

Were you to pick up the Gallatins and drop them into California, they would instantly, because of their diversity of original native mammals, be the wildest mountains in the state. The same would be true if you relocated them to Utah, Colorado, Washington State, Oregon, Nevada, Arizona, New Mexico, Idaho, Texas—any state outside of Montana and Wyoming.

If the Gallatins were a standalone national park they'd be wilder than any national park in the Lower 48 save for Yellowstone, Grand Teton and Glacier. They are the only significant mountain range next to Yellowstone without a major road bisecting them

At the bottom of the Porcupine where Koehler stood, the possibility had even been floated of putting in a golf course. Were it ever to materialize, one would be able to tee off into higher-elevation fairways with the backdrop of jagged summits and with exotic manicured grasses supplanting game trails where grizzlies and members of the Gallatin Herd still grazed and where cow elk gave birth to their calves. There was also talk of subdividing private 640-acre square sections of private land, part of a checkerboard pattern, into trophy homes, guest lodges and who knows what else.

The previous autumn, a motion picture had hit the big screen, a movie adaptation of Norman Maclean's novella, *A River Runs Through It*, produced by Robert Redford and starring among other actors, a young Brad Pitt. The film not only instantly popularized fly-fishing, but inspired a rush of well-to-do outsiders coming to Montana looking for land where they could secure their casting fantasy.

Koehler and his colleagues knew they faced a race against time. For purposes of full disclosure, Koehler on that morning many years ago set out with a topo map in hand, and as he whistled his fresh tune, a young reporter tagged along with him into the Porcupine. A year later, the same journalist joined him on a trek into another nearby drainage to the south, the Buffalo Horn: also a wildlife stronghold located just to the south and next to U.S. Highway 191.

That writer in Koehler's company was me.

Today, the Custer Gallatin National Forest is deciding the fate of the Gallatins with a management plan that proposes how much of the mountains will be protected with the highest level of safeguarding—"wilderness" status. Leaders of the national forest only make recommendations but it is up to Congress to advance legislation that ultimately must be passed by both the House and Senate and signed into law by the president.

This isn't a provincial "backyard issue" for denizens of Bozeman, Livingston, Big Sky and West Yellowstone to decide. The issue is being closely watched nationally The principal protagonists are not the usual suspects such as traditional natural resource industrialists on one side such as loggers and miners battling tree huggers. The conflict is internecine, pitting citizen conservationists concerned about wildlife against outdoor recreationists who want to use the Gallatins as their playground. And nearby is what conservation biologists call "the elephant in the room": Big Sky, the one time semi-quaint downhill ski resort destination that each day more closely resembles a large development complex like one would find in the Colorado Rockies.

For those who need a bit more geographic description the Gallatins are a bio-geographical extension of Yellowstone, which means they are a vital unbroken appendage, a highway for wildlife moving in and out of the park. Stretching beyond the artificial northern boundary of Yellowstone, these mountains extend into Montana and run between Paradise Valley to the east and the Gallatin River Canyon on the west—the latter today dominated by the bulging bustle of the resort complex of Big Sky that is causing many spillover effects on adjacent public land, including the Gallatin River.

In fact, it could be asserted, the fate of the Gallatins is a national *Yellowstonesque* test of our resolve, for *our time*. Call the terrain "wilderness," *wildness*, whatever you choose, even try to demean it as a reference, but one way of thinking about wilderness in the 21ˢᵗ century is it's a place where humans with conscious deliberateness make space for wild creatures that have a hard time thriving in human-dominated landscapes. Wilderness *is* where the wild things *are*. Wilderness is where *a lot of people*, moving fast-paced trying to cover as much ground as possible, are *not*.

One way to think about the high caliber of wildness in the Gallatins is that they still hold a full complement of animals that has disappeared from the rest of West because of land fragmentation, human intolerance and large numbers of people overwhelming their habitat. Based on that distinction alone, of what can still live there, the Gallatins are wild.

Where does the comparison to Yellowstone come in? In July of 2021 I had the honor of being invited by the Gallatin Wildlife Association to deliver a few words on the occasion of that local conservation organization turning 45 years old. The organization has proposed that at least 230,000 acres of the Gallatins receive wilderness protection, some two and half times more than the amount recommended by the Forest Service and twice as much as a group of environmentalists aligned with mountain bikers.

My short riff was about a derisive word that gets tossed around—"radical"—and who gets to tag others with the label. I added how I've seen farsighted courage manifested, set within the context of why the Greater Yellowstone is the last of its kind in the Lower 48. This region, considered the cradle of American conservation, is the product of radical thinking that proved to be ingenious over time.

Those who advocated for establishment of Yellowstone National Park were labeled impractical radicals by members of the Montana Territorial Legislature and local natural resource profiteers who had colonized Paradise Valley and didn't want park lands put off limits to their unbounded exploitation. Some were willing to keep hunting wildlife inside the park even if it meant killing off every last one.

Had the naysayers prevailed with their argument that protecting land would impair prosperity, liberty, freedom and progress, we would not have Yellowstone today or, at best, there would be a pale watered down imitation. And if we are being brutally candid, every momentous conservation accomplishment in America was borne by radicals willing to challenge and stand up to the status quo. Radicals who called out special interests that only treat nature as a commodity to be exploited, scraped out of the ground, bought or sold. Wild country, too, that can be "used up" by sheer numbers of people desiring to covet it, or possess it, in some way.

During my chat before the Gallatin Wildlife Association, I shared that some environmentalists in Bozeman had labeled GWA "radical" and "extremists" for believing that the Gallatin Mountains deserve to have the maximum number of acres possible set aside as federal wilderness. Imagine that, I said, wildlife advocates being disparaged by members of their own tribe because they wanted *more public land to remain as it is*.

Strange times, these.

In more than 40 years of activism, Koehler has walked in the canopy of half millennial-old giant spruce and hemlocks, sparing them from circular saws; he has seen wild salmon spawn in ancient streams fed by post-Pleistocene glaciers, ridden his horse into the most remote corners of the Lower 48 in Wyoming, and camped on red-rock mesas where indigenous peoples 500 generations earlier had the same sunset vantage. "I've had the privilege of helping to save some remarkable places from being ruined," he said recently. "And I would put the importance of protecting the Gallatins, especially now, right up there with the best of them."

With swelling development pressures in the northwestern tier of the

Greater Yellowstone Ecosystem and rising numbers of recreational users, together with the facts that Bozeman is the fastest-growing micropolitan city in America with more than a billion dollars in new construction happening at Big Sky, and with climate change already notching impacts, Koehler sees Wilderness as a chance for citizens, civil servants, and elected officials to place a positive bet on the future.

Together with Michael Scott, who oversaw the Northern Rockies Office of the Wilderness Society in Bozeman, Montana decades ago, Koehler was a conservationist on the front lines in an effort to essentially erase human boundaries drawn across the Gallatins and restore a more holistic conceptualization of their natural qualities. A reader might think of what transpired as a high-stakes chess game played on top of a carto-graphic checkerboard with the goal making the checkerboard itself disappear.

The kind of wildlife attributes found in the Gallatins, in particular the Porcupine and Buffalo Horn, Koehler observed, are superlative even by the already high standards of globally-recognized wildness that exists in Greater Yellowstone. The Porcupine is valuable because it's not topo-graphical rocks and ice.

"This wild spot isn't obscure or in the middle of nowhere. And it isn't in isolation as an island all by itself surrounded by development." After a long pause, he added, "the Gallatins are part of the life-support system of the very first national park on Earth."

Government wildlife officials and land managers in the early 20th century had long pressed to safeguard the part of the Gallatins—about three dozen linear miles worth—stretching beyond Yellowstone. From the moment it was created in 1872, architects of Yellowstone realized the 2.2 million-acre park, by itself, was not big enough to sustain the large "charismatic megafauna" that resided there and moved seasonally between high country and lower-lying winter range. Topographically, geographically, and ecologically, the Gallatins represent a seamless extension of parklike qualities.

In the years after the Civil War, the federal government gifted railroad companies alternating sections of land that they could exploit for timber as an incentive for building new track line across the interior of the West. Those parcels they were given, creating a checkerboard pattern mixed in with public sections of land—became lucrative in modern times as real estate holdings for development. During the 1990s a series of land swaps and cash deals enabled checkerboard lands in the Gallatin Range to be consolidated into public ownership and it set the stage for today's debate over how much of the mountain should be given the highest standard of protection. Koehler was a major player who helped secure land consolidation which involved delicate negotiations between private timber barons, the Forest Service, Congress, citizens and others.

Koehler went to Washington D.C. with Michael Scott who said the following that was put into the Congressional record: "This bill will facilitate future wilderness designations for the Hyalite-Porcupine-Buffalo Horn WSA," Scott said and emphasized that it would "provide an unbroken Wilderness Area from just south of Bozeman to Yellowstone National Park."

There was no question, no confusion, about what the intent of the legislation was in getting the land swaps expedited: *unbroken wilderness* to benefit wildlife, Koehler said. And the sound of that had appeal to lawmakers, he added. Members of both houses of Congress passed the Gallatin Range Consolidation and Protection Act of 1993 and President Bill Clinton signed it into law.

Scott and Koehler agree that the phrase *unbroken wilderness* wasn't presented solely for impact, to stir the imagination, but it spoke to a deeper ecological function: the Gallatins being a crucial cog in the Greater Yellowstone *Ecosystem* and a continuation of the caliber of unfragmented nature present and hailed in the backcountry of Yellowstone Park. The critical difference, once the mountains crossed the northwest park boundary and leaned northward into Montana, is that on the adjacent Custer Gallatin National Forest hunting was permitted whereas in Yellowstone it isn't. Hunters understand the premium importance of quality habitat that transcends borders and they referenced the Porcupine-Buffalo Horn as "the Holy land" for big game hunting.

In many ways, Scott and Koehler were a perfectly teamed dynamic duo, each bringing different strengths and both spending parts of their careers with both the Greater Yellowstone Coalition and The Wilderness Society. "We worked as friends with an abiding respect for one another," Koehler said, explaining they "knew what a good fight was and the Gallatins were as meaningful as any."

Known for his expertise in formulating environmental policy and strategy, Scott had worked in Washington DC earlier and was promoted to lead The Wilderness Society's Northern Rockies office in the 1980s because of its high profile and an array of threats to public lands. Koehler, adept at being able to relate to local people unpretentiously, had earned a master's in outdoor recreation resource management and planning from the University of Wyoming. He isn't just some garden variety greenie. He probably has more experience in the trenches than any staffer working today for any of the dozens of conservation groups in Greater Yellowstone today.

After matriculating the University of Wyoming, he became a young field staffer for The Wilderness Society and fell under the tutelage of Margaret E. "Mardy" Murie and her twin sister, Louise Murie MacLeod in Moose, Wyoming. They had been married to a pair of half-brothers who were biologists. Mardy Murie's husband, Olaus Murie, was a pioneering elk biologist and Louise's husband, Adolph Murie, was also a federal biologist well known for his studies of wolves and grizzlies in Denali National Park in Alaska and coyotes in Yellowstone.

Olaus Murie, decades earlier, had echoed the advisement from the U.S. Forest Service's first chief, Gifford Pinchot, a close friend of Theodore Roosevelt who had ridden a horse through the Gallatins, that the mountains, especially their southern section between present day Windy Pass and the Yellowstone Park border, needed higher protection to safeguard elk and mule deer.

All four Muries—wives and husbands—were friends with people like Aldo Leopold, Bob Marshall, and Sigurd Olson and were involved in the growth of the American conservation movement which represented a check against the legacy of robber barons who treated the West as a natural resource colony ripe for thoughtless exploitation.

Notably, Olaus Murie, too, was a founding member of The Wilderness Society, later becoming its national director. In the lore of the Society, the Murie Ranch in Moose was known as the organization's unofficial national headquarters. Following Olaus' death in autumn 1963, Mardy stood behind President Lyndon Johnson when he signed the Wilderness Act of 1964 into law.

The Murie clan has been closely associated with creation and protection of the Arctic National Wildlife Refuge in Alaska and in 1998 President Clinton awarded her the Presidential Medal of Freedom, the nation's highest civilian honor for her presence as "the grandmother of the modern American conservation movement."

Mardy and Louise in the 1970s mentored many young people, including Koehler and a who's who of others, women and men, who are conservation leaders today. "I'll never forget one of my first tasks of being sent into the lion's den. It was 1975 and I was tasked with going back to Washington DC to testify against Wyoming Governor Stanley K. Hathaway's nomination by President Gerald Ford to become Secretary of the Interior," Koehler shared. "Mardy gave me a hand-written note and told me to read it once I got on the airplane to DC. It said, 'I know you will be calm, objective, non-acrimonious, but armed with real facts—this will be hard hitting.'"

Murie closed it with a question and one sentence was capitalized for emphasis: "Do you remember Sir Galahad's words in Tennyson's *Idyll of the King*? 'MY STRENGTH IS AS THE STRENGTH OF TEN BECAUSE MY HEART IS PURE'. Fond best wishes travel with you, Mardy."

Hathaway was confirmed and he only served for the remaining short tenure of Ford in The White House. In addition to Murie's gesture of confidence bestowed in the young activist, Koehler says her point was always to stand on principle, to not willingly surrender that which should not be given away or is irreplaceable without first reflecting on what's at stake and resisting needless surrender. "Mardy would repeat this whether it was her arguing for protection of the Arctic or of the few untouched places in the Lower 48," Koehler says.

Her reference to Sir Galahad wasn't superficial. He had been one of the mythical knights of King Arthur's court who found the holy grail, which for her symbolized wildness, Koehler said. "She would always say the world already has plenty of people pushing to take what they want, but it's important to remind people of the animals and places that have no voice in the human world. They are counting upon us to make sure their interests are considered and defended."

Following that initiation with The Wilderness Society, Koehler became a co-founder of the Wyoming Wilderness Association and he worked for the Greater Yellowstone Coalition and returned to The Wilderness Society.

How much of the Gallatin that gets protected is really framed within the context of what's called the Hyalite-Porcupine-Buffalo Horn Wilderness Study Area, encompassing 155,000 acres and established in the late 1970s by a bill drafted by Lee Metcalf a U.S. senator from Montana. At the time, lands inside the study area were deemed of high ecological value and in such an untrammeled state as to be considered in the future for full-fledged wilderness status. The Forest Service, by law, was required to manage the lands with the same level of protection it would give to established wilderness. But Koehler says, that didn't happen. "It sure seemed when I left the Greater Yellowstone [region] in 1999 that eventually the Porcupine and Buffalo Horn would get what they deserved and be a lawful part of the National Wilderness Preservation System," Koehler said. "But the lesson is that if the public isn't constantly demanding accountability from federal land management agencies and pushing for protection where it's needed, holding their feet to the fire, you can lose any gains you thought you made."

What's different? The advent of mountain biking and its growth in terms of riders along with a mountain biking industry pushing to create more trails on public lands. Well organized, mountain biking advocates have told traditional conservation organizations that they not support public lands protection unless they can ride in it. Koehler has watched groups he used to work for morph from being very focused on wildlife protection to being advocates for outdoor recreation. The problem is, he notes, that rapidly rising numbers of outdoor recreationists are not good for wildlife and habitat protection. And scientific studies, he says, back him up.

In recent years, a group called the Gallatin Forest Partnership comprising the two influential organizations Koehler and Scott used to work for—the Greater Yellowstone Coalition and The Wilderness Society—along with the Montana Wilderness Association, the Southwest Montana Mountain Bike Association, and a few others, advanced their own plan for the Holy Land. It calls for designating 102,005 acres of the Gallatins as Wilderness and putting 31,000 acres of Porcupine and Buffalo Horn into a new "wildlife management area" classification so that mountain biking can occur.

Koehler believes that mountain bikers should not have political power to determine the management fate of two drainages like the Porcupine and Buffalo Horn. Back during the days of testimony on Gallatin range consolidation in the 1990s, Forest Service staffers working for the Custer Gallatin acknowledged that whatever was happening, the uses wouldn't disqualify those lands inside the WSA from being considered for full Wilderness status, Koehler said.

"Mountain biking certainly was not then a major recreation activity," he said. "I think a key point worth mentioning is that mountain bikes—how we visualize them as expensive backcountry machines today—were first created by a guy in Marin County, California in 1978. The Montana Wilderness Study Act was passed in 1977, before their official invention and even after that they were late to arrive in Bozeman."

Koehler points to Forest Service planning documents pertaining to the Custer Gallatin Forest that never mention mountain biking, not even once, in their description of recreational activities in the 1990s and early 2000s. The argument that mountain biking represents a pre-existing use that could supersede wilderness designation is false, he asserted. "There were no mountain biking advocates or activists who spoke out about the land exchanges or the wilderness bills in the 1980s and 1990s."

No representatives from motorized or mountain biking interests ever formally requested permission to blaze new trails into the Hyalite-Porcupine-Buffalo Horn Wilderness Study Area over the last 40-some years and, best as anyone can tell, no permission was ever granted by the Forest Service. If the agency had given a green light, it would have been in violation of law.

Yet what the courts would deem illegal trespass occurred in the WSA with mountain bikes and motorized users and the Custer Gallatin did nothing to stop it. Only after a lawsuit was filed by environmentalists to uphold the law and a court sided with the litigants, did the Custer Gallatin assemble a "travel plan," i.e., a document that spelled out exactly where certain mechanized and motorized uses could occur.

After the Custer Gallatin resisted closing trails, EarthJustice senior attorney Tim Preso, on behalf of litigants Greater Yellowstone Coalition, The Wilderness Society, and Montana Wilderness Association, brought another suit alleging the Forest Service did not adequately assess the impact of wheeled uses on wilderness character, as required by the National Environmental Policy Act. They won before U.S. District Court Judge Donald Malloy, though the judge acknowledged the Custer Gallatin is confronted with "a Sisyphean challenge."

Dozens of miles of trails were ordered closed, but not all: not those in the Porcupine and Buffalo Horn. A motorized access group called Citizens For Balanced Use sued, seeking to reverse trail closures, but in December 2011 the U.S. 9th Circuit Court ruled that the travel plan did not adequately protect wilderness character.

Even then, in the years since the travel plan was completed, illegal trespass has continued on the Custer Gallatin. The Forest Service has welcomed trail improvement projects from mountain bikers and motorized interests that have only increased user numbers, all of it happening without any serious or comprehensive agency analysis of impacts on wildlife.

According to Preso, whose office prepared a memo that lays out legal arguments for assessing compliance with the 1977 Wilderness Study Act statute, the focus really was on motorbikes as they were the mechanized state of the art at the time the law was passed and really doesn't address mountain bikes. Further, the law doesn't strictly require that WSAs be managed like designated Wilderness; it does, however, say that any uses allowed to occur cannot degrade wilderness caliber of the lands. Mechanized uses might be allowed in WSAs but neither are they afforded statutory protection that those uses be permanent.

A major criticism of the Forest Service is that it has exacerbated the conflict by allowing uses to occur in areas where, when the law is enforced, the agency must ban them, angering many.

"It's important to note that the Hyalite-Porcupine-Buffalo Horn Wilderness Study Area itself and its 155,000 acres was a result of earlier compromise, a whittling down of acreage. Other lands that might have qualified as wilderness were given away to appease the timber industry and other special interests," Koehler says. "With the WSA, given the law, the Forest Service was responsible for holding the line and obviously, as you can see by the court's finding, it didn't."

Let's be clear, the Gallatin Forest Partnership is working toward one kind of outcome that is intended to give all user groups a little bit of something. But what's been missing from the discussion of "balance" and "consensus" and "collaboration" is the opinion of wildlife, critics of the Partnership's position argue. They say wildlife is referenced, yes, but it isn't treated with priority or given the same level of status and influence as, say, mountain bikers. A prominent conservation biologist told me the Partnership's proposal should have undergone a rigorous peer review from scientists who would have pointed out that outdoor recreation, especially the intensity levels that exist today and are certain to grow, displaces wildlife. This is a problem of not a single use but cumulative effects and the sheer numbers of people moving through wild country. Mountain bikers, who have been notorious for trespassing into already-established Wilderness and boldly pioneering "user-created" trails throughout the national forests of Greater Yellowstone are able to ride faster, longer and cover more terrain than hikers.

Again, Koehler is critical of the Gallatin Forest Partnership because the decision that the Porcupine and Buffalo Horn should be open to mountain biking was owed largely to its alliance with the Southwest Montana Mountain Biking Association, which, he says, was given disproportionate defferance. Koehler says: "No shop that sells mountain bikes in Big Sky, Bozeman, or Livingston is going to go out of business or be seriously economically impacted if more land is made into Wilderness. No individual mountain biker will be seriously aggrieved if they can't ride in the parts of the Gallatin that should be Wilderness," he noted. "But more Wilderness will matter to wildlife. It will benefit the animals that live there."

Many scientists, including Dr. Chris Servheen, former national Grizzly Bear Recovery Coordinator for the U.S. Fish and Wildlife Service, say that mountain biking, because of speed, numbers of riders, quietness at which they travel, blind turns in trails and number of miles covered, is dangerous for people and grizzlies likely to be startled. It also results in displacement of animals from habitat and potentially opens the door for e-bikes, too. Illegal riding is occurring throughout much of the Gallatins, including on the crest. It is distasteful to some outdoorspeople to encounter bicyclists on the tops of mountains.

Colorado, where mountain bike participation has exploded, portends what is yet to come to Greater Yellowstone, wildlife biologists have predicted. Colorado does not have any place that holds the wildlife diversity present in the Porcupine and Buffalo Horn.

In the mountain biking hub of Durango, Shannon Borders, spokeswoman for the Bureau of Land Management, addressed illegal mountain biking trespass and trail building. "We're not talking small connector trails," she told a reporter. "We're talking miles of illegally built trails. And it's *not* like there's *not* a ton of recreational opportunities around town."

"Rule number one is you don't negotiate with a group of users who basically say, 'If you don't give us what we want, we're going to take it,' because that is condoning and encouraging lawbreaking. Imagine if poachers made that argument with state fish and game agencies about elk," Koehler said. "Rule number two is you don't compromise away, through collaboration, pieces of the landscape that are irreplaceable and should not be open for barter. Rule number three: if you couldn't trust the Forest Service before and you had to haul the agency into court to do its job, what makes you think things will be better this time around?"

In the spring 2020 issue of *Backcountry Journal*, the publication of the organization called "Backcountry Hunters & Anglers," mountain bikes and e-bikes appeared in the center of a bull's eye of scrutiny. "A growing breadth of scientific evidence is showing that recreational disturbance from mountain bikes and other uses is having a significant negative impact on elk populations in Colorado," hunter Timothy Brass, BHA's state policy and field operations director in Colorado, wrote. "Wildlife biologists are sounding alarm bells as wildlife habitat on our public lands is increasingly being fragmented by both sanctioned and illegal user-created trails, in some cases leading to population level declines."

Preso notes that legally the Forest Service cannot simply ignore increasing volumes of users if they are having a deleterious effect on wilderness character that includes solitude and wildlife. So far, no one from the Gallatin Forest Partnership or Custer Gallatin has provided evidence to refute Servheen's contention about impacts on bears from bikers. Nor has either entity spoken directly, except with vague references, to a significant body of scientific evidence showing the impacts of outdoor recreation on wildlife. It is known that on public lands not many hunters like going where there are large numbers of recreationists and vice versa. Koehler says the point isn't just that mechanized uses are technically illegal *today* under the terms of the 1977 Montana Wilderness Study Area Act; it's also what the use levels *will become* with growing numbers of people and short-time vacationers at Big Sky wanting to ride trails without understanding the cumulative consequences of their incursion.

And then there's climate change, which will make parts of the landscape warmer, affecting secure habitat and foraging areas and it means that wildlife will seek out higher elevations and remote backcountry to escape both people and the heat.

Someone who was intimately familiar with the quality of the Gallatins was the late Joe Gutkoski who worked for the Forest Service for 32 years as a landscape architect, a bulk of his tenure on the Custer-Gallatin. What mountain bikers today don't realize is how much harrowing effort went in to preventing the wild nature of the Gallatins from being transformed by human development and huge numbers of people.

On his kitchen table a few months before he died in summer 2021, Gutkoski unfurled a couple of topo maps and had, marked in pencil, the perimeter of land sections that met the land condition standards for inclusion in potential Gallatin Range wilderness designation in part of the land consolidation that happened in the 1990s. He identified other parts of the mountains where historic mining had occurred and where land could be healed and restored to high value for wildlife. Gutkoski believed at least 230,000 acres qualifies, including the biologically-rich Porcupine and Buffalo Horn drainages.

A member of the Gallatin Forest Partnership told me Gutkoski and his friends were "radical" and "extremist" for proposing 230,000 acres be considered for wilderness. Ironically, one of the Gallatin Forest Partnership members, the Greater Yellowstone Coalition, had once given Gutkoski its "conservationist of the year award" for his advocacy and commitment to wildlife protection.

Yes, Gutkoski did a couple of things that might indeed be considered radical, if not gutsy. One of them was that, as a man in his 70s and 80s, he personally hiked the entire circumference and crisscrossed the interior of the 230,000 acres of the Custer-Gallatin to ground truth their ecological condition and to make sure his conclusion was accurate. To the best of anyone's recollection, no other person went to such lengths and likely no one else better understood the Gallatin's high wildlife values. What he and others believe qualifies for wilderness is nearly two and half times what the Forest Service does.

"It may sound strange, but I don't trust the Forest Service. My whole career with the Forest Service involved trying to hold the agency to account," Joe told me, noting that he believed in its mission as a conservation agency but he ran headlong into superiors who were rewarded and received promotions for carrying out political mandates tied to resource extraction because it created jobs, won votes and political contributions. "Modern environmental laws forced the Forest Service to listen to science and not always tilt the scale in favor of extraction. I was a good soldier in that I didn't take my battles public until after I retired. I fought them inside [the agency] but some of the issues did reach the newspaper," he said.

One such internal run-in that didn't held enormous consequences for the fate of Gallatin Range as we know it today. The forerunning American ecologist Aldo Leopold who himself was a veteran of the Forest Service and who became a diehard believer in the value of wilderness, once remarked: "Ethical behavior is doing the right thing when no one else is watching—even when doing the wrong thing is legal."

Gutkoski pulled out another weathered and cracking map that detailed a proposed road, supported by the forest supervisor, that would've been blazed along Buffalo Horn Creek from the present location of the 320 Ranch along U.S. Highway 191 and stretch all the way over the Gallatin Crest, It would have connected with the current dead-end road rising from Paradise Valley into Tom Miner Basin. Had it been built, it would have given Greater Big Sky a quick back-door short cut route to reach the front door of Yellowstone at Gardiner.

"Can you imagine?" Joe mused in July, the same as he had done in other conversations we had. "If the road had been engineered, it would have been constantly improved over the years—all that money in Big Sky would have helped make it happen. And it would have cut the Gallatins in two."

Gutkoski learned that a powerful triumvirate had formed and the plan was to get the road approved in a way that significant public scrutiny would be avoided. Montana Power (today Northwestern Energy) approached the then Gallatin Forest requesting that an access road be approved to allow construction of a power line extending over the mountains. Burlington Northern Railroad, which owned checkerboard sections of land in the Gallatins astride of the proposed road and eventually became Plum Creek Timber, expressed interest is carrying out some significant logging and using the road to get the timber out. At the time, Congress was generous in giving the Forest Service ample money for building roads.

"I got wind of the plan and then I saw the rough map that laid out the proposed route and I was shocked and horrified," Gutkoski says. "I was, after all, the landscape architect on staff and I went to the forest supervisor and asked, 'How come I never heard about this?' I was told that I should just mind my own business, so I reminded him that this *is* my business. I am a public servant and the public will want to know about this."

After a series of tense internal meetings, the road was shelved. In a case of "what might have been," Gutkoski says, the consequences would have been game-changing for the Gallatins and Tom Miner Basin. Had the plan moved forward, the road would have likely become a through-way for Big Sky tourism promoters advertising it as a short-cut to Mammoth Hot Springs and back again.

"The part that scared me just as much is that Burlington Northern would have clearcut its holdings and then might have sold them to developers," Gutkoski said. "Those sections would have had trophy homes and guest lodges and subdivisions and who knows what else. If a road corridor had been opened up, the Gallatin Land Exchanges would never have happened. Instead of having the opportunity to save the Gallatins as we do today they would have been cut over and turned into a suburb of Big Sky." That was hardly the only time Gutkoski challenged his bosses or was a burr in their side. Gutkoski remembered being called into the supervisor's office of the Custer-Gallatin and asked the question, "Who's side do you think you're on?"

Gutkoski was told that being insubordinate, if he wasn't careful, might result in him being re-assigned to the most remote national forest office in Alaska. He looked back at his superior, calling his bluff, and said, "Alaska's probably a fine place to hunt to fish. When should I start packing?"

The Custer Gallatin does not refute Koehler's conclusions about rising threats from human users and the likelihood that a higher volume of recreationists will displace wildlife and degrade the wild character of the Gallatins. In fact, in its November 2016 report titled "Draft Assessment Report of Ecological, Social and Economic Conditions on the Custer Gallatin National Forest," authors noted that Custer Gallatin ranks behind only Yellowstone and Grand Teton national parks in terms of visitor numbers, with more than three million visits annually.

The report states that "...national forest use is rising faster than expected and recreational demands are becoming more varied and intense due to population growth and social changes. Management is also challenged as communities expand closer to the national forest. In the meantime, funding has fallen, reducing the ability to properly manage recreational resources as they currently exist, let alone if they change or if new recreational demands arise. And, of course, recreational demands must be balanced with other resource obligations, such as fish, water, and wildlife. Even with an increased reliance on partners and volunteers, the recreation opportunities offered on the Custer Gallatin may change as competing priorities emerge for limited natural and financial resources." That, scientists say, should warrant caution and analysis and applying the best science possible, even asking hard questions of what the word "balance" really means if more people are being encouraged to use the most sensitive wildlife habitat on the Custer Gallatin while knowing it will come at the expense of the animals.

In another report prepared by Backcountry Hunters & Anglers in Colorado, authors documented numerous instances across the state where recreation pressure has led to declines in large game species and it includes problems with mountain bikers entering areas with seasonal closures, which would be one management tool available in the Porcupine and Buffalo Horn.

"To be an advocate for the wild Gallatins does not equate to being broadly anti-mountain biking or anti-recreation. That argument, frankly, is silly, because it's not true. Let the mountain biking community try that argument of being anti-bike on me," Koehler said. "I find it ironic that three groups long associated with wildlife conversation and now affiliated with the Gallatin Forest Partnership would seem to side with bikers over rising impacts from human activity on wildlife," Koehler says. "Fortunately, and I mean this sincerely, bikers have plenty of other places, other than the Porcupine and Buffalo Horn, places with lower wildlife values— including in and around Big Sky."

The issue of mountain biking impacts may soon be coming to a head. "The Forest Service takes the position that mountain bikes can use WSAs that were accessed by motorized vehicles (e.g., dirt bikes) in 1977, so long as the aggregate level of use does not result in wilderness character being degraded below 1977 levels," EarthJustice attorney Tim Preso told me. "In practice, this would seem to envision substitution of modern mountain bike use for 1977-era dirt bike use. The courts have yet to squarely address whether this is a legitimate approach."

Many Americans, Koehler explained, do not realize a fundamental fact about Wilderness. All wilderness-caliber lands are not equal. "In terms of the wildlife values at stake, few come close to what you find in the Gallatins," he said. "The west and northwest sides of Yellowstone are the only ones lacking a significant layer of insulation that wilderness in the Gallatins would provide. It would be the last missing puzzle piece essential to protect the interior core of the Yellowstone ecosystem being put in place. If that's not an honorable conservation objective, then what is?"

The Greater Yellowstone Ecosystem is a product of innumerable decision, cuts and scratches, some large but most small. They involve some who refuse to accept limits on personal ambition and self-interest. And they involve the drawings of lines in the sand, defending pieces of terra firma that are considered inviolate.

Mike Clark was hired to be executive director of the Greater Yellowstone Coalition in the mid-1990s, taking over from Ed Lewis, and he would eventually hand off the reins to Michael Scott. Clark is best known for his role in scrutinizing and ultimately stopping the New World Mine from being built just off the northeast corner of Yellowstone near Cooke City. He says the Custer Gallatin National Forest would have permitted it, had it not been for public opposition and intervention from the President of the United States. Bill Clinton helped persuade the Canadian mining company, Noranda, it wasn't a good idea to pursue something that might harm a place as beloved as Yellowstone.

Clark had his hands full with the New World fight but he was also concerned about simultaneous development pressure that arose with timber baron turned real estate developer Tim Blixseth in Big Sky, founder of the Yellowstone Club, a gated community for the uber wealthy. Blixseth shrewdly had come into possession of the old railroad checkerboard lands and used them as bargaining chips to secure land in Big Sky he wanted, cash and the ability to acquire and sell other tracts to timber companies that then clearcut them. Blixseth had once played hardball, threatening to put subdivisions into the Porcupine drainage if he didn't get his way.

"When Blixseth parked the dozer and said he would strip everything [clearcut the parcels] or develop them in the Porcupine, that was about the time I arrived," Clark said. "The main thrust was to deal with the enormous amount of checkerboarded lands that would, if developed, fragment an important part of the ecosystem. Our goal was to make it possible to get wilderness protection on some of those lands. Two of the highest priorities were the Porcupine and securing the Taylor Fork in the Madisons that are an elk migration corridor. But first we had to get them into public hands. And we did that. However, it did not happen without having to give something up."

Many forget that the Forest Service gave up tracts of public land in the Bangtail Mountains east of Bozeman and the north Bridgers and those sections of land were clearcut. Important wildlife habitat was destroyed, and in some places, trees have been slow to grow back. "They got nuked and we knew they would. And we knew the land we agreed to trade out around Big Sky was going to get nuked with intense development. Nobody could have foreseen just how much more developed Big Sky would become," Clark said. "And that's why protecting the Porcupine and Buffalo Horn as wilderness now is even more important. The public gave up some quality wildlands and allowed them to be sacrificed so that more of the Gallatins would become Wilderness."

Clark, who grew up in the Appalachians where mountaintop removal coal mining decimated communities and watersheds, believes that "multiple use" as an attitude reflective of frontier-era thinking is a failed paradigm in the context of protecting wild places. As example after example has shown, landscapes are not good at accommodating multiple human activities at once and still maintaining their natural integrity.

Full-field energy development is not good for wildlife, nor is water spoiled by mining good for agriculture. People do not like to live in sight of clearcuts or oil wells. Similarly, he says, wildlife cannot persist amid a lot of human development or constant rushes of recreation activity.

"Be they Forest Service, Park Service, BLM or any government entity, we need to periodically force meek agencies and the people who work for them to not be mediocre," he said. "What we face, too, is a political problem. If we don't have Congressional support from people in the Congress who understand that the conservation legacy of this country has been bipartisan and there are heroes on both sides, then lots of stuff, the wild places we care about among them, will go down the tubes."

During the 1990s, another staffer from the Greater Yellowstone Coalition was drafting that first comprehensive overview of the Greater Yellowstone Ecosystem—Dennis Glick's *Sustaining Greater Yellowstone*.

Glick's FutureWest helps local towns grapple with growth-related challenges and deal with economic hardship in ways that help them maintain their culture and the health of the environment. The inspiration for FutureWest resides with what Glick witnessed in the past, through 40 years of conservation work that involved international land protection in developing nations.

Koehler was with the Greater Yellowstone Coalition, as a colleague of Glick's when the report was published. "The GYC blueprint, edited and approved by staff and board, called for nothing less than wilderness area designations for the Porcupine and Buffalo Horn," said Koehler, who was part of the GYC team that produced the Wilderness Proposal Section of the report.

While GYC was battling the New World Mine in the mid-1990s and working behind the scenes to get the land deals expedited, Glick said no conservation organization, not even his own group, GYC, was carefully scrutinizing the rapidly-expanding footprint of human development in Big Sky. It was about to erupt with the pending approval for construction of major homes, a lodge, roads, a golf course, private ski hill, trails and other facilities at The Yellowstone Club and adjacent developments.

Glick showed up at a meeting of the Madison County planning board when development plans for the Yellowstone Club were pending approval. He knew he would be the lone voice from the environmental community. "I was alone expressing concern basically about the impact that significant development would have over time on the Madison Range. I said we needed to look at this cumulatively, given what had already happened at Big Sky. You can't turn back the clock but you can be smarter looking forward," he said. "What I always say about Big Sky is it only has three problems—location, location, location. When you put major development in the heart of a narrow mountain range, as occurred in the Madisons, the wildlife habitat and passageways animals use to move can easily become fragmented. And that's exactly what has happened."

From a community of just several hundred permanent residents in the mid 1970s, there are today around 3300 permanent residents and 4300 housing units with almost seven of ten of those worth at least $1 million. Another 5700 residential units alone are planned for construction at the four major developments, according to the 2019 Big Sky Economic Development Profile. Growth problems abound. The Big Sky County

Water & Sewer District is obligated to serve 10,678 single-family equivalents (SFEs) however it can presently only serve up to about 8,000 SFEs and some would like to expand the sewage treatment plant and put treated effluent into the Gallatin River.

In Colorado, at Vail, which Big Sky often draws comparisons to, the town of Vail and an entity called The Vail Symposium hosted a forum on wildlife issues. Numbers of elk, deer and bighorn sheep are falling. "The decline we're seeing in the elk herd goes from Vail Pass to Aspen," Bill Andree, a wildlife officer for Colorado Parks and Wildlife said. "It's not too tough to figure out why when you're looking at the levels of development, recreation and roads."

That's the direction the Bozeman to Big Sky corridor is headed, Glick says, sharing the anecdote that many people have relocated to Montana from Colorado ski resort towns because their once intimate connection to nature has vanished from the bustle. He laments that over the years, with the exception of scrutinizing sewage spills in Big Sky and the possible release of treated effluent into the Gallatin River, none of the conservation groups in Bozeman (a burg that has one of the highest concentrations of paid conservationists per capita in America) has bird-dogged development in Big Sky and gauged its impact on wildlife, water and air quality, wildfire, and what eventual build-out will look like.

Glick says the current debate of Wilderness must consider context, not only what's happened but what is coming. You can't ponder what's best for the Gallatins in isolation from Big Sky and the aggressive efforts being made to exploit or monetize wildlands as much as possible. "We can't undo what has happened so far at Big Sky but Big Sky going forward as a community can prove that it respects its special setting and wants to be a good neighbor to Yellowstone and wildlife," he says. "To accommodate Big Sky, to accommodate developers like Blixseth, that part of the ecosystem has already given up a lot. Why would you want that kind of impact to have spillover effects across the highway into the Gallatins with industrial recreation? The answer is, no, you wouldn't," Glick says. "We're talking about mountains that anywhere else would be worthy of national park status because of the high wildlife values. It's kind of unbelievable that we would allow Wilderness status to be vetoed because mountain bikers hunger to ride there."

"Back in the 1990s people weren't paying as much attention to a place like Big Sky because conservationists were concerned about traditional resource extraction like logging and mining," he says. "I think it's been a big mistake that conservation groups haven't been applying scrutiny to Big Sky the way they would a hardrock mining proposal. And we don't apply the same level of scrutiny to our favorite outdoor recreation activities either," he said. "Today, viewing Big Sky objectively as this creeping complex of development with a long list of spillover effects, it is one of the greatest ongoing environmental challenges in the entire Greater Yellowstone Ecosystem."

The pause brought by Covid-19 should give citizens who feel a strong connection to Yellowstone Park and the quality of nature around it a reason to reflect. He encourages leaders in Big Sky to rally behind the findings of a recent opinion poll that found 47 percent of those surveyed said "the environment is what makes Big Sky, Big Sky."

"If it is really our goal to maintain the wild character of Greater Yellowstone as this place set apart from degraded settings elsewhere, places that have lost wildlife diversity as we have here, then we all need to become more familiar with the concept of cumulative effects. It's almost as if traditional conservation groups that inspired the public because of their commitment to wildlife protection have turned into mouthpieces for the outdoor recreation industry. We need to stop taking a blind eye to impacts we know are there," Glick said.

What does that mean? I ask him. "It means stop looking at efforts to greenlight mountain biking in Porcupine and Buffalo Horn as being separate from development trends in Big Sky. And stop treating development in Big Sky as being separate from water quality in the Gallatin River and rising traffic levels on U.S. Highway 191 that are causing people and wildlife to die. We need to stop separating the impacts of buildout in Gallatin Valley from Paradise Valley, and more deeply explore how growth issues in Jackson Hole are affecting Teton Valley and the Hoback."

Considering the impact of cumulative effects enables smarter thinking, he believes.

"On the other hand," Glick goes on, "if you are concerned about the future of grizzlies and wildlife in the Gallatins, and you recognize the

Porcupine for being exceptional, then not allowing mountain bikes could be one of the easiest ways to help preserve that piece of the puzzle. That's not a decision that will be made by conservationists. It must be made as a declaration of vision by the Forest Service and communicated to Congress, just as the case was made for the land consolidations to do what is best for the Gallatins. But it starts with citizens saying, 'I put the protection of these mountains ahead of my own personal desire to take every square inch of terrain I possibly can.'"

Koehler observed that the Forest Service does not comprise nameless faceless people who wear uniforms belonging to a distant government bureaucracy. Many Forest Service employees started with the agency because of their affection for the natural world. He has many good friends who made careers in the Forest Service and he speaks of them with glowing respect. Forest Service employees need to be called out when they violate the public trust, Koehler advised.

Given recent headline-making climate change reports delivered by scientists about the future of Greater Yellowstone and the world—as well as the obvious inundation of people that has happened in Greater Yellowstone with the Covid pandemic—Gutkoski and others argue the Forest Service and environmental groups promoting less wilderness protection need to reassess their conclusions because they are outdated. "With all the people here now, wild country isn't growing, it's shrinking," Gutkoski said

Koehler agrees. The Gallatins are a place that inspires the public to understand, in real, not abstract ways, the dividends of conservation, he believes, reciting more lyrics to the old song he shared 27 years ago about "Elk Valley" when we arrived at the Porcupine Creek trailhead. The Gallatins, he said, have every species that were there before Europeans arrived on the continent. Think about how and why a composition like that has disappeared from most every other corner of the Lower 48, except the Northern Rockies.

"We need to think big because this is our legacy we're talking about. Because of this opportunity in history, we have a once-in-a-lifetime attempt at a do-over ... a second chance to do the right thing, do it with honor and respect this wondrous place—the wild heart of the Gallatins—by finally safeguarding it as an unbroken wilderness," he said. "Those who set the boundaries of Yellowstone knew they weren't big enough and it's caused problems we're still trying to fix. In the future, no one will regret having more wilderness over less. They'll thank us. For the sake of wildlife, let's not repeat the same mistake made in Yellowstone. Let's not sell the wild Gallatins short."

Twilight of the Winterkeepers

S TEVEN FULLER HAS WELCOMED a half century's worth of consecutive New Year's Day mornings in Yellowstone. In years' past, he's often greeted a new annum by skiing into a whirl of falling graupel and trees jangling like wind chimes. With fumaroles billowing geothermal steam around him, he's glided solo into the far "back side" of Hayden Valley when the thermometer reads -20 degrees (or even cryogenically brisker), his silhouette quickly fading into diaphanous light.

Bound for his favorite cluster of prismatic paint pots that shall not be named, Fuller's course often intersects with fresh furrows of a bison trail, tracks of a wolf pack and branches of fir covered in hoarfrost. Stopping to admire these patterns of "animal calligraphy" scrawled in the crystalline snow, it's been his tradition to honor his natural muses by raising his camera to make yet another portrait of his homeland. It's a place that everyone has heard of, but none know as intimately.

Yellowstone is changing—it's climate and the volume of people passing through, in ways more profoundly since he first arrived in the early 1970s. What he senses—generally warmer winters and fewer extended deep-freeze conditions, wetlands shrinking in their outlines, whitebark pine in the high country turning to ghost trees, longer fire seasons and warmth and dryness lasting longer—is more than gut instinct. It's confirmed by scientific readings going back to long before he arrived. In the northeast corner of Yellowstone there are now, on average, 80 to 100 days more above freezing than there were in the 1960s.

As the "winterkeeper" at Canyon Village—a development that sits nearly astride of the Grand Canyon of the Yellowstone in the park's geographic heart—Fuller has one of *the rarest* occupational titles in a warming world. The other day while catching up, he told me he had witnessed more than 14,000 sunrises in Yellowstone "and looking out my front windows I have been thrilled by what I have seen every time. Each one holds greater meaning."

In his bones, Fuller knows that change is coming as the clock of nature and temporal existence keeps ticking. Old Faithful's eruption seems predictable, reliable and eternal; his tenure in Yellowstone—it's been a longer one than any of his peers in the park's storied history—is ephemeral, he admits, as seasons of memories flash by.

On our spinning, increasingly-crowded planet with 7.5 billion human souls, Fuller is, in extraordinary ways, one-of-a-kind—a modern anachronism. He is a jack-of-all-trades engineer keeping Canyon's buildings operating during the busy summer season. But philosophically, he is a throwback—a mixture of Henry David Thoreau, Henri Cartier Bresson, Ansel Adams, and with pinches of Lao Tzu, Edward Abbey and Noam Chomsky thrown in for good measure.

None of them, however, have courted solitude as he has. When it comes to Fuller's reclusive relationship with winter, he has cultivated a tapestry of poetic idioms—his own *Fullerian* language—for describing snow and atmospherics that would make even the Inuit proud. Some are meteorological allusions; others architectural; still more customized to describe the otherworldly realm that is his wild backyard which brushes up against more than four million annual tourist visits.

Mountain Journal was founded to illuminate the spirit of America's last best ecosystem in the Lower 48. Greater Yellowstone, for which Yellowstone Park is its spiritual center. We can think of *no one* better suited to help make sense of the reasons we celebrate it.

Since Fuller also began writing a column in 2018 and which appears when he has time, *MoJo* readers have enjoyed an insider's perspective of Yellowstone. The septuagenerian has filed visual dispatches, chronicling not only his contemporaneous encounters but sharing imagery and vignettes of inspiring, sometimes harrowing encounters going back to his arrival in 1973.

Appropriately, Fuller's column is called "A Life In Wonderland." Operating like a journal, it will speak to a kind of hermetic geographical experience that has all but vanished in the Anthropocene—or at least from the Lower 48 states.

I first met Fuller and his former wife, Angela, in 1982, upon taking a summer job during college working as a cook at Canyon Village. I credit them with deepening my own sense of connection to the park and this region. Angela would go on to gain distinction as a world-class hotelier, overseeing Jenny Lake Lodge in Jackson Hole and the revitalization of the historic Pollard Hotel in Red Lodge, Montana. The couple also raised two daughters at Canyon.

As for Steve, he's never left Yellowstone. A Mojave-Desert-born son of a National Park Service ranger, Fuller studied history at the San Francisco campus of Antioch University. Then he spent two years in Europe, studying in England, where he met UK-born Angela.

Eventually tiring of European cities, the young couple set off for Africa, a continent that continues to pull Fuller back every year. In Uganda, Fuller taught in a Shiite Muslim middle school. He sailed to India and Southeast Asia, the only American traveling in steerage class on his boat. Returning to the States, he interned for The Associated Press, covering the U.S. Senate. He also worked as an emergency-room technician at Massachusetts General Hospital in Boston. Then he and Angela made their way to West Yellowstone.

Winterkeepers mentioned in the lore of Yellowstone were an eccentric lot, a mixture of antisocial, hard-drinking libertarians who wanted to get away from people (and suffered occasional mental breakdowns) and bearing the traits of hardy, rugged individualists.

"Going back to the nineteenth century, winterkeepers tended to be basically backwoods good ol' boys, and not necessarily with a high level of education. They were looked upon as refugees from civilization, trying to get away by hiding out as hermits," retired Yellowstone Park historian Lee Whittlesey told me years ago. "Steve Fuller has done a lot to change that prosaic image, but he has his own Thoreauian place as an anomaly in the twenty-first century."

Yellowstone's first winterkeeper was George Marshall, who spent the winter of 1880-81 at his now long gone Marshall Hotel in the Lower Geyser Basin. By 1887, there were also winterkeepers at Old Faithful, Canyon, and Norris.

Until the advent of motorized transportation—snow planes in the 1940s, and snowcoaches and snowmobiles in the 1960s—there was no winter tourism to speak of in Yellowstone and travel to the interior did not happen. It was the sole domain of its winterkeepers and parallel to what researchers in Antarctica know today but even they have far more access—physical and digital—to the regular world.

Fuller inhabits an historic wood-framed, cedar-shingled house (circa 1910) that is set maybe a quarter mile above the rim of the Grand Canyon of the Yellowstone—the place where Thomas Moran stood and sketched in 1871, ultimately inspiring masterworks that, in turn, inspired Congress to set aside Yellowstone as the first national park in the world a year later.

Notably, Fuller's rustic quarters are also a stone's throw away from the site of the historic Canyon Hotel, designed by architect Robert Reamer that, in its day, was considered the most inspiring guest lodge in the world, superior in its charm even to the Old Faithful Inn.

Once upon a time, tourists staying there could watch grizzly and black bears being fed in nearby open-pit dumps. But today the hotel is long gone, its remnants having returned to the earth but its departure significantly improving Fuller's views, some stretching for 150 miles.

When the Fullers arrived in the park in 1973, and subsequently raised and home-schooled their daughters, Emma and Skye, wolves had been eradicated and grizzlies were on their way toward extirpation. In some ways, Fuller says, Yellowstone's frontcountry today is paradoxically more harried and yet its backcountry wilder considering the restoration of those apex predators. The fact that more people aren't yet invading and over-running the outback is vital to wild Yellowstone's persistence and its only hope for staying that way, he notes. Yes, it's true that 99 percent of Yellowstone's visitors are found along a road network that covers 1 percent of the park, that road system in the most visited months, and heavy traffic loads moving through it, fragments Yellowstone. And it's doubtful that were the wildlife ever asked if they believed the Yellowstone backcountry was "underutilized" or would benefit from having more intense levels of dispersed recreation involving those on two legs, they would disagree.

The lack of inundation by humans in the Yellowstone backcountry is one reason why the park still has all of its original mammals and birds that were there in 1491—before Europeans came to the continent and before the park became a pleasuring ground for tourists. For millennia, it was home to a band of the indigenous Shoshone known as "the Sheepeaters" and other tribes that came seasonally or passed through.

Megafauna in diversity and abundance and which move long distances seasonally in migration are only able to persist in a modern world where lots of people are not—be it human settlements or vast numbers of outdoor recreationists. As seemingly big as Yellowstone and adjacent Forest Service wilderness areas flanking it seem, Fuller says, they are actually quite small, and rare, growing more so with each passing year.

"His situation has allowed him to spend an immense amount of contemplative time in a wild landscape in order to develop his way of seeing," Doug Peacock, the noted author, Green Beret medic in Vietnam, environmental activist, and friend of Fuller told me more than 20 years ago in a story I wrote for *The Christian Science Monitor*. "Fuller's great value to us is his way of being the shaman who goes out into ... *the other world*."

Fuller has a photo portfolio of hundreds of thousands of images of Yellowstone. He has visual impressions of the park's wildlife and landscapes in all seasons, representing a library that is likely unsurpassed.

Fuller's eye and technical skill first gained national attention when his pictures appeared in a *National Geographic* magazine feature, "Winterkeeping in Yellowstone," in 1978. The story, unprecedentedly long for the time, made him a bit of a folk hero. Later, a photograph titled "Garish Moose, Yellowstone Lake" won the prestigious International Wildlife Photographer of the Year Award and earned him invitations to give public talks at both the National and Royal Geographical societies in both the U.S. and U.K.

"Through Steve's photographic vision, we all get to experience Yellowstone in a way that few of us will ever witness, regardless of how many times we visit the park," says Dubois-based nature photographer Jeff Vanuga. Vanuga, who has led safaris around the world and taught and shot with some of the biggest names in photography, says Fuller's perspective is novel among photographers, past and present. Vanuga instead groups Fuller with nineteenth-century romantic landscape painters like Albert Bierstadt and Thomas Moran—luminists who exalted in portraying panoramas glowing in the backlight of sun, mist, and moon.

"Steve's work has influenced my own vision of Yellowstone by allowing me to see the nuances often overlooked by the casual observer," Vanuga says. "The predatory spider in a thermal pool, a bone fragment from an expired animal lying in a crystal-clear thermal feature, a backlit orb web covered with dew, or the luminous grand landscape."

"Through Steve's photographic vision, we all get to experience Yellowstone in a way that few of us will ever witness, regardless of how many times we visit the park," noted Award-winning nature photographer Jeff Vanuga.

The way Fuller treats landscapes is often in juxtaposition to the landscapes themselves. "I've always been drawn to stark, fierce landscapes," he says, "whether in the sunburned deserts of Africa or the deep, cold, albino winter landscapes of Yellowstone, especially when either is animated by archetypal wildlife."

Fuller's favorite expanse of land on earth is Hayden Valley; next are the Norris Geyser Basin and the mosaic of forests and meadows flanking the corridor of the Firehole River. Animals in his viewfinder—and wildlife does frequently appear—are never fierce or imposing. He is not a sharp-focused, headshot opportunist interested in portraying wildlife as trophies. Instead, creatures more often are smallish—reference points for conveying the scale of a vast landscape. In Yellowstone, he has particular reverence for bison. In Namibia, his favorite getaway, he has encountered lions, elephants, rhinos, and hyenas, on foot and next to his tent. Though at opposite ends of the temperature gauge, he craves what these stark landscapes represent: fast-evaporating wildness.

"The older I've become, the more I've begun to appreciate the sentient connections between living things here and the places they inhabit," Fuller says. Standing in his quaint living room, the walls dominated not by his own photographs but row after row of several thousands of books he's read, Fuller glances out the window. On a clear day, he can see the Tetons, one hundred miles distant. He recalls the day a treasured acquaintance, an old bison bull, died in Hayden Valley. Long part of the neighborhood, the bull succumbed to the elements and old age.

Afterward, Fuller watched as another old bull came to the carcass sand stopped, appearing to contemplate the lifeless body and the loss. When that bison moved on, the park's scavengers—coyotes, foxes, and ravens—moved in. They made quick work of the remains. Fuller says people who dismiss this anecdote as groundless New Age anthropomorphizing—he isn't a New Ager—need to spend more time in nature. He points out there are similar accounts of African elephants saying "goodbye" as he witnessed in these Yellowstone bison.

Fuller tells of cow moose and cow elk that lived in the meadows around his home. Each year, they bore calves. In recent years, though, they've vanished. The consequences of growing wolf and grizzly populations as well as climate and habitat changes have been profound for some of the things he loves. "One day, I returned home on my snowmobile and came upon a pack of wolves standing over the steaming red meat of those elk. Alas, gone was a poor elk cow, whom for years I knew well. I appreciate the importance of predator and prey, but this was personal," Fuller says. "I take pleasure in the wolves' return, the sonic texture they add to the night, and the ecological intactness they bring to the ecosystem, but I'm not a wolf groupie."

In more than four decades at Canyon, Fuller has had countless close calls with lightning, with wildfire, and with blizzards that forced him to bivouac miles from the nearest human. During Yellowstone's 1988 fires, trees burned near his cabin. He has busted skis and had snowmobiles break down when he's been miles from safety and shelter and temperatures are fifty degrees below zero. Then there was a grizzly bear incident in Hayden Valley which he'll write about in his column.

"You live here, stuff can happen, you accept it, but is it any different, really, from anywhere else?" he asks, saying he prefers his perils—the possibility of avalanches, hypothermia, being mauled maybe by a bear, getting gored by a bison—to being run over by a truck while crossing an urban street or dying of a heart attack in an office cubicle.

Joe Sawyer, a Bozeman engineer and one of Fuller's closet friends, has accompanied him on skis, horse rides and hikes through the Yellowstone backcountry as well as sojourns through the remotest corners of Namibia. "Steve's gift is his ability to illuminate the magic of the ever-changing natural world around us. His integrity, devotion to form and place give us hope that one day we will all be able to bathe in the beauty of *that* place he so wonderfully illustrates through his prose and imagery," he explains. "I guess this is my attempt at saying Steve is a dream keeper of special moments in time."

Does Fuller have any regrets as he skis along depositing tracks that will only melt away while leaving behind only the artifacts of such moments glimpsed by naked eye and viewfinder? His reply: "Where could I possibly go on Earth that would be more spectacularly unique than this place?"

After a long pause, he adds: "Unfortunately, I think we are losing it. I feel it sleeping away. There are no other Yellowstones where a person might retreat. To save it, it's going to take all of us doing our part to hold the line."

Smoke Signals from the Future

I N LATE JULY I AM DRIVING along the course of the Upper Madison River, one of the enchanting near mythic trout waters in the West and synonymous with the Greater Yellowstone Ecosystem. I stop at a fishing access site and there is a sign that announces "hoot owl restrictions," informing that casting for trout can only occur in the morning hours because fish are stressed by low water and warm temperatures. I drive on, headed to a hiking trail on the southern end of the Madison Mountains near Montana's border with Idaho, and am greeted by another sign that notes all motorized backcountry travel and campfires are prohibited due to tinder dry conditions. Eventually, continuing on, I reach Hebgen Lake, a reservoir on the Madison, where I want to take a swim with my dog. A sign there warns of harmful pea-soup-looking algae being present.

What? *Toxic* algae blooms in some of Greater Yellowstone's headwater river systems for the country capable of making people, pets, livestock and wildlife deathly ill? Yes, combine that with mountain snowpacks a fraction of average loads vanishing sooner in late spring heat resembling conditions you'd find in the desert. Along with it, angling on some streams being closed and low flows pushing trout and other fish (as well as fly-fishing guides) to the edge of survival? Streams being completely dewatered, with the top priority being irrigation for alfalfa to feed cows though diverted flows pulled out of the drainage prevent recharge of underground aquifers, leaving drinking water wells of some homeowners dry? Yes, that too. And wildfires breaking out long before they typically erupt? Water use restrictions being imposed upon residents of Bozeman? Woodsmoke muting the horizon for weeks on end of 90-degree-plus days, making it unhealthy to exercise outdoors?

These are not hypotheticals. They are not happening in the future. The future is now. They are already happening, harbingers of the new normal in the idyllic West, punctuated by jarring disruption of the way things *used to be*—those former predictable passings of seasons that enabled ecology and economy to thrive in a kind of waltzing synchronicity. Pieces of the new normal that converged, all at once, in these 2020s, events astutely predicted by scientists working on multiple parts of the Montana Climate Assessment and other studies. Some skeptics said, "How can you predict something that hasn't happened yet." Those dissenting voices were silenced as megadrought expanded across much of the West.

There's a lot of attention directed toward Greater Yellowstone because it is viewed as the watery wellspring for the western half of the nation. Three major river systems—the Yellowstone-Missouri; Snake Columbia; and Green-Colorado originate here, products themselves of innumerable veins of creeks that nourish the ecosystem like blood flows through a body. The solution to confronting climate change, adherents of science and skeptics of climate change both agree, rests with the economy. However, the costs involve a polemic of trying to take corrective action now vs. deferring and letting future generations deal with the consequences of our inactions. So far, we've chosen the latter as our non-strategy, invoking the word "adaptation" as a fix. How exactly will that work when there isn't enough water to go 'round?

In Jackson Hole, you can gaze across Jackson Lake toward the rise of Mount Moran, one of the venerated Teton summits without realizing that it's in part, an illusion. Potato farmers and other crop growers as well as municipalities far downstream along the Snake River system in Idaho are able to drain the tarn dramatically whenever they want to call for the water they own by right. The city of Bozeman is blowing through population levels that represented the threshold for water supply being able to slake the thirst of people and their lawns in this growing mini-metropolis. Secondary streams that serve as prime spawning areas for wild trout were transformed into barely trickling lanes of dry smooth-worn cobble.

The abundance or lack of water and what form it takes is what thinking about climbing change really comes down to. As surface expressions of water desiccate, livestock and wildlife head for rare remnants like animals gathered around water holes in Africa. If precipitation falls as rain instead of snow a ski season might be a month or two shorter. If runoff of snowmelt happens a month (or two) earlier, agricultural operations already getting by barely on the margins may be left financially high and dry but down for the count. Are we capable of taking action as a society to make changes with everything we love about the West on the line?

Yvon Chouinard believes we aren't. Chouinard, who is now in his eighties, may, at this moment in time, be the most radically blunt-talking, non-Pollyannish, successful business entrepreneur on the planet. A proud denizen of the Greater Yellowstone, he spends a good part of every year at home in Jackson Hole not far from the Snake River that is suffering from its own low flows. Chouinard doesn't mess around and he speaks as if there's nothing to lose by being honest. He says, "We're f—ked." Chouinard is one of the fiercest proponents of the region's wild salvation and yet, factoring in current trends, he believes we're doomed until something proves him wrong.

That's different, he says, from being a complete cynic, of not having hope, or not believing in karma, or in embracing the conceit that all companies are in business to tell their customers only what they aspirationally want to hear and need to buy in order to make a buck—even if for them it means putting a lot more carbon into the atmosphere. Chouinard and the company he founded does none of those things and its customers are willing to patronize a brand that does not sugar coat the truth. What he says, what his company does is a demonstration of what businesses need to do, observers say, because business is what drives politics and systemic change. Ironically, Patagonia's imperfect success is evidence that citizens are attracted to companies and willing to spend dollars buying their products if they tell them the truth.

Chouinard has been a patron saint of funhogs but these days he is telling those self-obsessed with pondering only what to do with their leisure time to get serious and start thinking of others—as in other species that are going to suffer because of our own self-obsession on doing nothing—our refusal to inconvenience out fluffy lives of luxury.

A rabid fly fisher, Chouinard will be out blissfully casting for trout on a Greater Yellowstone stream and comment that he's convinced there is no future for cold-water fish given water challenges and warming temperatures. To get a rise out of people he meets, he'll say that doing anything about climate change is a lost cause. He may play the role of dire messenger but in his heart he's not truly a cynic; he's worried about his grandkids and he believes in the power of people to come together and act on their values.

"Of course, *that* is our only hope. We have nothing to lose by viewing this as the most serious threat we've seen, apart from maybe nuclear anni-hilation or an errant meteor crashing into us, to our survival. We haven't been approaching it this way but we need to," he says, using irreverence for happy talk to try and get a rise out of people who angrily may want to prove him wrong.

The radical changes needed to confront climate change, he says, must be met with radical thinking. "The same kind of thinking that got us into this mess is incapable of getting us out of it," he says. "That applies to a lot of things, not only climate change but how we've been approaching conservation. We're not thinking big enough. We're not thinking bold enough. Many of the conservationists I know are too afraid to say anything that might offend people, including the funders who are given them money and want to keep them silent—but look where that strategy has gotten us."

Chouinard, author of the best-selling business book, *Let My People Surf*, is also noted for being counter-intuitive and brilliant in getting people motivated. He has endorsed advertising campaigns at Christmas time telling faithful adherents of the Patagonia clothing brand not to buy new attire. (It resulted instead in a season of brisk sales and in Patagonia handing out millions more in profits to conservation organizations, groups promoting diversity, equity and inclusion, re-generative agriculture, and Patagonia provided crucial seed money to help jumpstart *Mountain Journal*).

In the summer of 2021, Chouinard and Patagonia's leadership announced that it would not allow its products to be sold in outlets at Jackson Hole Mountain Resort after its owner held a fundraiser for three political candidates who keep repeating the false claim of former President Trump that the 2020 election was stolen.

Chouinard has a way of provoking, pairing ambitiousness with mod-esty, adventure with an ethic of saying it's not cool to wreck the places that give you meaning, and challenging those who wear the wares of his socially-conscious-driven outdoor clothing manufacturer to do something good for the earth that will one day make your offspring proud to have had you as an ancestor.

Espousing values like that, he's still profoundly disappointed in the people we elect to public office and the monied set who build big second or third or fourth homes in Greater Yellowstone and are clueless about the environmental threats. He calls out inhabitants of the tony Yellowstone Club in Big Sky and captains of industry who think that by escaping to Jackson Hole they can stop thinking about the woes of the world. Climate change is his top priority and he's been out on the stump trying to rally other business leaders to take a stand.

Here are four observations he shared recently pertaining to the paralyzing challenge we all feel in thinking about climate change.

"There is no such thing as sustainability. The best we can do is cause the least amount of harm." (Translation: With regard to unspoiled public wild lands, save them all, now).

"You've got to change the consumers first and then the corporations will follow and then government will follow the corporations. They [governments] are last in line." (Translation: Don't let those in government set any agenda. Citizens need to create a new political reality and it begins with how they spend their money and who they keep or run out of business).

"If you expect victories, then you're in the wrong business. Evil never stops. And it's just a matter of endless fighting … the fight is the important thing." (Translation: Don't worry about creating enemies. Hang out with likeminded happy warriors and don't worry about getting into heaven if its populated by earth destroyers because you wouldn't want to go there anyway).

"The solution to depression is action, and I've got a clear idea what I need to do. A lot of people want to do something about global warming, but they don't know where to start. It's a lack of introspection, imagination, and courage." (Translation: The most impactful things we can do begin by moving out of our own comfort zones and doing something that benefits the preservation of Nature because when you do that you do things that benefit everything else).

Regarding karma, goodwill, empathy, altruism, magnanimity, whatever you want to call it, Chouinard is firmly convinced that whatever good you send out into the world comes back. What Greater Yellowstone needs most right now is advocates who either live in the region or visit here and can lean on politicians to think beyond the self-interest of their own re-election cycles and connect the dots to the future—even if it means them not being re-elected.

No company with a CEO like this in the history of the world has, on a ratio of earnings to philanthropy and employee to customer, devoted a higher percentage of its profits to engaging on environmental issues with most it revolving around climate change than his company.

Mr. Chouinard told *The Guardian* newspaper that "People who deny climate change are *evil*."

At present we are unable to travel backward in time, and we are living in the future created by people who came before us, whose decisions forged the world we live in today, for better or worse.

Similarly, our actions are shaping what the world, the United States of America, and the Greater Yellowstone Ecosystem will be, later in the 21st century.

Should we care what that will look like? Do we have any kind of moral, ethical, and economic imperative to consider how what we do today will impact others? Even if you are not a parent, even if you and your partner choose not to have children, does that let you off the hook? Is it only your rational self-interest and self-indulgence in the here and now what matters? Or are you, are we as a society, really capable of thinking beyond our own time?

Imagine that we are the ancestors, here and now, of people looking back in time at us. Had they the opportunity to communicate with us, what might they recommend we should be doing? And if messages were being whispered to us from a time when we are long gone would we heed them? Would we care? Is our species capable of imposing limits on how we consume Nature, via the space and resources we use and the material products we buy? These are not questions asked by an anti-capitalist; they are among the ponderances coming from Chouinard, other executives and leaders from across the political and academic spectrum. And it even includes philosophers who wonder if modern humans have the intelligence to take corrective, preemptive action to avoid a catastrophe. This isn't a fiction of a comet headed for Earth, as portrayed in the film, *Don't Look Up*. It is real.

In 2021, a group of scientists and conservationists released the findings of the first-ever climate change assessment for Greater Yellowstone. Want an example of another ripple effect? Here's one articulated by Yellowstone Park Superintendent Cam Sholly who joined the authors:

"Warmer temperatures have already led to decreased snowpack at elevations ranging from 5000 to 7000 feet, drier conditions conducive to fire, widespread die-offs of mature whitebark pine trees, invasive species outbreaks, and changes in the timing and rate of snowmelt are affecting fish spawning and the health of aquatic systems," he stated. "Grasslandhabitats are altering bison migratory patterns, and rising temperatures are affecting food availability for songbirds. Protecting and restoring corridors—passageways that connect habitat patches—and connectivity across landscapes will require strong collaboration with partners and programs—public and private—throughout Greater Yellowstone and beyond. These partners must share knowledge, ensure the survival of native species, and develop meaningful cross-jurisdictional conservation priorities and tools to address climate change threats across the ecosystem."

The authors said that by the end of this century temperatures could be on average 10 degrees warmer, bringing a wholesale change to ecosystem plant communities that evolved with cold weather being important in shaping forests and grasses. They noted that while annual precipitation increase by 9 to 15 percent, the combination of elevated temperatures and higher evaporation rates will likely make future conditions drier in summer. Reduced soil moisture in summer will be an additional stress on plant communities making drought and wildfires more common. There will be between 40 and 60 more days each year exceeding 90 degrees Fahrenheit in Bozeman, Jackson Hole, Pinedale and Cody, Wyoming, if there is little to no mitigation of future emissions. The statistics are daunting but they are hard to translate.

Pretend again, that you can time travel. Imagine that you are not you but a young person not yet born in this time; rather, you are a twentysomething staring in retrospect at us from the future. Try to let you, here, now, reading this book, empathize with those in the future, and the best way to do that is by putting yourself in their place. You are in the Greater Yellowstone Ecosystem. It's between the middle and the end of this century. You are alone in an attic, rummaging through a trunk that's been handed down across the generations. You happen upon a dusty scrapbook. Intrigued, you open it. Flipping through its fraying pages, you discover a series of candid poses featuring your great-grandparents's generation—that's us—back in those distant years of the 2020s, when they were roughly the same age you are now. Something about the look in their eyes strikes a chord: a mixture, you think with hindsight, of wonderment and concern in regard to how they present themselves. They had the good life. And then you make ask yourself: what were they thinking?

Decades before you were born, these hale, frosty-faced distant relatives—us—evincing grins from their snowy past, stand in vaulted white ramparts, the curves of topography recognizable to you and yet those landscapes rimming your home valley seem so strangely different. From the sixth or seventh decade of the 21st century. But there your ancestors are in the last real winters in the first few decades of the New Millennium, bundled contentedly against the elements, riding packed trams to the legendary powderamas of yore; ascending with their skis and snowboards to destinations like Rendezvous Bowl in Jackson Hole, Wyoming; the black diamond runs of Grand Targhee along the Wyoming-Idaho border; to the crest of Lone Peak towering over Big Sky, Montana; mugging for cellphone cameras along the ridge at Bridger Bowl and the slopes of Red Lodge. Or maybe they were in Colorado, the Wasatch, Sierra, or New England.

Their snapshots offer a vicarious glimpse. Savoring what old-timers called "downhill skiing's golden age," they hit the piste in late November as we do now and didn't quit until mid-April. Then, like clockwork come springtime, they'd pull out their boats, and greet the first insect hatches on annual river pilgrimages, and delight in leaving the first set of tracks by foot and bike. They convinced themselves it would always be like that. And now, judging by the images in front of you, it looked like they lived a charmed carefree life indeed, if you were privileged enough to have it before *the changes* set in. They loved their lives and they were willing to defer action on climate change as part of your inheritance.

Now in your own future time it's the latter weeks of winter in the late 2060s or what *used* to be called that *cold*-weather season. You find the notion of a "downhill ski industry" and lives ordered around nothing more than outdoor leisure to be peculiar and frankly ridiculous given the misery now in the world with millions upon millions of refugees seeking water and food. Coral reefs are bleached and no longer oceanic ecocenters; coastal cities are in ruin from constant flooding brought by storm surges; desert cities have emptied out due to water shortages; Hudson Bay no longer has polar bear watching but in summer you can bathe in a bikini.

Where once the newcomers who came to your Greater Yellowstone hamlet with plenty of cash and designs on owning a trophy home or ranchette to allow them to socially distance and still have a horse in the backyard during the age of Covid-19, more recent arrivals in the decades afterward have been home-grown American *refugees*. They fled the desert Southwest where water ran out, from the coasts where tidal surges happened and other areas where "the new normal" was not conducive to supporting urban populations.

On this afternoon in the Greater Yellowstone Ecosystem, circa late 2072—the 200th anniversary year of Yellowstone's creation—it's drizzling, same as it was in late January and now in February the thermometer is pushing past 60 degrees. The intermittent snow, which accumulated for just a couple of weeks in the valley, disappeared more than a month ago. Tulip sprigs and crocuses have been pressing out of the soil for weeks and very soon, lilac blooms. (None of this may sound *too* horrific, dear reader as you imagine time travel to the future to join your descendants. Most forward-thinking computer models say it may not be abrupt change but steady incremental like the allusion of a frog being cooked in a pot of boiling water. Of course, this is not considering what happens if the thermafrost disappears in the Arctic North, setting off an unstoppable surge of carbon dioxide into the atmosphere, creating a truly catastrophic feedback loop). But forget that for a moment. Try to relate to young people in the future who are examining photographs. Intrigued by the haunting white backdrops, they set out to find the elusive snow line where depth this time of year, according to historic records, was measured in feet.

As they wheel in a driverless autonomous car through Greater Bozeman/Gallatin Valley, population 500,000, they think nothing of the scattered subdivisions stretching for 40 miles because it's all they've ever known: farmland that octogenarians say gave way to a ceaseless grid a generation before. It's hard perhaps to fathom that the vista in front of them was ever touted as the best pastoral cropland in the state and that Bozeman one of the country's "it" micro-cities.

Dryland agriculture became unworkable in unrelenting heatwaves; square footage and real estate lots were worth far more as tradable commodities than beef raised on the hoof or wheat shipped out by the bushel. Of course, then, too, came the contentious never-ending battles over water, the years when personal green manicured lawns went away with the advent of mandatory water restrictions, when ranchers and farmers no longer sold crops but made fortunes in the water and real-estate development business.

Summers with only a few days of temperatures that soared into the 90s in your forebears' era now broil over 90 degrees for months. (Those temperatures actually happened for weeks on end in the summer of 2021). The haze of woodsmoke that tinged their air in July at the turn of the century wafts in now from the west two months earlier (as it did in 2021), obscuring views of the mountains on many days and lasts until early November.

Few could've predicted that when extreme heat events (high temperatures routinely in the 120s) coupled with shortages of fresh water caused social unrest a thousand miles away in the desert Southwest, from Vegas to California's Mojave, to Phoenix and Tucson, it would also set off an exodus to here.

Nor, correspondingly, could anyone have grasped a different chain of events that linked Greater Yellowstone to the oceans: rising seas pushed by tropical storm surges causing hundreds of billions of dollars in damage to coastal developments, submerging some, sending huge numbers of residents scrambling inland when insurance companies no longer were willing to pay policy owners to rebuild or the companies were bankrupt.

Yet it *happened* and the only evidence those in the future have of things being different is a trove of images and news clips they pulled from the trunk. More than a million desperate "environmental refugees" poured into different corners of Greater Yellowstone on top of the others who once came seeking the good life.

Greater Yellowstone's famous wildlife migrations, once likened to an American version of the Serengeti, are only rumored to have existed. They were squandered by people in the past who refused to alter their lifestyles and plan ahead, for the benefit of those in the future. Yellowstone Park's forests are converted to scrub after wildfires burned most of the trees and rangeland is covered in cheatgrass and other exotics that supports only a fraction of wildlife that once existed and is contending with competition from, of all things, invasive wild hogs. The Yellowstone celebrated in 2022 at its 150th anniversary is unrecognizable.

Now, along the route to Big Sky, a travel route three times as wide as the Gallatin River itself, they find every bend of the Gallatin River on this March day strangely crowded with masses of gray-headed diehard anglers waiting their turns to cast; each knows the current will be dipping fast as another short fishing season is brought to a close. They're catching bass and catfish and carp. It's an odd ritual they do in remembrance of a pastime that long ago lost its meaning. They are akin to indigenous people who kept returning to old buffalo hunting grounds in the late 19th century after the slaughter of the species by colonists nearly left those animals extinct. They kept going back because it was part of their tradition, culture and spiritual connection to the Earth.

Just as it is difficult to conceive of a "ski industry" as once being a major pillar of the "winter economy" in the Rockies; so, too, is it a weird notion to ponder there ever being a thriving multi-million-dollar "fly-fishing industry." Up at Hyalite Reservoir south of Bozeman, that in the 2020s was among the busiest Forest Service recreation sites in the Rockies and provided a huge percentage of Bozeman's public water supply, the artificial lake dries up by July.

No matter, they can still fish, in their own living rooms, simply by slipping into your Virtual Reality suit and catching any fish species or observing any animal you desire. They look into the pages of the old scrapbook and that distant world in the past is gone and they wonder, what were their great grandparents thinking? In fact, you knew this punchline was coming, *we are* their great grandparents.

Such a future, what some might consider dystopia, isn't a jeremiad coming from the mouth of a radical environmentalist. Rather, it's a future readily predicted by studies and experts, who are paid to anticipate the future, when they examined likely scenarios for climate change in ski and trout towns, whose winter economies were built on two water mediums—frozen and liquid flowing—and the expectation they would always exist; the predicted scenarios are very different and their likely transformation, in a warming West, became omens. But they were dismissed and they went unsupported because apathetic citizens looked the other way.

If we're asking our great grandchildren and others who come after us to embrace vague "adaptation" as a response to the scenario above, what does it say about us, about our values, our ability to critically think and act altruistically? Are we worthy of veneration or concerned only about what is good for us now? Since America and the U.S. Congress still largely thinks of this country as a "Christian nation," well, let's invoke the Bible and ponder that if presented with all the evidence before us, What Would Jesus Do?

In our time, we have decisions to make that go far beyond protection of Yellowstone and the Greater Yellowstone Ecosystem but the choices hold symbolic value for the larger world. In 2020, University of Utah law professor Robert Keiter, an expert on public policy published a paper, "The Greater Yellowstone Ecosystem Revisited: Law, Science, and the Pursuit of Science in an Iconic Landscape." In it he wrote: "Any description of the Greater Yellowstone environment today must also include the impact of climate change on the region's ecological integrity. Thirty years ago, the term 'climate change' rarely appeared in the vocabulary of conservation, nor was it mentioned in connection with the Greater Yellowstone Ecosystem management debate. Today, discussions about conservation regularly include references to global warming and corresponding management adaptations."

Keiter goes on: "In the GYE, temperatures are expected to rise, and more precipitation is expected to fall as rain rather than snow. These climatic changes will alter seasonal start dates, accelerate spring runoff in mountain streams, and dry out area vegetation during summer months. These changes will, in turn, modify animal migration patterns, impact native trout habitat, increase as well as intensify wildfire events, alter forest habitat, and endanger habitat-specific wildlife, like the wolverine, which depends on deep snow cover. Indeed, climate change impacts are already evident in the GYE, where a raging pine bark beetle epidemic has killed large numbers of whitebark pine trees, an important seasonal food source for the grizzly bear. Although current and forecasted climate change impacts vary across the ecologically diverse Greater Yellowstone, there is little doubt that the region's wildlife, water, and vegetation will experience notable changes, which will also affect nearby communities that depend on the region's natural attributes for their economic sustenance and identity."

Climate change *is* and will continue to disrupt everything; the only hopeful buffering agent is a big, resilient protected environment. Forests and rangeland that benefit wildlife migrations are good for clean water and they trap more carbon.

Every day we are presented with an opportunity to generate a positive or negative ripple effect. Flip, for example, through the menu of our favorite sushi restaurants that today offering several varieties of raw and cooked ocean fish, all of which in the future may be extinct or so rare as to be obscure. Saltwater environments now are in trouble. Consider this perspective from the Scripps Oceanic Institute based in San Diego: "Climate change impacts have been identified as one of the greatest global threats to coral reef ecosystems. As temperatures rise, mass bleaching, and infectious disease outbreaks are likely to become more frequent. Additionally, carbon dioxide (CO_2) absorbed into the ocean from the atmosphere has already begun to reduce calcification rates in reef-building and reef-associated organisms by altering sea water chemistry through decreases in pH (ocean acidification). In 2007, the Intergovernmental Panel on Climate Change noted that the evidence is now 'unequivocal' that the earth's atmosphere and oceans are warming. They concluded that these changes are primarily due to anthropogenic greenhouse gases, especially the accelerating increase in emissions of CO_2."

Simultaneous to the warnings that sounded about accelerating impacts to the most prominent terrestrial ecosystems, Greater Yellowstone, something analogous is occurring in the oceans off the coasts of America, in the tropics and rimming island chains like Hawaii. "Coral reef ecosystems are some of the most valuable ecosystems on Earth," scientists at Scripps wrote. "They provide billions of dollars in economic and environmental services: food, protection for coasts, and tourism. As home to the richest marine biodiversity, coral reef ecosystems are beautiful and awe-inspiring. Coral reefs face serious threats, especially from the impacts of climate change (including ocean acidification), fishing, and land-based pollution. A 2008 Global Coral Reef Monitoring Network report says 'The world has effectively lost 19 percent of the original area of coral reefs.' Disappearing coral reefs means loss of underwater buffers that reduce wave strength during storms, loss of nature's nurseries for fish species that generate 200 million jobs and food for a billion people, and loss of the home for plants and animals used to treat cancer and HIV and other viruses."

Dr. Cathy Whitlock, a member in the National Academy of Sciences, professor emeritus in Montana State University Department of Earth Sciences, and one of the lead authors, along with Scott Bishke of the multi-volume Montana Climate Assessment, told me the reason for creating the documents was to deliver a science-informed, peer-reviewed regional overview of likely climate-related outcomes in Montana pertaining to forestry, agriculture, water and human impacts, such as from wildfire smoke. Her colleagues said the findings could generally also be extrapolated to the neighboring states of more arid Wyoming and Idaho. However, elected state legislators in Montana, Wyoming and Idaho appear to refuse to accept the science. They send warnings to public land grant universities that if they turn out documents the legislators do not agree with, they may punish the universities by reducing funding. This is, and has been a real issue, for university researchers who feel muzzled.

In Cody, Wyoming, a school board member sought to have mention of *human-caused* climate change stricken from books. In Laramie, at the University of Wyoming, an art installation meant to draw attention to the impacts of climate on forests, was ordered taken down after legislators from that coal-producing state complained and issued rhetorical warnings about funding. The arid West, where rural economies and, by extension, the stability of water coming from snowpack, has much to lose.

The Intergovernmental Panel on Climate Change has prepared a number of global assessments that identifies macro-issues. It should be noted that professor emeritus Dr. Steven Running, at the University of Montana, was part of a team, separate from Whitlock's, that received the Nobel Peace Prize in 2007 for its pioneering work in pondering the cause-and-effect of climate change. Ironically, those who deny climate change is a serious existential challenge claim to support the military, those serving in uniform and their devotion to protecting the American home-land and its interests abroad.

One might suppose, then, that elected officials would heed what the military is saying. The U.S. Department of Defense, in the Pentagon's regular Quadrennial Reports for the four branches of the military, referred to climate change as both a serious national security risk and a major challenge to American interests around the world.

Relatedly, the first volume of Montana Climate Assessment involved a comprehensive congealing of historic temperature, crop, and water data, a thorough review of existing peer-reviewed science and it used sophisti-cated computer modeling, given trendlines, to project likely scenarios as it relates to greenhouse gases entering the atmosphere. Whitlock said Montana had experienced an average rise of between two and three degrees since 1950. She and colleagues concluded that temperatures going forward would warm between four and six degrees more by the middle of the 21st century.

To put this in perspective, even a small rise in temperature can result in "average" low precipitation years plunging into full-on drought conditions; meanwhile, "normal" drought conditions can quickly escalate into the severe category when streams feeding rivers run bone dry or are reduced to trickles. It also affects the "recharge" of underground aquifers that are fed by surface water which normally passes nearly unseen through the landscape.

That can make all the difference between having a successful harvest and crop failure. And let us not forget that most small-scale agrarians, who dryland farm or depend upon flows from irrigation, are financially struggling. The offspring are moving away and not coming back, large industrial entities are buying out mom and pop operators, they are earning less from what they produce while facing rising costs of production. Much of the rural West, ironically, continues to empty out. Climate change may destroy the rural arid West that already is mourning and grieving the loss of communities.

In the three decades that followed the 1990s, when climate change data first started to accumulate and droughts became called "the new normal" in the West, impacts to farmers' crops and ranchers' livestock inflicted billions of dollars in negative economic impact and costs associated with federal disaster relief. On top of it, billions of dollars annually during the first two decades of the new millennium were spent by the U.S. Forest Service fighting wildfires, consuming half of the agency's operating budget and hobbling its ability to do other things.

In a different breathtaking analysis published by the National Academies and echoed in the second Montana Climate Assessment that predicted ecological chaos in the Northern Rockies, it suggests forests as we recognize them today will vanish: "Continued warming could completely transform Greater Yellowstone Ecosystem fire regimes by the mid-21st century, with profound consequences for many species and for ecosystem services including aesthetics, hydrology, and carbon storage," the authors wrote.

"The conditions associated with extreme fire seasons are expected to become much more frequent, with fire occurrence and area burned exceeding that observed in the historical record or reconstructed from paleoproxy records for the past 10,000 years. Even in years without extreme fire events, average annual area burned is projected to increase, and years with no large fires—common until recently—are projected to become increasingly rare."

Scientists with the National Academy of Sciences also stated that since 1979, climate change is to blame for half of the drying forests in the West, expanding wildfire areas by 16,000 square miles. In addition, research spelled out in a recent U.S. Department of Agriculture report said that for every couple of degrees the Fahrenheit rises, wildfire areas would quadruple in the West.

Still, some claimed that climate change meant good news, that warmer temperatures would yield longer growing seasons. That's true so long as it is accompanied by adequate moisture. Such sanguine thinking also was rebuffed by forerunning geographer John Wesley Powell in the late 19th century who warned that homesteaders who believed rain would, by the providence of God, follow their plows were fools. And for much of the 20th century, many rural areas of the West emptied out, especially after the Dust Bowl years. William deBuys, the great Powell historian, wrote in his biography, Seeing Things Whole: The Essential John Wesley Powell: "Many thousands of families made a go of trying to farm without irrigation in the arid lands, and they suffered extremely. It was a bitter double-cross on those hopeful people, and Powell saw it."

With climate change, irrigation ditches in the 2040s, crucial to growing food and crops for livestock, could run dry by June and even slightly more rainfall won't offset the consequences of more heat. Over time, rivers chronically will have their flows squeezed tighter and tighter. Sorting out who will get priority in water use—agriculture/irrigators, municipalities (flows at the tap, lawn and garden watering), developers buying up rights, or ecology (such as keeping enough water in streams to ensure fish populations can persist) are likely to bring major conflict, Whitlock predicts. With only so much water to go around, current pillars of Greater Yellowstone's economy will be pitted against each other, more powerful states will be looking to buy or steal water.

A new report called "The Greater Yellowstone Climate Assessment," part of the Montana Climate Assessment's ongoing series, was released 2021 and it focuses on hydrology—i.e. snowpack and stream flows in the Greater Yellowstone region. Greater Yellowstone, again, is the headwaters for three major river systems in America: the Snake-Columbia which heads to the Pacific Northwest; the Upper Green-Colorado that winds through the desert Southwest; and the Yellowstone-Missouri that ultimately marries the Mississippi. Many tens of millions of people downstream have a connection to Greater Yellowstone based on the water flowing out of their taps, in their garden hoses, what they do recreationally, the water they need for agriculture and business.

While growing seasons for the rest of this century will be longer in all major Greater Yellowstone river basins, it will be matched by huge reductions in snowpack. The Yellowstone, Big Horn, Upper Green, Snake and Missouri headwaters are expected to see temperatures rise, on average about 5 degrees F, be facing snowpack declines of between 38 percent and 43 percent, and see spring runoffs—crucial to agriculture—one-third or more less than today.

This, of course, correlates, as a negative ripple effect, to an extended wildfire season and weeks of valleys being cloaked in unhealthy woodsmoke. And then there is the phenomenon of people rapidly moving into the so-called "wildland-urban interface," i.e. places at the forested edge that are highly prone to burning by wildfire. Will insurance carriers stop offering policies to homeowners who build there, the same as carriers have stopped insuring people who unwisely build in river flood plains or coastal areas prone to destruction by hurricanes.

There's an important ecological element, too. The "wildland-urban interface" is, in Greater Yellowstone, a place where important wildlife habitat resides—habitat that will be even more essential in the future as public lands are altered and wildlife needs more space to survive.

More Americans than ever before are dwelling in the fire zone. The trendlines are stunning. In the western U.S. the average fire season is 84 days longer than in the 1970s, notes Dr. Kimi Barrett with Headwaters Economics, and between 1985 and 2017, the number of fires classified as severe increased 700 percent. Since 2005, over 90,000 structures have been lost and nearly 2,000 communities have dealt with a wildfire of 100 acres or greater within two miles of town. In the 2018 Camp Fire in California, more than 18,000 structures were destroyed. In 2018, wildfires in the U.S. caused more than $24 billion in property loss.

Since 2000, 75 percent of western forests have become significantly drier, tied to winnowing snow packs, less rain and earlier heat waves every year. By the middle of this century, additional fire suppression costs attributed to climate change alone are expected to reach at least $2 billion.

Today, notes Barrett, fully half of the West's population lives in the wild-land-urban interface, where 97 percent of all wildfires are human-caused.

In just 20 years between 1990 and 2010, the number of new houses/structures built in the wildland-urban interface topped 40 million, representing 41 percent growth. In many areas of the West the percentage is much higher, according to a study led by Voker Radeloff published by the National Academy of Sciences.

Sobering is that within the perimeter of recent wildfires there were more than 100,000 new houses and the pattern is only accelerating. "When houses are built close to forests or other types of natural vegetation, they pose two problems related to wildfires. First, there will be more wildfires due to human ignitions," the authors write. "Second, wildfires that occur will pose a greater risk to lives and homes, they will be hard to fight, and letting natural fires burn becomes impossible."

Unfortunately, most county commissions in the rural West, citing freedom, liberty and private property rights above all else, are vehemently opposed to planning and zoning that would prevent such risky and costly development from happening.

Again, ironically, those county commissions, which claim to be fiscally conservative and opposed to "big government," gladly accept federal and state disaster relief—funded by taxpayers—when wildfires tear through the wildland-urban interface. Who is ultimately responsible? Voters and taxpayers are, citizens who demand accountability, who want to know why someone else's personal bad choices becomes a debt foisted upon them.

Startlingly, Whitlock warns: if the status quo of CO2 emissions in the 2020s continued unabated *or increased* as a result of burning more fossil fuels, the end of the 21st century could actually see a temperature rise of around *nine* to twelve degrees. For dryland farming in Montana, it means catastrophe. "If those temperature increases happen, it will literally be a different world, unlike the one we presently know," she told me. Again, her imploring and that of colleagues who have no agenda other than providing the best information, have been ignored by lawmakers in the Greater Yellowstone states of Montana, Wyoming and Idaho.

Nobel Prize winner Steve Running told me that southwest Montana's climate within two human generations will resemble that of Salt Lake City's and arid stretches of the Great Basin. In the rural interior of

Wyoming, away from the mountains, where summer temperatures are already scorching, conditions will become far more problematic, waterwise. Plus, there are the major metropolitan areas with political influence— LA, Phoenix, Denver, Las Vegas, Salt Lake—pushing to sink straws into water in the inland West and piping it, like oil, to serve their needs.

Running scoffs at notions that spending millions of dollars in cloud seeding, as some states are doing, will make an appreciable difference against declining snowpacks. And, he chuckles at the irony that the same science-denying politicians who *embrace* manipulative cloud seeding (that has a flimsier scientific bases) and they reject the notion that human influence affects climate.

The rapidly growing city of Bozeman, along with Gallatin Valley, is today blowing through its original water capacity. And there are sidebar discussions that new dams may be needed on creeks to hold back water in mini-reservoirs. Warmer temperatures, as mentioned earlier, mean less snow and more rain. "The snow season we currently experience have won't last as long and it will likely end abruptly," Whitlock says.

And yet, the U.S. Forest Service in Greater Yellowstone has continued to approve or consider expansion of ski resorts on public lands which also is accompanied by more development on private land, including development in the wildland-urban interface. This, with the best science predicting snowpacks will be half of what they are now in decades to come. Despite the negative impacts to ecology, community, and the evidence of climate change, the Forest Service seems to think, based on its actions, that public lands exist to help private entities record more profits in the short term without pondering the long-term consequences. To most people, the changes until recently were almost imperceptible, but the gradual deepening effects are becoming transformative: in the altered timing of runoff, the pollination of plants, when green-up happens, when trees die and burn, when humans are forced to give up what they used to know and do. Of course, such a massive disruption, that turns the world upside down, is something that indigenous people in the West know well. Today, tribes are savvily managing their water rights as a way of preparing for what I coming.

If you flip through the National Climate Assessment prepared by the National Academy of Science you will find a few highlighted stats:

We are living in the warmest time in the history of modern civilization and it is heating up; some 24 of the warmest years on record globally occurred in the first 25 years of the 21st century.

Since 1980, the cost of extreme weather/climate events for the U.S. has exceeded $1.8 trillion and it will triple in the 2030s.

Global average sea level has risen 7 to 8 inches since 1900 with half of the rise occurring since 1993 and is greater than any rise going back 2800 years. Global average sea levels continued to rise—by at least several inches into the 2030s and by 1 to 4 feet by 2100. A rise of as much as 8 feet by 2100 could not be ruled out. In your time, many cities along the American coast are underwater.

Substantial reductions in western U.S. winter and spring snowpack is happening now.

The rate of ocean acidification is unparalleled in at least the past 66 million years; Arctic sea ice loss is speeding up and by the 2040s the northern polar region was ice-free, spawning a rush amongst the U.S., Canada, China, Russia, and Scandinavian countries to extract oil and gas and open megamines to get at gold deposits in landscapes snow-free for the first time in 100,000 years.

Remember the hypothetical letter penned by the President of the United States about Yellowstone's death? Now, dear reader: does it really seem so far-fetched?

One might assume that land, wildlife and water agencies, combined with elected officials would have a plan. Or the business community would have learned from the 19th century era of Western resource boom towns that go bust; that it would demand forward thinking plans. Unless citizens demand it, for planning is a positive ripple effect that leads to a common strategy, it won't happen.

Urgency, as businessman and environmentalist Yvon Chouinard notes, is nowhere in sight. Ski towns because of their location in the higher elevations may be buffered *for a while*. And it's poignant to mention that people who can afford to take ski vacations are less likely to have their lives disrupted much, for now. One ski industry expert sounding the alarm is Auden Schendler. He works for one of the best-known outdoor snow sports corporations in the world, the Aspen Skiing Company.

What Schendler and others describe as Greater Yellowstone's possible climate-related future-shock can be applied to other hamlets throughout the Rockies. "Climate change isn't coming," Schendler explains. "It's *already here*; it's been here. We're at the front-end now. But we can alter the future for those who will be looking back. The only question is: will they be praising us for taking action or cursing us for what we didn't do?"

An ardent recreationist and a family man with bills to pay, Schendler has been labeled a cognitive dissident, conscientious objector, like Chouinard, and, to ski destinations that want to keep pretending there isn't a problem of culpability, he is a gadfly. He actually gets paid to think defiantly about not only the connection between climate change and business but the relationship between economy and ecology, and how the health of the latter supports the former.

The warnings about needing to scale back fossil fuel development are still going unheeded even as the coal economy in Wyoming collapses. Some in Congress are still vowing to radically alter the management of public lands in the West, gutting environmental laws and unleashing an unprecedented push to extract oil, gas, and coal in order to secure "American energy dominance," code for burning a lot of fossil fuels.

Who controls Congress and who is in the White House represents an existential question. During the Trump Administration, environmental laws were rolled back administratively because Democrats controlled Congress and wouldn't let the codes be undone. In addition, when Republicans controlled Congress during the Obama years, public hearings on Capitol Hill pertaining to climate change came to a stop. Climate change was treated as a hoax allegedly concocted, like Covid-19, by the Chinese.

The combination of radical Republicans controlling Congress, the White House and shaping the courts has huge implications. It could result in not only landmark environmental laws that made protections of ecosystems like Greater Yellowstone possible, but it could throw any progress being made on cutting carbon emissions in reverse

In a speech delivered to the oil industry, former Interior Secretary Ryan Zinke from Montana, while in that cabinet position for the Trump Administration, said that anyone working in government uniform who questioned the push for fossil fuel energy dominance was "disloyal." He and colleagues also were part of efforts to silence scientists. One of Zinke's young associates muzzled a staffer for the U.S. Geological Survey who circulated an agency study chronicling the shrinking of glaciers in Glacier National Park.

During an interview with Fox News, Congresswoman Liz Cheney from Wyoming declared that "the science [of climate change] is just simply bogus, you know, we know that temperatures have been stable for the last 15 years." Noteworthy is that Congresswoman Cheney, one of the few Republicans to call for an investigation into the attempted insurrection at the U.S. Capitol on January 6, 2021, is now one of the most moderate members of the GOP.

If pressure is going to happen, the paradox is that it must be led by the business community which traditionally has fought regulations and has exploited the rhetoric of freedom and liberty to bolster its bottom line.

Schendler agrees with Yvon Chouinard that we are not ready for what's coming. Besides being the senior vice-president of sustainability for Aspen Snowmass, he has served as board president of Protect Our Winters, a no-holds-barred nonprofit group that has hundreds of thousands of supporters around the globe. Its primary target is trying to get the ski industry and outdoor gear manufacturers to become more outspoken, but these groups still hesitate for fear of alienating politicians and customers who claim climate change is a fairy tale.

Protect Our Winters founder Jeremy Jones noted that as the first decades of the 21st century set temperature records, more than a million square miles of snowpack—an area equal in size to three times that of Texas—had disappeared since 1970. The organization released a report stating that: "Low snow years have negative impacts on the economy. We found that the increased skier participation levels in high snow years meant an extra $692.9 million in value added and 11,800 extra jobs compared to the 2001–2016 average. In low snow years, reduced participation decreased value added by over $1 billion and cost 17,400 jobs compared to an average season."

What happens when low snow years become chronic? The outdoor recreation industry still suffers from a major blind spot: it continues to promote the consumption of public wildlands, by promoting more public access, more trails and the buying of more stuff, so that manufacturers record more profit. But their market shares come at the expense of wildlife. Outdoor recreation and expanding access to wildlands does not equate to better wildlife conservation prospects for animals who call the backcountry home. Numerous scientific studies confirm this.

Here, a confession: I am an outdoor recreationist. Being in the outdoors lit my passion for Nature early in my life and served as a gateway for me becoming an environmental writer. I have ridden snowmobiles, ATVs and mountain bikes, I have paddled boats on rivers, skied mountain slopes, hiked, camped, hunted, fished and skated across lakes. Recreation is good for our mental well-being and physical health. That's a no-brainer. It is good for people to get into the great outdoors but all outdoor settings are not equal.

Moab, Utah, calls itself the mountain biking capital of the world but the level of intense recreation there would not be compatible with the needs of sensitive wildlife in Greater Yellowstone. In fact, it is the mountain biking community, as mentioned earlier, that is against the designation of more wilderness because it prevents bikers from riding in it. How is that promoting conservation? And why are the traditional conservation groups hardly speaking up, given that wildlife are going to need as much protected space as possible given the effects of population growth, more recreationists pouring into the backcountry, and climate change?

A point of reckoning is coming for outdoor recreation and its cumulative impacts on wildlife. Each of us musk ask: is my personal desire to recreate in an area essential for wildlife more important than the need of the animals that live there to have safe, secure habitat? Some have called outdoor recreation a form neo-Manifest Destiny—a last wave of human colonizers, greedily eying the last gasp of the rare, truly wild West, are desiring to take their own piece of it—*for fun*.

There is no scientific evidence supporting the contention that more outdoor recreation in a given area benefits the wildlife living there. There is no study that says more people floating and wading rivers like the Madison and Gallatin—add into it standup paddleboarders, packrafters and inner tubers—are good for wild fish in the stream and nesting birds. There is no study that says copping more po in unexploited areas of the mountains is good for the scarce number of wolverines or bighorn sheep. Outdoor recreation does not equate to better wildlife conservation outcomes. This is a myth.

The only thing that safeguards the rare assemblage of wildlife, of the kind that miraculously still exists in Greater Yellowstone, is fewer people moving less intensely through the habitat wildlife needs. Yes, limiting the way we humans consume wild places *is* wildlife conservation. It comes down to what are we willing to give up and what do we consciously choose *not* to take? It requires honest reflection, with we outdoor recreationists looking ourselves in the mirror and confronting the question of when is enough, *enough?*

Will groups like Protect Our Winters, the Greater Yellowstone Coalition, The Wilderness Society, Montana Wild, the Sierra Club, Backcountry Hunters and Anglers, the Rocky Mountain Elk Foundation and others have the courage to call out the negative impacts of outdoor recreation on wildlife, and the way some public lands are turning into fragmented human ant hills?

Part of making landscapes more resilient is saving all of the parts, including wildlife, especially in a world-class place like Greater Yellowstone and the threats it is facing. Conservation organizations, whose staffers are comprised of young, zealous outdoor recreationists, must decide: do they come down on the side of mountain bikers who want in, or the needs of wildlife that cannot tolerate human inundation of their last strongholds? Human words like "balance" and "consensus" and "collaboration" mean nothing to a grizzly, a wolverine or a migrating elk herd.

We are not going to build or play our way to greater ecological prosperity. The skiing industry, Schendler says, could find itself in a death spiral; at first resort towns will try to transition to becoming warm season recreation meccas, but how will they cope with water challenges? Whether *we* are able to ski, boat, cast a line or not, experts say, that will be the least of our worries.

Even a seemingly small rise in average temperature can have big effects, ecologist Mike Tercek noted in a special climate change edition of the journal *Yellowstone Science*, "... the planet will experience about as much warming in the next 100 years as it did in the 8,000 years at the end of the last ice age, but this time it will be 30 to 80 times faster."

Professor Andrew Hansen, who oversees the Biodiversity Lab at Montana State University, was among four lead authors of a 2016 book, *Climate Change in Wildlands*, which offers a comprehensive overview of documented impacts and likely consequences for wild ecosystems. He recently elaborated on what it means for the Greater Yellowstone Ecosystem.

According to Hansen, the number of days below zero (Fahrenheit) in Bozeman averaged 20 during the 1950s, yet only 14 in the last decade

(2006-2016) and is trending toward fewer and fewer. And the decline in snowpack has reduced river flows by about 25 percent in the Yellowstone River since then. Due to the current low flows and warmer water temperatures, summer fishing restrictions are now the norm in rivers.

And Dr. Jesse Logan, a retired Forest Service entomologist, a national authority on mountain beetle outbreaks, describes the unprecedented scale of insect attacks occurring on western forests.

Some 80 percent of whitebark pine trees in Greater Yellowstone have already vanished from blister rust and epic infestations of mountain pine beetles fueled by warming temperatures that allow them to more easily reproduce. Seeds in whitebark pine cones have been an important food source for grizzly bears prior to denning and the collapse of whitebark pine is causing bears to range more widely, increasing the number of conflicts with humans, and could be resulting in smaller cub litter sizes and rates of reproduction in female bruins. The Forest Service says it is working to develop new, hardier varieties of whitebark pine that are more drought- and disease-resistant. But what good will it be if most of the forests are predicted to burn and it takes decades before whitebark pine become mature and produce cones with seeds in them that grizzlies can eat.

For a long while, Greater Yellowstone has been regarded as a primo place to escape and play. It's wildlands are viewed by many as the last great wild frontier. Schendler recounted in a news story how he was asked to give a talk at an Outdoor Industry Association convention in Denver. As he prepared his remarks, organizers wanted him to tone down his call to action in seeking reductions in carbon dioxide outputs among outdoor product manufacturers. They asked him to focus not on swift attitude adjustments companies must make to slow climate change, but instead on how business can still grow and thrive in a warming world that is exacting a tremendous toll on wildlife.

They wanted him to paint a sanguine portrait, he notes, to suggest bullish investment conditions for real estate in ski towns await while the getting is good, and to gloss over reality; they wanted him to tout better snowmaking and recycling gray water, to say that the answer will simply be shifting the focus of outdoor recreation from winter to summer and to shoulder seasons; they wanted him not to mention the ecological challenges that are coming for species that will be pushed to the edge.

Schendler said the Outdoor Industry Association wanted him to not cause waves because he was sounding like a Negative Nelly, dampening their marketing plans and attempts to recruit new generations of fun hogs. "I told them, 'No. I won't do it. I don't sugar-coat." And when he remained defiant, they tried to get Aspen Ski Company to fire him but it wouldn't. "That head-in-sand perspective is pervasive and it feeds into the perception that climate change is only a silly preoccupation of a radical fringe instead of being the greatest challenge for civilization of our time," he told me.

He isn't alone in his rabble rousing. What he and others, including former Black Diamond mountaineering CEO Peter Metcalf, who has been a trustee of the Outdoor Alliance, makes many in the outdoor recreation industry uncomfortable. Young people want companies to step up and be socially-environmentally responsible on climate change and protecting wildlife. And yes, as Patagonia demonstrates, having an environmental ethic, is good for business.

In his travels across the West, trying to engage citizens, Schendler explains that young people want to work for companies that not only believe in promoting human diversity and sustainability but evince an environmental consciousness in their business practices. And he added that companies demonstrating social responsibility, like Patagonia, attract smarter, more committed employees and win more customers.

Businessman Michael Bloomberg, the former mayor of New York City and an outspoken promoter of sustainability, corporate altruism in addressing climate change, and healthy environments, was featured in *National Geographic* magazine in an interview with *National Geographic*'s editor-in-chief, Susan Goldberg. When Goldberg asked Bloomberg what role big employers play in the environment, Bloomberg replied, "Why will a corporation be environmentally friendly? Today, if you go and recruit on campus for the best and brightest, *they* [young people] interview *you*. They ask, What are you doing for the environment? Employees want to work for an environmentally-friendly company. And then there are investors. If you talk to the managers of the big pensions and endowments, they want socially responsible investing. We don't buy coal stocks, gun stocks, tobacco stocks."

Some companies are heeding the call. Some 14 ski resorts in Utah sent a letter to former Governor Gary Herbert pointing out that 70 percent of Salt Lake City's drinking water comes from snowpack and 80 percent of the state's freshwater goes to farmers and ranchers. They noted that by 2050, Utah's population is expected to double to six million. (Salt Lake is the closest big city to Greater Yellowstone). In an interview with a reporter, Metcalf, who earned a position chairman of the Salt Lake City branch of the Federal Reserve Bank, asked, "Do I find it a little ridiculous to be pondering whether we'll have a ski season 50 years from now given what other more serious priorities will be? Completely. But whatever it takes to motivate people. If businesses with the most engaged passionate audiences don't step forward, there's no hope."

Many say that names need to be named, that leading CEOs need to be relentlessly called out because sitting silent or being a denialist has been too easy. Metcalf led the effort to move the Outdoor Retailer convention out of Utah based on the state's regressive land use policies and denial of climate change science. That was a $100 million economic hit to the state, and boon to Denver.

Still, Chouinard is skeptical about the willingness of Americans to disrupt the way they are sabotaging their own future. "We're self-centered consumers, not citizens concerned about a greater good," Chouinard declared to a magazine writer. "We're electing people who are actually voting against our survival. It's just like being an alcoholic and being in denial that you're an alcoholic. And until we face up to that, nothing's going to happen."

"This is a crisis of our own creation that will not go away on its own," wrote a panel of authors who completed a report on climate change, titled "Unnatural Disaster, for the National Parks Conservation Association."

There needs, in America today, to have honest discussions about the importance of wildlands and wildlife conservation. One area, presently fraught with contradiction, is the claim that activists pushing for more justice, equity, diversity and inclusion—in the outdoor retail industry and the conservation movement—are not conversant about the ecological factors necessary to sustain, say, grizzly bears or elk migrations. A parallel criticism is that the human social justice movement is only interested in the human world and making the divvying up of resources more equitable. In fact, the cause of human diversity should not be at odds with the cause of preserving biological diversity. They are not mutually exclusive. Just as white people, especially white males, need to ponder what the world is like through the eyes of a Person of Color, or person of different gender identity, why can't the human social justice movement try to understand what the world looks like through the eyes of a grizzly or wolf or bison that suffers from its own form of persecution? Shouldn't we also, in a place like Greater Yellowstone, be extending or compassion and empathy and assistance to perpetually the survival of other species? Indigenous people are already way ahead of American society in understanding this, and the fact that when we treat Nature and other beings with a cruelty, injustice and lack of respect, it represents the worst of us.

So, the question is: what can society do? It applies to climate change and everything else. Apart from phasing out old coal-fired power plants, regulating methane emissions, shifting to electric cars with better batteries, and having government and the private sector invest in a Manhattan Project to develop non-carbon emitting energy, and give serious consideration to nuclear power generation, humans must do the hardest thing of all. We need to limit what we take and adopt it as an ethic. We need to change our collective slacker attitudes, vote with our wallets for change and go to the voting booth. Rallying for wildlife can be a great unifier, because what's good for wildlife is good for our health and well-being, our economies, our conscience, and it can be a strategy that better enables us to prepare for climate change.

"We were bearing witness to the start of a collapse," Metcalf warns. "In light of the profound, uncomfortable, and challenging truths and policy implications we have to come to grips with, incrementalism will not suffice. It's been a delusion being reinforced by a well-funded fossil fuel industry to distort the science. But we've been accomplices. What we need demands leadership, guts, and a forward-looking attitude that goes deeper than what's convenient for us in the immediate now."

Schendler weighs in. "The farce of those advancing the argument 'we'll just adapt' is that you can't adapt to a 4- or 5-degree rise because it's a pathway to a 9-, 10- or 11-degree rise," he said. "All bets are off if you believe that adaptation can be easily managed in order to assure some kind of *orderly* transition."

Schendler, like Chouinard, refuses to capitulate. He noted the legendary selfless attitude of the so-called "Greatest Generation" during World War II. He says there is no retirement age by which an elder stops trying to leave behind a better world. And he points out that when Earth's essential protective ozone layer was vanishing two generations ago, policymakers took action based on the science, and phased out the chemicals imperiling our survival at the time. "They took brave action because they refused to accept the prospect of doomsday," Schendler says. "They put everything on the line because they knew there was so much more to lose if they didn't."

Epilogue

J UST AS *EVERYTHING IN NATURE* is interconnected, or barely apart by a few degrees of separation, all of the major challenges in Greater Yellowstone—climate change, population growth and recreation pressure, wildlife diseases, co-existing with predators, protecting the wildness that remains, trying to restore ecosystems and species that have been lost—are interrelated.

Ignorance is not bliss. Once you open your heart and mind to caring about the natural world and a region as magnificent as the Greater Yellowstone Ecosystem—which belongs to you, and to which *you* belong—you cannot go backward. Your intelligence and personal integrity will not allow you to forget what you know. Love for nature is innate in all of us but elevating that into consciousness and personal responsibility is another thing.

Right now you are probably wondering, *"What can I do?"*

The stories in this book are heavy, in that they address serious topics that matter and ought not to be considered piecemeal. We need to stop living, behaving, thinking, and acting in such a fragmented fashion because it is registering on the landscape.

I embrace hope. I embrace the enthusiasm of young people and, after all, all of us have been young. I embrace human justice, equity, diversity and inclusion in a new America. I embrace extending the same passion to Nature and non-human beings. I embrace heeding the wisdom of elders and pushing aside our ageist dismissals. I embrace agreeing to disagree, passionately, respectfully, and civilly. I embrace conflict and tension, knowing that throughout human history differences have been the grist for ushering forward new ways of thinking, including ecologically. I embrace the truth that there are limits to "collaboration" and "consensus" and that there are some things, like protecting Earth's life-support systems, that should not be bargained away. I embrace people who live closest to the land. I embrace admitting to my own ignorance and trying to correct it. I embrace that there is sentience in our world and spirituality inside each of us that cannot be expressed and does not reside in a holy book. I embrace the notion that each of us is looking for meaning in life, and affirmation of our individuality, our good intentions and desire to feel and be loved.

I embrace the truth that many of us often feel alone, and isolated, that it's easy to feel overwhelmed and paralyzed and scared, that it's hard to care for the environment when we are trying to make ends meet, and give our kids a better life, and suffer less. There is something we all can do together that addresses all of the above. It is not dependent upon how much we give back, but that we *do it*. That each of us possesses something of important value, and that the stone we toss into the water, creating ripples, matters.

What can we do? We can rally. We reside on a miracle in the universe and the Greater Yellowstone Ecosystem and still parts of the wild West represent one of the pinnacles of life. That we are holding it in our hands together at this moment is a big responsibility, yes, but we ought to embrace it as our honor to defend.

What can you do? I have one modest suggestion that serves as a starting point, where there exists a community of people who care. *Mountain Journal* was formed to keep you informed, arm you with facts, and share stories that will inspire you. It is a non-profit, public interest journalism site devoted to the conservation of nature, and it can be found at mountainjournal.org. *Mountain Journal* has prepared a list of options and set up a portal for action. Please visit it. *Mountain Journal* provides free content but cannot exist without financial contributions from you. Help us do better. We believe there is still a chance to protect the things that make the Greater Yellowstone extraordinary and not allow it to slip away. I embrace hope in our ability to rally. Let's send out positive ripple effects together.

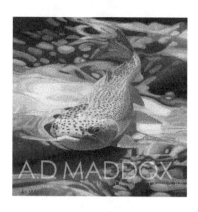

ABOUT THE ARTIST

Born **Amelia Drane Maddox**, A.D. has spent over 30 years with her paintbrushes wet and creating canvases full-time.

A.D. apprenticed under Flournoy Holmes and Kamy Deljou of Deljou Art Group. Unlike many of her contemporaries, she carefully spends hundreds of hours creating her original canvases. Her Alla Prima technique builds the vibrant colors of her trout skins and creates the depth of character and detail in her fish and wildlife art.

Maddox paints in oil, mainly on Belgian linen. She is fascinated by the brilliant hues of nature's trout and the movement of water. Her original works display both her talent for photographic realism as well as abstract art in the interpretation of water. Constantly evolving over the years, her creations have been featured on the covers of over 40 magazines including Gray's Sporting Journal, The Cormac McCarthy Journal, and LL Bean's Fly Fishing Catalogs, in addition to articles in prominent publications such as Cowboys and Indians Magazine, The Virginia Sportsman, and Sporting Classics. Her art can also be found in merchandising lines through Montana Fly Company, Cognito Brands, and many others.

Embodying her purpose to inspire and uplift the spirit with her art, A.D. is a Ducati-riding, fly fishing, blonde firecracker dedicated to her craft. She is also a philanthropist who spends her time inspiring young artists and supporting anti-drug and criminal education programs.

Her gallery and current residence is in Livingston, Montana. Check out www.admaddox.com for new originals, fine art prints, merchandise and updates.

ABOUT THE AUTHOR

Todd Wilkinson is an award-winning American journalist and author whose work has appeared in dozens of prominent newspapers and magazines. Today, he is a Bozeman, Montana-based correspondent for *National Geographic* and *The Guardian*, and he serves as founder of *Mountain Journal* (mountainjournal.org). Among his acclaimed books are *Grizzlies of Pilgrim Creek*, a story about famous Jackson Hole Grizzly Bear Mother 399 featuring photographs by Thomas D. Mangelsen; *Last Stand: Ted Turner's Quest to Save a Troubled Planet* that explores Turner's legacy as a conservationist, entrepreneur, humanitarian and promotor of nuclear de-proliferation; and *Science Under Siege: The Politicians' War on Nature and Truth* that features the harrowing stories of more than a dozen different whistleblowers involved with trying to protect the environment. Wilkinson also has authored several art books, among them: *George Carlson: The American West; Seasons of Yellowstone* featuring the photography of Thomas Mangelsen: and *Conserving America's Wildlands: The Vision of Ted Turner* showcasing photographs by Rhett Turner.

Wilkinson is available for speaking engagements. He has lectured at college campuses across the country and given a number of sold-out public talks on topics ranging from nature and journalism to the American West. Visit toddwilkinsonwriter.com

Acknowledgments

CUSTOMARILY, PUBLISHERS are mentioned last in book acknowledgments. Nancy Cleary, founder of Wyatt-MacKenzie Publishing in Deadwood, Oregon, warrants words of praise in the first sentence. She not only toiled to ensure *Ripple Effects* made it into print, and persevered through Covid and continuous necessary updating on my part, but she strongly believes the Greater Yellowstone Ecosystem is worthy of receiving special attention because it is a national/international treasure—and it is at risk. Wyatt-MacKenzie is one of those rare, courageous, independent publishers operating with the conviction that the West need not be interpreted through the lens of urban, wild-Nature-deprived editors in the distant East. People who understand the West best are those who live in it, are conversant about it, and who realize the most exciting kind of storytelling about the West happening today is by artists in the West. What motivates Nancy Cleary? She wants to safeguard a better world for her children, Wyatt and MacKenzie. How many publishers have that as a priority?

Next, I thank Tom Spruance for his foreword. It is a moving example of how a nature-loving right-of-center businessperson, upon gleaning insight into how a special place is threatened, refuses to deny the sense of personal responsibility that he must assume. Spruance absorbed the information as a matter of duty and continues to take action to help prevent destruction from happening. We are all capable of being a Tom Spruance—of vowing to give more than we take. Tom is motivated by doing right for the common good and trying to leave behind a healthy, diverse world for his children, Preston and Chelsea.

So, too, it is with me. My motivation is trying to imagine the future world of two bright conscientious young people who go by the names of Zooey Carter and Natalie. You don't need to have offspring to care for protecting things bigger than ourselves. If the impetus for becoming a conservationist is not done on behalf of another human, well, then do it for the animals who have no voice. Give them one. Lend them yours.

In the opening pages of this book you will read that profits from the sale of this book will go to *Mountain Journal* and its hopes of expanding its reporting staff. *Mountain Journal* was born in 2017, based on the rapidly materializing reality that, right before our eyes, we are losing the things that set Greater Yellowstone apart from any other region in the Lower 48 and most of the world. Back then, I had been a freelance writer putting together stories for a variety of different publications such as *National Geographic, The Guardian, Christian Science Monitor* and others. Assignments took me to different sometimes far-flung places. I had just written a couple books about the land ethic and eco-humanitarianism of Ted Turner, and collaborated on another with noted American nature photographer Thomas D. Mangelsen on a volume about Grizzly Bear Mother 399 in Jackson Hole, the most famous ursid matriarch in the world.

I realized, however, that urgently needed in Greater Yellowstone was a centrifugal force of focus, something that would make public understanding of what's at stake an urgent priority. Something that was not happening and, for the most part, still isn't. The late Rick Reese and Mike Clark, both leading conservation figures in Greater Yellowstone, served as catalysts. *MoJo* was launched as an experiment on a shoestring and its future is uncertain. As the commercial media world was crumbling, we set out as a non-profit public interest journalism site and encountered naysayers who insisted we could not command a significant audience. A giant, unexpected readership—our stories are free but we rely upon contributions who see journalism as an investment in the public good—proved the skeptics wrong. People around the world care about Yellowstone and Grand Teton National Parks, wild species like grizzlies, wolves, bison and others that make the region a cradle of American conservation. If we don't get it right here, we're in trouble. A sidekick in *MoJo's* early development days, who deserves praise, is a big-hearted young man named Angus "Gus" O'Keefe and Valorie Drake who gave us our bookkeeping.

Instantly, people found us. Our following steadily grew. During the next summer, I had a chat with friend Ted Roosevelt IV, businessman and great grandson of President Theodore Roosevelt, who was out West visiting from New York City. He said there ought to be a *MoJo* devoted to bioregional thinking—and the human role in nature—in every corner of the country. People cannot treat the environment as an "other," he said. We are extensions of Nature and we are paying the consequences of trying to ignore that fact and defy the will of ecological forces far more intricate, complicated and powerful than we realize.

As of Earth Day 2022, I've been a journalist/writer for 37 years (yes, unbelievably, it's been that long) and it's been a journey filled with the extraordinary good fortune of encountering extraordinary people who hail from across gender, racial, socio-economic, cultural and language spectrums. To those I've had the luck of engaging in conversation and learning, know that I am grateful.

In 1985, when I began as greenhorn violent crime reporter, working for the City News Bureau of Chicago, I was presented with an operational mantra: "If your mother says she loves you, check it out." What my boss at City News added was, "and provide at least verifiable sources to prove it's true." We need to return to a fact-based world. Insist upon facts, hold people to account who abuse them or try to claim that alternative facts will do. We won't have a functional democracy if we don't defend scientific truths and the scientists who bring them.

Before I start listing human names, let me say that I in debt to the wildlife—the sentient beings—that give us so much yet depend upon us being wise and compassionate for their existence. With that, I thank Jeanne Carter, the children we raised together, Zooey Carter and Natalie, Jeanne's family and mine. They endured a lot living with a constantly scrambling writer trying to make ends meet. I thank my parents—my mother, Mary, and my late father, Dick who, as restauranteurs taught me the meaning of hard work and how to succeed when the odds are stacked against you. I thank my brother, Steve, and his family.

I thank a group of steadfast pals: Rick Peterson, Steve Fuller, Dennis Glick, Tim Crawford, Mark Shuman, Fritz Anderson, Tom Mangelsen, Steve Fuller, David Quammen, Susan Clark, Dan Hart, George and Pam Carlson, Joe O'Connor, Sue Simpson Gallagher, Sue Cedarholm, Marshall Cutchin, Steve and Cindi Kestrel, John Felsing, the late Alex Diekmann and many others. I thank my staff colleagues and board members at *MoJo*:

Sarah DeOpsomer, Emily Saunders, Paula Beswick, Joanne Dornan, Jackie Mathews, Shane Doyle, Mike Finley, Roger Lang, Lisa Diekmann, Hank Perry, Sandra Lambert, Chris Edelen, Will Price, Mike Person and Mike Sutton.

I thank my colleagues at the *Manitou Messenger, Kanabec County Times, Northfield News, City News Bureau of Chicago, Jackson Hole News and Guide,* editors at *National Geographic, The Christian Science Monitor, Denver Post, High Country News, The Guardian,* and dozens of other newspapers, magazines and the book editors who have made my writing better. I thank Ted Turner and the people working alongside him who forced me to think bigger about the interconnected world.

I thank my pals in writing for your friendship and inspiration: Besides Quammen, there is Terry Tempest Williams, Scott Armstrong, Ted Kerasote, Rick Bass, Doug and Andrea Peacock, Tom McNamee, Hal Herring, David McCumber, Carter Walker, Ed, Betsy and David Marston, Greg Hansom, and news people in the region: Scott McMillion, Bob Ekey, Rocky Barker, Angus Thuermer Jr., Ted Wood, Mike Sellett, and Kevin Olson, among others.

There are many more too numerous to name in total. A few courageous souls who have deeply affected my thinking about conservation: John Varley, Paul Schullery and Marsha Karle, Amy Vanderbilt, Joan Anzelmo, Dan Wenk, Cam Sholly, Jane Goodall, Kris Tompkins, Yvon and Malinda Chouinard, Peter Metcalf, Auden Schendler, Mike Finley, Tim Wirth, Mike Phillips, Doug Smith, Dave Hallac, Franz Camenzind, Deb and Susan Patla, Anne Smith, Lisa Robertson, Anne Smith, Brooke Williams, Don Bachman, Dave Mattson, Louisa Willcox, Chris Ser7veen, Dave Mech, Dan Ashe, Andy Hansen, Ray Rasker, Ed Lewis, Jeff van Ee, Al Espinosa, Jeff DeBonis, Phillip Evans, George Wuerthner, Conrad Anker, Cathy Whitlock, Bob Gresswell, Todd Koel, Ralph Maughan, Bruce Babbitt, Merrill Lynch, Mark Kossler, Russ Miller, Steve Dobrott, Tom Waddell, Danny Johnson, Laura Turner Seydel, Rutherford Seydel, Teddy Turner, Rhett Turner, Beau Turner, Sally Ranney, Rob Ament, Caroline Byrd, Phil Knight, Tom Skeele, Dustin Long, Lori Ryker, John and Melody Taft, John Hansen, Lee Whittlesey, L Keith Benefiel, Bob Crabtree, Bert Harting, Chris Wood, Val Asher, Rolf Peterson, John Vucetich, Michelle Sullivan, Lance and April Craighead, Steve Cain, Bob Smith, Bill and

Joffa Kerr, Tony Angell, Kerry Gunther, Reed Noss, Jody Hilty, Monte Dolack, Harvey Locke, Bart Koehler, Peter Aengst, Scott Bosse, Michael Soule, Dave Mattson, Luther Propst, John Heminway, Randy Newberg, Gloria Flora, Michael Osterholm, Al Simpson, Brent Brock, Brian Yablonski, Lee Nellis, Doug Leen, Jeremy Bruskotter, Dune Lankard, Bob Sitz, Chuck Schwartz, Phil Hocker, Hank Phibbs, Leslie Petersen, Pete and Jean Jorgensen, Meredith and Tory Taylor, Colleen Tretter, Chris Servheen, Randy Carpenter, Phil Round, Beth McIntosh, Ben Sherman, Mark Haroldson, Richard Sherman, Lori Pourier, Howie Wolke, Dave Foreman, Oren Lyons, Phil Brick, Don Snow, Craig Matthews, Alan Front, John Muhlfeld, Tom Sadler, Jeff Lazslo, Brian and Raelene Jarvi, Tim Lawson, Bill and Pam Bryan, Pat Bigelow, Ann Harvey, Jan Brown, Sandy Nykerk, Eva and Duncan Patten, Dwight Minton, Chuck Preston, Jim and Karen Averitt, Bill West, Jim and Valerie Webster, Robert Keith, Bruce Farling, Dave Sweet, John F. Turner, Holly Pippel, Robby Keith, Dwayne Harty, Steve Gehman, George Wuerthner, Tim Swanson, Buddy Drake, Ben Lomeli, Angela Beaumont, Julie Napier Moss, Marshall Gingery, Laney Hicks, Lloyd Dorsey, John and Deb Robinette, Eric Ladd, John Potter, Kent Ullberg, Betsy Robinson, Michelle Ereaux, Eric Cole, Holly Fretwell, Charlie Ereaux, Pat Byorth, Chuck Peterson, Ken Barrett, the late Mardy Murie, Jim Posewitz, Len and Sandy Sargent, Gil Ordway, John and Frank Craighead, Dick Knight, Stuart Brandborg, Bob Anderson, David Brower, David Ross, Jeff Ruch, Walkin' Jim Stoltz, Louise Murie Macleod, Joe Gutkoski, Bob Barbee, Jean Hocker, Bill Tall Bull, Nikki Price, George Horse Capture, Tim Shinabarger, Mike Barlow, Curly Bear Wagner, Virginia Huidekoper, Michael Soule, Jack Stark, Joy Belsky, Erica Lockridge, Tom Graf, Bob Kuhn, Floyd DeWitt, Don Richard Eckelberry, Bert Raynes, and Tom Watkins, among others.

I thank the great nature painter A.D. Maddox for granting us permission to use her marvelous painting for the book cover.

I thank the generations of federal and state public land and wildlife management employees who are upholding the public trust, who helped me learn and gently reminded me when I made a mistake relating facts. If you know a civil servant, call them up today and say thank you. They deserve it and they'll appreciate it. I also thank the constellation of plucky conservationists in Greater Yellowstone who do hard work on behalf of things greater than themselves.

CPSIA information can be obtained
at www.ICGtesting.com
Printed in the USA
LVHW111657020822
725011LV00002B/5